Southern Africa Since 1800

Southern Africa Since 1800

Donald Denoon

with Balam Nyeko and the advice of J. B. Webster

PRAEGER PUBLISHERS
New York • Washington

BOOKS THAT MATTER
Published in the United States of America in 1973
by Praeger Publishers, Inc.
111 Fourth Avenue, New York, N.Y. 10003

© Longman Group Ltd 1972

Library of Congress Catalog Card Number: 72–93016

Printed in the United States of America

Contents

List of maps

The publishers are grateful to the following for permission to reproduce photographs:

John Hilleson Agency pp. 72, 75(t), 137, 188, 204(b), 216; Camera Press pp. 126, 177, 192, 198, 203; Mansell Collection pp. 51, 101, 118; Radio Times Hulton Picture Library pp. 80, 204(t); De Beers pp. 68, 75(b); Popperfoto p. 82; Thomson Newspapers p. 194; National Archives of Rhodesia p. 92.

Authors' note

As far as possible, the contemporary names of political and geographical areas have been used. Moshoeshoe's state, for example, has been termed Lesotho until it was annexed as Basutoland Protectorate, and Lesotho once again after independence. Zambia, Malawi and Tanzania have been used to describe those states only after the new names were adopted. The term Rhodesia has been used to refer to Southern Rhodesia since the arrival of Rhodes's Pioneer Column. This usage is open to dispute but has the merit of convenience. The terms Namibia (for South-West Africa) and Zimbabwe (for Rhodesia) should perhaps be adopted in this text, but once again the writers have preferred the terms which are more widely used. In short, the writers have attempted to balance accuracy against convenience, rather than absolute and pedantic accuracy.

Chapter 1

Southern Africa in 1800

So many great changes have taken place in Southern Africa during the past two centuries that it is unusually difficult to describe life in that area before the changes occurred. The reader must abandon most of what he already knows of Southern Africa today, in order to understand conditions in the early nineteenth century. Before the far-reaching revolution of the Mfecane years, in which many new and powerful African states were born, life for most people was more secure and uneventful than it would ever be again. Before the expansion of white settlers and the foundation of industrial activity in the interior, the European impact on African life was very slight indeed. Moving back to 1800 in Southern Africa, we not only pass into a different age, we also pass almost into a different country.

Before the mineral revolution, almost everyone of every colour depended upon the land for a living: even Colonial Governors and African rulers were supported directly by taxes and tributes paid by those on the land; and merchants depended upon the productivity of land and people. The nature of the land, therefore, had a much greater influence upon the way people lived, than is true today, when so many millions of people depend upon industrial employment. Geographical features are therefore of immense importance in understanding the people of the early nineteenth century. Of these features, the most obvious is perhaps the fact that the east coast enjoys plentiful and reliable rain, and that the quantity and dependability of the rainfall declines very sharply as one moves westwards. The west coast itself – sometimes known as the Skeleton Coast – is desert. Portuguese authority was never effective further south than Angola, and there were very few natural harbours or broad river estuaries to attract foreign shipping. Variation in rainfall encouraged people to adopt different ways of living. On the wet and fertile east coast, for example, a large and relatively dense population could make a living throughout the coastal belt below the Drakensberg mountains. West of the mountains the climate would not support so dense a population. On the edge of the desert country itself, life was only possible for hunting and gathering people, since the climate was too harsh either for crops or for domestic cattle.

Yet we must not suppose that geography was the sole cause of every event or every way of life. The people did not simply behave as the climate

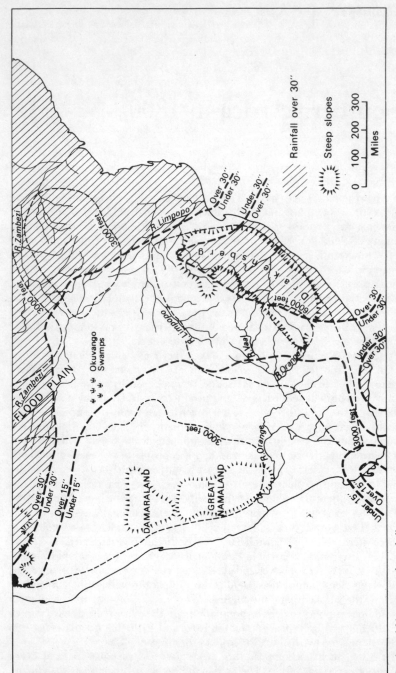

Southern Africa: geography and climate

suggested they should, but made their own choices so far as the climate would permit. The environment provided opportunities, but did not dictate to the people. None of the Nguni coastal people, for example, were willing to eat fish, so they ignored the opportunity of catching food from the sea, and never took to the water. These same people, though living in country well suited to agriculture, preferred to keep cattle as well – even though the drier country to the west was better suited to a pastoral way of life. West of the Drakensberg mountains also, some communities preferred the excitement of hunting to the tedium of cattle-keeping, and so they remained hunting communities.

Who were these people? Through many centuries there have been movements in search of more profitable or secure country, intermingling of peoples, and sometimes the conquest or dispersal of the weak by the strong. Because of the multiplicity of these contacts and movements, it is misleading to think of any of the communities as being self-contained or 'pure' ethnically. The people are normally described by the language which they spoke, and it is certainly true that language gives us a clue to the origin of the people, but never more than a clue. It is also important to realise that different cultures and languages were not limited by clear boundaries, but on the contrary often merged into each other. These warnings should be kept in mind when considering who the people were, and where they came from. It is now generally agreed that the first of the present inhabitants of Southern Africa to arrive in the region were Khoikhoi and San. It would therefore be logical to consider them first. However, by about 1800 these communities had been so greatly changed by their contacts with more powerful societies that it is clearer to consider those other communities first.

At the beginning of the nineteenth century, as now, the most numerous communities were those described as Bantu, since their languages belonged to the Bantu family. It is possible to guess at their dates of arrival, since many of these Bantu communities were associated with metal-working and building in stone. The Khoikhoi and San have no such tradition, and therefore the archaeological dates may be taken as evidence of Bantu occupation and activity. Possibly the Bantu arrived before they learned how to be technologists in metal and stone, and so the dates are not the earliest possible for Bantu settlement. Some copper mining took place in the northern Transvaal as early as the eighth century A.D., though it is possible that this mining was undertaken by non-Bantu or non-African miners. Certainly by the ninth century A.D. there was Bantu settlement in the northern Transvaal, and there is a continuous iron-age culture in that region from the ninth to the twentieth centuries. At any rate, if we imagine a south and south-eastward expansion out of Rhodesia and northern Transvaal from the ninth century onwards, we may not be very inaccurate. The communities knew how to make iron implements, and in the interior they also developed a considerable technology in stone.

The Bantu-speakers who moved furthest to the south-east have become known as 'Nguni'. By the sixteenth century they had established themselves so securely along the well-watered coastal belt that ship-wrecked white sailors sometimes chose to settle amongst them, in their peaceful and well-organised communities. Although Nguni-speakers later acquired a reputation for producing fierce, large-scale military states, ruled over by powerful monarchs, their way of life until the beginning of the nineteenth century gave no indication of later development. As they had lived for many decades before, they continued to live in small political units, which seldom (if ever) exceeded 35,000 citizens. The famous Xhosa chief Hintsa, in the early nineteenth century, had a following of some 10,000 people, which was unusually large for the times. These political units were collections of clans, within which the chief's clan had greatest prestige and power. The chief was not expected to exercise arbitrary authority, nor was he able to do so even if he so wished. Ordinary people could – and sometimes did – transfer their allegiance from an arbitrary and unpleasant chief to a rival who promised to be a more generous patron. It was also within the power of the people to break up a community by deciding to abandon the chief and set up a separate community under a younger brother or a cousin of the ruler. The chief was therefore obliged to keep a close check on public opinion among his subjects if he wished to continue in his office. The Nguni were cattle-keepers and cultivators. The relatively poor country of the Zuurveld, to the west of Xhosa settlement, discouraged them from expanding too fast in that direction, and the Drakensberg mountains behind them tended to discourage frequent or large-scale movement into the interior. Living in fertile country in any case there was little incentive to move elsewhere. The economy was amply sufficient for the needs of the people, and trading also in a small way with the Portuguese at Lourenço Marques, the Nguni were able to live a life of considerable comfort and security. They were not tempted to join in the slave trade, nor was there sufficient dissatisfaction or poverty for crime to be prevalent. Literate travellers through Nguni country commented very favourably on the security of life and property. The historians may find such dullness disappointing; but there are worse afflictions than dullness.

West of the Drakensberg mountains, the Sotho and related Tswana communities inhabited a region admirably suited to pastoralism. It was relatively dry, largely free of tsetse fly, and also of human diseases such as malaria. The country had probably been chosen by the Sotho for precisely these reasons. Cultivation was also reasonably good, especially to the east, where numerous streams emerge, later to join the Orange or the Limpopo. Unlike the Nguni, the Sotho – and especially the Tswana – tended to converge in large-scale settlements often exceeding 10,000 inhabitants and deserving the description of towns. Urbanisation may have been encouraged by the fact that water tended to be reliable only in riverine regions. At any rate, in these urban settlements it was possible for economic specialisation and political centralisation to take place on a considerable scale. It was easier for chiefs to exercise authority over closely-settled subjects, than over an evenly distributed population. Similarly, large numbers of workers could be mobilised for metal and stone working, and

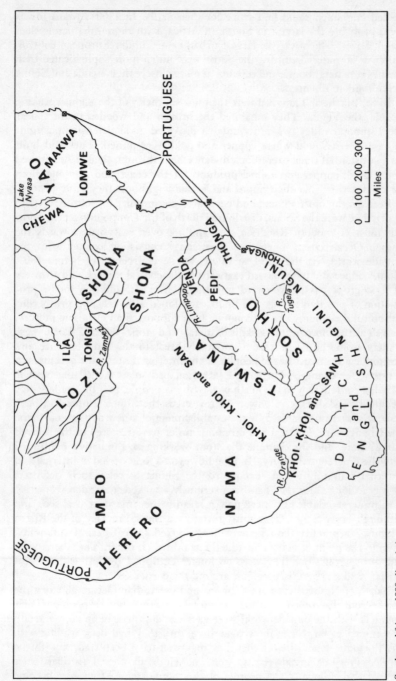

Southern Africa c. 1800: linguistic

skilled craftsmen could find scope for their skills. In 1800 Tswana towns were probably the largest in Southern Africa, with more inhabitants than Cape Town, which was the largest urban centre under European control. In terms of material culture, the Sotho were much more sophisticated than their Nguni neighbours, and resembled more closely their Venda and Shona neighbours to the north.

In the northern Transvaal were the most southerly of the Shona speaking people, the Venda. They inhabited the broken and wooded country near the Limpopo valley, where mountains provided good defensive positions in case of crisis, and where copper and gold were mined. They had built up a substantial trade over a long distance, and through their hands passed ivory, gold, copper and animal products for the coast, and iron and cloth for the interior. Like their Shona and Sotho neighbours they built in stone.

Perhaps the most affluent and contented community in Southern Africa at this date were the Shona, distributed north of the Limpopo river throughout most of modern Rhodesia, and spilling over eastwards towards the Indian Ocean coast. There had been fairly consistent contact with the outside world, via the Zambesi valley, for several centuries before 1800. Gold, copper and ivory passed eastward to the coastal traders, and a variety of food crops passed westward into the interior. In addition to the production of precious metals, the Shona developed a diverse and prosperous agricultural economy. That economic base supported an elaborate pottery, as well as the more ordinary skills of metal- and stone-working. Portuguese traders from the coast were a potential threat to the independence and economic advantages of the peoples of the interior. Late in the seventeenth century, for example, Portuguese intrusion had so weakened the Mwene Mutapa confederacy to the north of the Shona people, that the confederacy declined very sharply in power. In this crisis the Shona people had been re-united and re-organised by the establishment of a new dynasty of rulers, the Changamire. Political and economic order were restored in the revived Rozwi state, and for example the stone-working at Zimbabwe continued into the nineteenth century. By 1800 however, a long period of internal and external tranquillity had encouraged the Shona to relax their defences. It was so long since they had been seriously attacked, that such relaxation was understandable. Political power steadily became decentralised, and although every Shona community recognised the supremacy of the Rozwi Mambo, in practice the regional rulers enjoyed a great deal of autonomy, even to the point of being able to fight against each other. The Shona were still prosperous, but they were no longer equipped to deal with a great crisis – and a great crisis was just around the corner.

North of Nguni, between the Shona and the Indian Ocean, all along the coast from Lourenço Marques to Sofala, were Thonga people. Their contacts with the outside world were greater than those of any other group mentioned so far. Since the sixteenth century they had been trading with the Portuguese, and before that they may well have been trading with the Arabs. Precious metals, ivory, iron and cloth all passed through their hands; and – alone of the peoples of Southern Africa – they had become involved in the slave trade, providing war captives to the Portuguese buyers. The coastal belt where they settled was rather unhealthy, and not at all suited to cattle-keeping, so that it seems to have been necessary for them to explore a variety of unusual ways of making a living. Slavery and other trade was one, and fishing in the coastal lagoons was another which was unusual amongst the southern Bantu. Though they differed linguistically and culturally from their Nguni neighbours to the south, they did share with them a preference for small-scale political organisation. By the beginning of the nineteenth century they had produced no large-scale political system, nor any widely remembered hero.

To the west of the Shona and Sotho lay very difficult country, which impeded communication in that direction with other Bantu people. The elaborate Lozi kingship system in the Zambesi flood plain was approaching an internal crisis; and communication across the flood plain was difficult for non-Lozi people who lacked the canoes required during the long flood season. South of the Zambesi valley, the country rapidly degenerates into semi-desert, and then into the Kalahari desert itself, covering most of modern Botswana and South-West Africa. The Bantu communities spreading southwards from modern Angola, therefore, had little knowledge of events in the rest of southern Bantu Africa, and over time their language diverged greatly from that of related peoples. The southernmost of this wing of the Bantu expansion were the Herero, cattle-keeping people whose pastoral skills were admitted even by the later colonial intruders. Moving southward from the Kaokoveld late in the eighteenth century, they came to high land in central South-West Africa which was difficult but possible for cattle. Politically they were loosely organised under their leader, Maharero. Occupying the only substantial 'island' of good country in the neighbourhood, they were destined to play a major role in the struggle for that country after the Partition. North of them, closely settled in the north of modern South-West Africa and south of modern Angola, were the Ovambo and Okavango communities. Since they have been sealed off from the outside world for the past eighty years, and have been used simply as a reservoir for unskilled labour, we know very little indeed about their traditions and their organisation. Their traditional social organisation was matrilineal, they were herdsmen and cultivators, and they have no tradition of unity amongst themselves.

It is over-simple, but very convenient, to conceive of the Bantu expansion into Southern Africa as happening along three fronts. To the west, the Herero penetration was limited by the semi-desert country and the Nama people between them and the southern coast of the continent. In the centre, Shona, Venda and Sotho penetration was restricted to the interior plateau, and very few moved down into the coastal belt. In the east, Thonga and Nguni occupied the coastal belt as far south as the eastern Cape, and were inhibited from further expansion by the poor quality of the country west of their area of settlement. This distribution left a substantial area in the extreme south-west of the continent uninhabited by Bantu people. Very few Bantu groups lived on the coast – except the Thonga – so that contact with the outside world was very limited. Whereas the dry plateau of the interior facilitated contact with the rest of Africa, the inhospitable coastline inhibited contact with naval powers.

Until late in the seventeenth century, European presence in Southern Africa was almost entirely a naval and commercial phenomenon. Sheer distance impeded European influence, and the absence of commodities valued in Europe discouraged commercial activity so far from home. In the late fifteenth century the Portuguese had rounded the Cape on their way to trade in the East Indies, and later they planted trading communities along the coast. On the Angolan coast, a thriving slave trade permitted the Portuguese to establish a fairly firm control over the neighbouring interior, from the ports of Luanda and Benguela. In Mozambique, however, their hold was far less firm. On occasion the Portuguese were able to intervene successfully in the affairs of the Mwene Mutapa kingdom; but by 1800 they were once again restricted to the coast, with their valuable trade dependent upon the goodwill of African communities in the interior. Their successful trading ventures in the East Indies, however, attracted competition from the Dutch and the English, especially in the seventeenth century when both countries boasted expanding and aggressive naval power, and were challenging the old naval supremacy of the Spanish and Portuguese, throughout the world. The Dutch traders, deciding that the risks and the profits of the East India trade should be shared amongst the traders, formed themselves into the Dutch East India Company; and it was this company which in 1652 established a permanent post at Cape Town. The intention of the post was not white settlement, but to ensure a regular supply of fresh food and water for ships passing the Cape on their way to and from the East Indies. Medical facilities would also be provided for the sailors who found the long, slow voyage a great strain on their health. At first, supplies were obtained by barter with the Khoikhoi and San communities in the vicinity, whose herding, hunting and fishing activities enabled them to supply a large range of goods to the tiny garrison-settlement. However, that relationship soon broke down in the face of the inability of the Khoikhoi and San to provide regular supplies at prices which the garrison considered suitable. Within a decade, the small white community found that it had created something of a racial problem, and increasingly the members of the garrison came to regard the indigenous people as inferior, and gave them the insulting names of Bushmen and Hottentots, as a badge of inferiority.

To solve the related problems of labour and food supply, the Company resolved upon a policy of encouraging a limited number of white farmers to settle near the garrison. Farmers were imported from western Europe, and soldiers in the garrison were permitted to retire into civilian life as farmers in the same region. These were the first white colonists. Very quickly, however, the white community began to exhibit a preference for supervising work rather than performing it themselves. This preference has characterised white economic activity in southern Africa ever since. To cope therefore with the continuing problem of labour supply, the

Company further resolved to import African and Malayan slaves: the former mostly from eastern Africa, and the latter from Indonesia. The Khoikhoi and San, though occasionally entering service as employees of the colonists, proved too weak physically for the hard work required of them, and too unskilled to compete with the craftsmen in the white and slave communities. Though communities in the further interior continued to supply cattle on occasions, in general the 'Hottentots' came to be regarded as a nuisance to the colonists, rather than economic collaborators.

The growth of the resident white community was very slow, though it was boosted by the arrival of a few hundred French Protestant refugees – the Huguenots – in the early eighteenth century. These new arrivals brought with them some knowledge of grape and wine production, for which the Cape's climate was well suited. Nevertheless wine production did not offer great rewards to the white colonists as a whole; nor was wheat-growing very profitable except in the immediate vicinity of the market at Cape Town. As the colonists expanded further into the interior, they discovered (what the indigenous people already knew) that pastoralism was the most profitable way of using the land. Pastoralism further enabled the colonists to move great distances into the interior, since cattle (unlike wheat or grapes) could walk to market. Against this intrusion the Khoikhoi and San had little defence: European diseases, European alcohol and European firearms all made significant inroads upon their numbers. Until the colonists confronted the more densely settled Bantu people further east, they were able to expand along the southern coastal belt without much opposition. That country was good for cattle, and gradually the colonists became overwhelmingly a pastoral community. Despite the fact that the colonists brought from Europe no relevant experience of pastoral techniques, in such large areas it was possible to keep cattle profitably without very much knowledge of the subject, and by employing individual Khoikhoi or San herders who did know about cattle and sheep. Once pastoralism had been discovered as a means of supporting white settlement, white settlement began to flourish, despite the lack of encouragement by the Company. By the end of the eighteenth century there were about 10,000 colonists, probably a similar number of slaves; and the Khoikhoi and San population within the borders of the Company Colony had declined from perhaps 200,000 to perhaps a quarter of that number – partly through migration, but partly also through mortality. Only from the 1770s onwards did white colonisation encounter the Xhosa in the east of the settlement, and by that time the colonist community was very well entrenched from Cape Town to the neighbourhood of Port Elizabeth. By that time also, the tradition of sparse pastoral settlement was deeply rooted in the white community.

The movement into the interior, and away from the control of Company officials at Cape Town, provoked trouble with the authorities. The Company, being a profit-making organisation whose interest in the Cape was severely limited, looked askance at expansion of settlement and of Company responsibilities. It was not prepared to provide social services such as schools and defence-posts for so scattered and unrewarding a group of colonists. On the other hand, the Company was keen to extort taxes from its subjects to cover the costs of the settlement itself. Since the Company was both grasping and unhelpful to the Colonists, they steadily developed an acute suspicion of any authority emanating from Cape Town. Towards the end of the Company's reign, in 1795 the Colonists (or burghers) of Swellendam rebelled and established an independent republic for themselves. They were already keen, and believed themselves able, to do without any Company or external European control over their way of life. It was this potentially troublesome community which came under the authority of the British from 1795 onwards. They were of European origin but adapting to an African environment, few in numbers but rapidly increasing through natural increase, and rapidly acquiring the characteristics of a racial aristocracy.

In 1795, once again, the European situation impinged upon Southern Africa. During the course of the Napoleonic wars, the Netherlands were conquered by France, and Britain occupied some Dutch possessions, including the Cape. The occupation continued until 1803, when there was a three year period of Netherlands authority under the Batavian Republic which had succeeded the monarchy in the Netherlands. In 1806 the Cape was re-occupied by Britain on the outbreak of further war in Europe, and in 1815 the Cape became a permanent British possession. British interest in the Cape, during the occupations and thereafter, stemmed from the Cape's strategic position as the most useful and well-developed port along the trade route from Europe to Asia. With most of the neighbouring ports – Luanda, Delagoa Bay – in Portuguese hands, and thereby in alliance with Britain, possession of the Cape prevented any hostile European power from challenging British supremacy in the Europe–Asia trade route. Since British interest was predominantly naval and strategic, British officials looked at the interior without much knowledge and with even less enthusiasm. Clearly the rebellion at Swellendam had to be suppressed (and it was), but the officers in charge of the occupation were singularly lacking in ideas of what to do with the substantial land area attached to the naval bases. When occupation was replaced by permanent possession, British officials were obliged to consider the interior more seriously; and to impose their ideas of social and political relationships upon the new British citizens of the colony. Even then, however, policy was still determined very largely by strategic interests, the desire to run the colony with a minimum of expense, and a determination to avoid unnecessary trouble. The power of the Empire was immense but it was seldom exercised, and the initiative in the interior continued to lie, in normal circumstances, with the white settlers. British interests would be expressed as a rule only when a crisis had already been provoked by the settlers or the frontier African communities.

In these respects British Imperial influence was similar to that of Portugal, the only other European power directly involved along the coast of Southern Africa. Portugal, too, remained predominantly a naval and trading power, represented by military garrisons and traders in the harbours of

Sofala, Beira, Lourenço Marques, Benguela and Luanda. White settlement in Portuguese East Africa was on a trivial scale, and the prazo estates seldom did more than add a layer of European feudal landlords to the indigenous economic and political systems. The Portuguese lacked the capital, the technology and the manpower to transform the interior except by the destructive influence of slave raiding and trading. The traders depended upon African production and collection (of ivory, slaves, hides and skins) in the interior; the garrisons seldom had the power to control African communities in the hinterland of the ports, though they sometimes intervened in civil wars to ensure a favourable monarch's victory. The later British settlement at Port Natal (now Durban) in the 1820s was in a very similar position. Imperial and commercial interests, in other words, were largely restricted to the harbours, and seldom influenced events in the interior.

Meanwhile the earliest inhabitants were facing immense difficulties imposed by the expansion of Bantu from the north and colonists from the south-west. The Khoikhoi and San, living in small communities, unable to make their own iron, and dependent upon hunting and herding for a living, had neither the technical power nor the massive numbers to resist those intrusions upon their territories. Curiously, the colonists rather than the Bantu proved the most dangerous to these small communities. Certainly the expansion of a relatively dense population of agricultural Africans had forced the earlier inhabitants to abandon much of their land, but the progress seems to have been neither very abrupt nor necessarily very bloody. Between the Khoikhoi and San, and the Xhosa (the southernmost Nguni) there must have been prolonged inter-action. The Khoikhoi and San languages are characterised by clicks, which make those tongues immensely difficult for foreigners to learn. Several forms of clicks, however, had been absorbed into the Xhosa language, and a smaller number even into the language of the northern Nguni and southern Sotho. It must have required a number of generations of contact for one language to affect another to that extent. The southern Nguni also learned, from Khoikhoi and San herdsmen, how to train, to ride and to use oxen for agricultural, transport and military purposes; and those techniques too, could hardly have been transmitted in less than a number of generations of close contact. Some southern Nguni also depended upon San for making iron; and there was – at least for a while – a useful trade between the two communities. The Khoikhoi and San needed iron from the Nguni; and in exchange provided ivory and feathers and other hunting products which were unobtainable in Nguni country. What may well have happened was at first a close settlement of the two communities amongst each other, and later the steady expulsion of the economically inefficient by the economically strong. In the process of dispersion, individual Khoikhoi and San families seem to have attached themselves as clients to powerful Nguni and Sotho individuals, with whom they co-operated economically and technically. On the other hand, they were ultimately dispossessed and dispersed: their rock-paintings are found in many areas now occupied by Nguni and Sotho, as evidence of prior Khoikhoi and San occupation. Finally, even when these small-scale communities were dispersed from Bantu areas, there remained large tracts of country along the southern and south-western coast which were unoccupied by Bantu communities, and where the Khoikhoi and San continued to flourish until the seventeenth century and in some areas even later. The most south-westerly of the Nguni communities were also, probably, composed of Nguni and large numbers of Khoikhoi and San, who thereby entered into the world of agriculture, pastoralism and Bantu languages, losing their old languages and activities, but finding economic security instead.

The colonists were interested neither in the clicks nor in the technology of these small communities, nor were they anxious to mix with them. Colonist requirements in terms of land and cattle were also considerably greater than those of the Bantu, and their expansion was correspondingly much faster. Very swiftly the Khoikhoi and San communities found themselves driven eastwards and northwards, in the face of colonist encroachment. Some of the communities – like the Charigariqua near Cape Town – were disbanded, and individuals sought to attach themselves as clients to the colonists. Many other communities, rather than be ground between colonists and Bantu, moved away northwards into the semi-desert and desert areas of the northern Cape and Botswana and western South-West Africa. Some of these communities were reinforced by runaway slaves and people of mixed blood, and even by white adventurers eager to break away from the boredom of colonial life. Despite the insistence of the colonists upon their own racial purity, a Coloured community did grow up in the Cape, many of whose members found discrimination irksome, and preferred the uncomfortable but free existence of the refugee Khoikhoi and San.

Of all the communities owing their origin to the western Cape, in 1800 it was the Coloureds and Khoikhoi and San whose impact on the interior was greatest. A striking example of this influence is the Griqua community. They were predominantly descendants of the Charigariqua, but after prolonged contact with the colonists they had acquired familiarity with firearms, with the tactical methods of the white frontiersmen, and with Afrikaans, the modified Dutch of the frontier colonists. There were so many people of mixed race among them that they described themselves at first as Bastards, until they realised the insulting implications of the word. By the early nineteenth century the Griqua had settled beyond the borders of white settlement, at Griquatown in what is now Griqualand West. Individual white adventurers, such as Jan Bloem, led Griqua expeditions to raid into the interior; but as a rule the Griqua were prepared to accept the leadership of Adam Kok and his successors, and to lead a relatively peaceful and prosperous existence in their new territory. Similarly, a community later described as the Kora (or Korana) resulted from much the same sort of racial mixture, and led much the same kind of life beyond the borders of white authority. In order to establish themselves in their new territories, both Griqua and Kora had to expel pre-existing Khoikhoi and

San communities. Since the Coloured emigrants were armed with muskets, that was not a difficult problem. Their military superiority over the small indigenous communities was quite clear.

A similar process was taking place further west, where a number of clans which later came to call themselves the Nama, were settling along the banks of the Orange River and in high country further north. They were also a mixed population, speaking Afrikaans and armed with the Dutch Bible and European weapons. Unlike the Griqua, they became united only in the late nineteenth century, by which time the Griqua had fallen apart as a single community, and had been further dispersed. All these communities represented the first major migration out of the Colony, and foreshadowed the later migration of the colonists themselves. Meanwhile, they played a curious intermediary role, whether in the colony or outside it. Within the colony, they normally performed semi-skilled or skilled work which the Bantu were untrained to perform and which was beneath the dignity of the colonists themselves. Well into the nineteenth century they also served as military allies of the white government and colonists. Beyond the colony, they were expected (by a series of Cape Town officials) to act as a buffer between black and white and to spread Christianity and western ideas to the Bantu, while keeping the two major races apart from each other. It was an impossible role to play, since the Bantu regarded the Coloured communities as white, and the colonists regarded them as black. Only during the early nineteenth century was the role worth playing at all. As colonist power expanded, so the independent life of the Griqua, Kora and Nama came to an end. But that is for a later chapter.

Meanwhile, by the beginning of the nineteenth century, another kind of inter-action had begun, between Xhosa and colonists on the borders of their respective areas of settlement. By the time inter-action began, the colonists had formulated and hardened their opinion of all Africans whether Khoikhoi, San or Bantu. Africans were seen to be an alien, feeble community, deficient in technology, military strength and the attributes of western civilisation. Whatever Xhosa leaders thought on particular occasions, compromise was not really possible. Steadily – though more slowly than before – the border of colonist settlement expanded at the expense of the politically disunited Xhosa. When that happened, individuals and families who had lost land often moved westward to seek their livelihood in the dominant white community. There they were employed in unskilled work, and the social distinctions built up between white and Khoikhoi were applied also to relations between white and Bantu. Though each colonist's property included a multi-racial collection of people, racial distinctions continued to be enforced, and the Africans remained Africans even when absorbed into a society and an economy dominated by white colonists. Paradoxically, the expansion of the borders of white settlement, from a very early date, intensified the inter-racial contacts which took place. The frontier, which is often conceived as a military border separating colonists from Africans, was in fact also a filter through which Africans moved into a white-dominated community. As they crossed the border, or moved through the filter, it was the Africans who had lost their land and their cattle and their means of livelihood who came through, and who were obliged to accept whatever terms were offered them by the expanding white community. Though it is convenient to consider Southern Africa in 1800 as a collection of separate ethnic groups, already inter-ethnic contacts had begun to take place on a massive scale, and already it was possible to perceive the origins of a multi-racial society.

Chapter 2

The Zulu nation

A casual observer of the northern Nguni-speaking people at the close of the eighteenth century would not have expected any great revolution to occur in that area: yet during the first two decades of the nineteenth century a revolution did take place which changed the quality of life not only among the Nguni themselves, but also in a vast area from the Transkei to Tanzania, and from Barotseland to Beira. That revolution encouraged the growth of large-scale and centralised kingdoms throughout Southern and Central Africa, facilitated the movements of white settlers into the Southern African interior, and had a decisive effect upon relations between peoples for many decades thereafter. Much of the history of Southern Africa throughout the rest of the century was the working out of historical trends which originated in northern Nguni country. To understand that history, it is necessary first to begin with the revolution itself. Why the revolution took place at all, and why it took place among the northern Nguni, are extremely difficult questions to answer. Perhaps it will help to provide the main events of the revolution, before attempting to explain it.

One of the northern Nguni communities was the Mthethwa, located very near the coast in what is now Zululand. Dingiswayo came to the chieftaincy of this community during the 1790s, on the death of his father and after expelling his brother. Dingiswayo was an ambitious man, anxious to expand the borders of his chieftaincy – but such ambition was not unusual in a young chief. What made Dingiswayo remarkable was not his ambition but the fact that he achieved it to a remarkable degree, and that he employed new techniques in order to do so. Abolishing the circumcision rituals of the Mthethwa, he enrolled the young men of the community into age-regiments instead of age-grades. These regiments, which may be compared with National Service in the twentieth century, provided the young men with a channel for their own ambitions, and Dingiswayo with something like a standing army. This innovation gave him an immense advantage over his neighbours, and quite swiftly his authority expanded over them. Normally these neighbouring communities paid tribute to Dingiswayo but remained otherwise intact. The young men of these communities were often attracted to join Dingiswayo's regiments, thereby strengthening

Dingiswayo's control. The chief stopped short of any further innovation, however, and it cannot be said that any great political revolution had taken place before his death in 1818. His achievement had, indeed, been rivalled by a very similar process going on in Ndwandwe society, where Zwide emerged as a dominating figure comparable with Dingiswayo.

In about 1809, a new recruit joined Dingiswayo's regiments, called Shaka, the illegitimate son of chief Senzangakona who ruled the small Zulu community which had become tributary to Dingiswayo. Shaka was not only a very astute military thinker, but also a man of immense ambition – possibly as a result of mockery at his unrespectable background. Dingiswayo's army represented Shaka's only hope of personal success, and he threw his mind and body into the new life. Very rapidly he distinguished himself by courage and tactical skill, and became commander of one of the regiments despite his alien origin. Dingiswayo's regimental system, in other words, provided opportunities which Shaka seized with both hands. In 1816, when his father died, he was imposed as chief upon the Zulu tributary community as a result of Dingiswayo's support. Once he achieved political power in his community, he began a further revolution in military and political organisation. The regiments were now armed with short stabbing spears which made them immensely dangerous at close quarters, especially against men armed with the traditional throwing spear which could only be used once. Military training became much more rigorous: sandals were discarded, since they impeded quick movement even though they made travel more comfortable; and the regiments were trained to use the new enveloping tactics, whereby wings (or horns) of the Zulu army surrounded the enemy while the main body of the army attacked them from the front. The regiments also became the units of social life as well as military service. Men lived in the regimental headquarters until such time as Shaka permitted them to marry and retire from active service, when they were obliged to marry women from the equivalent female regiment. Since military service was drawn out for many years and men retired only in their forties, the regiments were a focus of social and political life in the way the old lineage-groups had been before the military revolution.

It is doubtful whether Shaka could have remained a subordinate of Dingiswayo for very long, since his personal ambition was so great and Dingiswayo so close a neighbour. It has been suggested that Shaka conspired to betray Dingiswayo to his enemy Zwide. At any rate in 1818 Zwide did capture and execute Dingiswayo, thereby leaving Shaka as the stronger military leader in the old Mthethwa confederacy. Just as Dingiswayo had imposed Shaka on the Zulu, so Shaka now imposed one of his followers on the Mthethwa, and consolidated his authority throughout Dingiswayo's sphere of influence. The following year he led Dingiswayo's old armies in a successful and devastating war against Zwide, and so extended his power over all the Nguni in what is now Zululand, and his influence over a vast area from Swaziland in the north to the Transkei in the south, and from the Drakensberg mountains to the sea. Military control had been established, and the way cleared for the political revolution which was about to begin.

What distinguishes Shaka from Zwide and Dingiswayo is not so much his military power (though his was certainly greater than theirs) as the use which he made of that power to bring about political change.

Many of these changes had already been attempted on a small scale in the pure Zulu community. Even then they had a different effect when applied on the large scale of the whole Zulu state. The regiments, for example, had been organised before: but now they served a nation-building purpose as well as a military one. Recruits from all over the new state were mixed up together in each regiment, where they built up a loyalty to the regiment and to Shaka as king, and tended to forget their separate individual origins. By living and fighting together, they grew to understand and to trust each other. In addition, promotion could only be achieved through the military organisation, so that ambitious young men devoted their efforts to zealous service under Shaka as commander-in-chief. Moreover, since most of the able-bodied men at any given time were to be found in these regiments, local chiefs were unable to build up any dangerous organisation against the state itself. Since the regiments were so often successful in the following years, the members steadily developed a pride in the regiment and in the state which it served, to the exclusion of prior political identity: Mthethwa and Ndwandwe young men could take common pride in belonging to the most powerful state any of them had ever encountered. Very quickly therefore a degree of political and social unity was achieved which replaced the political fragments of the earlier era. The Zulu dialect of Nguni became standard throughout the country; the traditions of the Zulu dynasty became the traditions of all the citizens; people thought of themselves as Ama-Zulu instead of the remnants of the earlier political units.

At the same time, military and social unity were accompanied by a centralisation of the economy. Each barracks of a regiment was also the location of one of the royal herds. Cattle and captives from the raids were distributed by the king himself. External trade was strictly controlled by him. The problem of feeding so large a standing army made it necessary to establish state control over food-production. Though each soldier had a home to go to on retirement, he spent most of his active life entirely dependent economically upon the ability of the state to organise food supplies, and the homesteads were no longer the focus of economic activity and interest. Not only the economy, but also the religious beliefs were transformed into instruments of nation-building. Shaka, making himself ritual as well as political and military head of the system, devoted his attention to rooting out sectional religious beliefs and exterminating sectional religious officials. The famous 'smelling-out of witches' exercise emphasised the fact that the king was supreme even over the religious institutions. That supremacy was symbolised when the annual first-fruits ceremony became a national event; an event which also symbolised the new economic centralisation. Naturally, Shaka also took care that his local chiefs (some of whom had ruled before the conquest) remained absolutely loyal, by bringing them frequently to his own court, and by dismissing or executing potential and real enemies of the new state system. Loyal subjects could win prestige and wealth through service to the king: those suspected of disloyalty ran the risk of swift execution. Chiefs were further controlled by the fact of having to spend much of their time at the royal court and in any case Shaka's female relatives were often posted to provincial centres.

The most striking attribute of Shaka was the thoroughness which marks all his most characteristic decisions. Having decided upon his ends, he was unswerving in pursuit of them. He was fearful of fathering sons, since these might eventually turn against him and succeed him: but unlike any other ruler of his day, he made sure that he had no children. His mother, who had quarrelled with his father, occupied a massive place in Shaka's consciousness. When she died, he found it difficult to express his grief adequately. That in itself is not unusual; but what is most unusual is Shaka's determination to make everyone else mourn, and his willingness to sacrifice other lives to make sure that mourning should be complete. As regards the army, it was sensible to insist that the men in the regiments did not marry, but it was remarkable that Shaka was prepared to over-rule human nature in his soldiers (and in himself) in order to create an effective military machine. Finally, he set no apparent limit upon his ambitions for his new Zulu nation: there were no neighbouring communities which could be left to themselves. No doubt it was sensible to keep the regiments fully occupied, lest they turn their attention to internal politics, but it is nevertheless striking that the Zulu state had no external allies whatsoever. Neighbours of the Zulu state could be enemies or they could be vassals, but no friendly equality was permissible. Ultimately the Zulu paid a great price for Shaka's policy, since none of their neighbours were prepared to assist them, and some were prepared to join the incoming colonists in alliance against them. Such singleness of purpose is probably necessary in the creation of a new and unprecedented political system. However, it is difficult to see what Shaka would have done had he not been assassinated. His neighbours were beginning to learn Shaka's own military tactics and to use them against his regiments; and the regiments themselves were growing discontented with their lives. It may well be the case that his death spared Shaka the necessity of re-considering his attitudes – just as it spared him the knowledge that his army in the Gaza empire had failed in its mission. It is doubtful whether any community can indefinitely accept such thoroughness, even in the course of revolution and external conquest.

To turn now to the complex problem of explaining the emergence of the Zulu state, it must be said that it was not the personal and sole creation of Shaka. Dingiswayo and Zwide before him had been moving in the same direction. The Nguni people were also, apparently, in a mood to tolerate this immense change in their manner of life. Had their mood been different, Dingiswayo and Shaka would have worked in vain, since soldiers can be trained but cannot be made to fight with enthusiasm, and people can be ruled but cannot be forced to welcome their rulers. In poorer agricultural country, there would have been neither the food nor the man-power required to operate such a system. To account for the rise of the Zulu state, several explanations have been advanced, none of which is entirely satisfactory.

One idea is that Dingiswayo was consciously imitating the white settlers in the Cape. That idea was advanced by the settlers themselves, anxious to derive reflected glory from the Zulu achievement, and there is no evidence whatever to support it. Furthermore, Dingiswayo's state and Shaka's bear very little resemblance to the white communities. A second idea is that there was population pressure at the time, and that it was necessary to reorganise the economic structure in order for everyone to make a living. There is probably some truth in this explanation, but it is not by itself convincing. Population pressure was greater among the southern Nguni, whose expansion was curtailed by the Drakensberg mountains and the white colonists to the south; yet the southern Nguni did not develop similar institutions. A third idea is that Zwide, Dingiswayo and Shaka were attempting to control the trade route flowing to Delagoa Bay. This is possible, though the evidence is scanty and the trade to Lourenço Marques at this time was very small in scale. In any case, the Thonga were closer to the trading community, and they did not attempt to centralise their political authority; and anyway much of this trade was in slaves, whereas the Zulu did not indulge in that kind of trading arrangement. Fourthly, it was probably an advantage that northern Nguni-land was influenced also by Sotho culture, since that mixture provided Shaka with a choice of social systems to work with. The most that can be said is that trading and mixed cultures and population pressures may have contributed towards the revolution. More important than these factors is a unique combination of circumstances in the area at the time, whereby Shaka was enabled to build upon the achievement of Dingiswayo and Zwide, and had his genius in the right place at the right time, in the right climate of popular opinion.

It is not enough, however, to enumerate the factors which may have assisted Shaka in the construction of the Zulu kingdom: his understanding of the situation and his ability to turn factors to his advantage are equally important. To grasp this point, we may briefly refer to the southern Nguni, where the various factors involved were all present, and who nevertheless remained politically fragmented.

If population expansion – and therefore increased pressure on the land – was important in northern Nguni-land, then it was even more important in the south, where the climate was equally favourable to population increase, where the mountains presented a deeper barrier between the coastal belt and the interior, and where the growth of a white farming population exacerbated land pressures. If 'imitation of the white political and military organisation' was important in the north (and it probably was not), then it should have been more important in the south, where it was much easier to observe what the white population was doing. If trade is the crucial factor, then it is curious that the southern Nguni were in much closer, more complex and more consistent trading relations with the outside world, than the northern Nguni.

It could perhaps be argued that the crucial factor was that Shaka was born in the north, not in the south. Here again, the argument is incomplete. A generation after Shaka, the southern Nguni had a leader – Maqoma – who was probably as able a diplomat, as clever a political analyst, and almost as competent a soldier as Shaka. Maqoma failed to unite – or even to combine in alliance – the southern Nguni, while Shaka succeeded in Zululand; but his personal qualities can hardly be blamed for this difference. Among the southern Nguni the political traditions seem to have been better entrenched than in the north, and the social structure more durable. Maqoma therefore failed to transform himself from a leader of a section into the leader of a people, because the citizens and chiefs of the other sections refused to co-operate. He even failed to retain power in his own section after the period of his regency came to an end. It seems difficult therefore to avoid the conclusion that Maqoma's failure was largely the result of the deep-seated and unchangeable political and social structure of the people he hoped to lead. In that case we might perhaps suggest that the crucial factor explaining the success of Shaka in Zululand was the fact that the political and social traditions of the northern Nguni were crumbling at the relevant time, and that people were therefore unusually willing to accept charismatic leadership and the construction of a very different political regime. Why the people were so willing, however, is a question beyond our power to answer.

It would be difficult to exaggerate the effects of the creation of the Zulu state. The Nguni speakers describe the period as the Mfecane, and the Sotho speakers as the Difaqane, both meaning the crushing of peoples. In the immediate neighbourhood of the Zulu themselves, other communities could only feel secure if they had a safe place of refuge. To the south, the white traders at Port Natal stayed close to the shore, hoping to find refuge in ships if a Zulu impi – regiment – approached. The African communities in the open country inland from the Port were either absorbed into the new nation, or retreated into the foothills of the Drakensberg mountains, or fled south into the territory of southern Nguni peoples. To the south of the Tukela river, therefore, there stretched a belt of country which was almost depopulated. The Hlubi, for example, had retired further into the hills; the Bhaca had crossed the Mzimkhulu river to establish themselves near the Mpondo. To the north-east, the Thonga were very vulnerable to Zulu raiding parties, and were in fact raided, but since they possessed very few cattle and presented no interesting military challenge, they were less harried than they might have been. To the north, beyond the Pongola river and partially sheltered by the Lebombo mountains, refugees were able to establish themselves over and among Ngwane people, where they built up the Swazi nation which will be considered in the next chapter. To the north-west, the open pasture country of the interior table-land offered an attractive raiding ground, whose Sotho inhabitants were obliged to move away from their grazing lands and seek refuge in the mountains or further away to the north. To the west, the Drakensberg offered a refuge in which the Sotho could and did find security and established one of the most interesting and successful political systems of the nineteenth century, under Moshoeshoe who will also be considered in the next chapter.

The area affected was very much larger than the area directly raided by any of Shaka's raiding parties. Refugees from this rule fled the country,

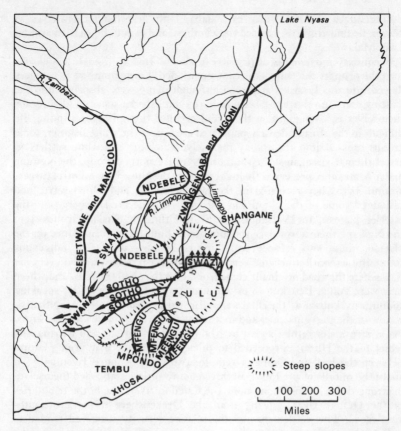

Main movements during the Mfecane

taking their immediate followers with them, often travelling immense distances, and almost always adopting the military system which had originally driven them away. In about 1823, for example, one of Shaka's generals – Mzilikazi – having failed in an expedition, thought it best to flee from the wrath to come. He was unusual in being also the chief of one of the pre-Zulu communities and therefore enjoyed a personal following. He and his followers, who were very familiar with Zulu military and political methods, fled onto the interior plateau, and eventually settled beyond the Limpopo river in what is now Rhodesia. They were described by the Sotho name for all Nguni speakers, Ndebele. Their numbers were expanded by conquest and absorption of the conquered people into the Ndebele community. Similarly Soshangane, a Ndwandwe refugee, in about 1820 fled northwards with a few dozen followers, and established himself as ruler of the Gaza kingdom, over conquered Thonga and Shona peoples in the hinterland of Lourenço Marques. Two similar groups of Nguni, one led by

21

Zwangendaba and the other by Nqaba, both describing themselves as Ngoni, fled northwards, crossed the Zambesi, and eventually settled around Lake Malawi.

Secondary movements of people can also be traced, though less clearly than the primary movements already mentioned. Large numbers of refugees flowed into the Transkei area; and although many were absorbed into the existing communities, most seem to have established a separate identity for themselves as Mfengu (or, as the colonists called them, Fingo). Finding life difficult in the already densely populated areas near the white frontier, some groups crossed into the colony themselves, helping the white settlers to assert themselves against the southern Nguni. Another group, the Ngwane under Matiwane, preserved their old identity despite a very eventful career; around 1818 they retreated in the face of Zwide and Dingiswayo, and dislodged some of the Hlubi who then crossed the Drakensberg onto the interior plateau. In 1822 another raid – this time by Shaka's armies – sent the Ngwane themselves over the mountains onto the plateau. Once on the plateau, these two refugee communities in turn displaced indigenous communities, until it became very difficult to grasp precisely who everyone was, where they had originally come from, how they had travelled and where they were going. Best known of the displaced peoples is a Sotho-speaking community known as the Tlokwa, and ruled at that time by MaNthatisi, widow of the previous chief and mother of the later chief Sekonyela. Three major streams of refugees – led by MaNthatisi, Matiwane and Mpangazita (chief of the Hlubi) – proceeded to pillage the southern interior plateau, between the Vaal and Orange rivers, for two years or more. Eventually, in about the middle of the 1820s, all three communities established themselves in strong defensive positions along the Caledon river, one of the tributaries of the Orange river, flowing from the Drakensberg mountains south-westwards. This settlement and the relative security it offered tended to reduce the severity and frequency of raiding activities. Nevertheless the *Mantatees* has become an English expression to describe any desperate and ruthless roving band. The Sotho communities had been disastrously affected by these movements, and many of these little communities, in turn, fled to the west or the north, spreading the dislocation even further. Only in the area which is now the northern Transvaal were the Pedi and the Venda able to defend themselves successfully and consistently, making use of the mountainous country in which they lived. In the whole country between the Limpopo and the Orange rivers, between the Kalahari desert and the Indian Ocean, only communities blessed with natural defensive positions were able to withstand the flood of raiding and flight. Moreover, the refugees were often obliged to adopt Shakan tactics in order to survive. In this way, people who might never have heard of Shaka nor of the Nguni peoples, found themselves profoundly affected all the same.

While all these movements were taking place, the original agent of the changes was assassinated. Shaka had taken care that no son should be able to challenge his position, but had neglected to take sufficient precautions against his father's other sons. In 1828, during one of Shaka's campaigns to the north – this time against Soshangane in Gaza – two of his half-brothers absented themselves from the army, returned to the capital and assassinated Shaka at his own home. These two brothers – Dingane and Mhlangana – then turned against each other, and Dingane organised Mhlangana's assassination as well. Having already killed another brother, Ngwadi, (a maternal brother of Shaka), Dingane was reasonably secure in possession of the kingdom by the time the army returned from the Gaza campaign. That was the crucial moment of the coup, since the army might well have revenged Shaka's death. However, finding the coup accomplished and Shaka dead, and being in any case discouraged by the failure of the military campaign, the army was in no mood to attempt a counter-coup. Shaka's campaigns had imposed a great strain on them, and since Dingane promised some relaxation of the campaigns and a reign of peace, the regiments were prepared to accept the new state of affairs.

However, it soon transpired that Shaka's revolution was incomplete. Perhaps even Shaka himself could not have completed it, but the un-warlike Dingane certainly could not. The military campaigns which he did conduct were often unsuccessful, and the army grew demoralised. It was dangerous to leave the army idle; on the other hand many of the neighbouring communities had adopted Shaka tactics and were difficult to defeat. Internally, one of the component groups of the Zulu nation – the Qwabe – rebelled and escaped to the south, while Dingane's regiments were powerless to prevent them. Dingane decided that the solution to these problems lay in acquiring firearms from the traders at Port Natal. It is doubtful whether that course of action did represent a solution to the internal political problem, but in any case Dingane's relations with the white traders at the port were not very happy. Increasing numbers of refugees from Dingane's rule sought refuge around the white community: this encouraged Dingane to regard the traders as a possible focus of discontent, and naturally the refugees painted a very unflattering picture of conditions within the kingdom. Despite Dingane's resolution to govern peacefully, he found himself ruling with greater reliance upon fear than Shaka had required. Many political organisations have survived an incompetent monarch, and perhaps the Zulu might also have preserved Shaka's achievements despite Dingane's reign. Unfortunately the Zulu state was about to encounter its most serious challenge so far, in the form of white settlers migrating from the Cape into what later became Natal. In 1837, when they arrived and sent a deputation to meet Dingane, the Zulu state was in sad disarray. Power was centralised in the hands of a monarch whose political control was both arbitrary and unsure, and whose military limitations were such that he could devise no sensible plan to deal with the trekkers. Where Shaka might possibly have devised successful tactics and would probably have kept the community more united, Dingane failed on both counts. He had, in addition, alienated the sympathy of the white traders at the port, whose support would have been very useful. As it was, neither missionaries nor traders saw any reason for trying to avert the destruction of the kingdom. But the greatest weakness of the Zulu state on the eve of the great crisis of 1837 was its failure to form any friendly alliance with neighbouring communities. Neither Swazi nor Ndebele, Sotho nor Mfengu, were prepared to mourn the misfortunes of the Zulu, much less to assist them in their time of trouble. The Zulu state was the only one in the sub-continent which could have led a confederacy of African communities. Because of the manner of its creation, such an alliance was unthinkable, and neither the Zulu nor their neighbours thought of it.

Chapter 3

Defensive nation-building

As we have seen, the emergence of the Zulu military state created a crisis for the neighbours of the northern Nguni. Different communities, of course, reacted in different ways, but one reaction may be described as that of building up a nation strong enough to withstand the pressures applied to it by the Zulu impis. Another reaction, to be dealt with in the following chapter, was to imitate the Zulu achievement in the process of conquering people far removed from the scene of the action. As regards defensive nation-building however, it is convenient to examine the development of two such states – the Swazi under Sobhuza and Mswati, and the Basotho under Moshoeshoe. These will be considered in some detail, and other similar examples will be mentioned briefly at the end of the chapter.

Moshoeshoe was not an innovator in the manner of the Zulu monarch. All his major policies and attitudes, and almost everything he did, had good precedents in the traditions of the southern Sotho people. What was the hall-mark of his greatness was the thoroughness and completeness with which he applied traditional Sotho tactics to the new Difaqane situation. This is not very surprising when one considers that he was born probably in 1786, was initiated into Sotho society, and had imbibed traditional Sotho political culture before the effects of the Mfecane were felt in his homeland to the west of the Drakensberg. His early career seems entirely typical of the life of an ambitious young Sotho of that generation. He and a close friend, Makoanyane, who was later to become a leading general, acquired an early reputation as cattle raiders among the Kwena community into which they were born. Since Moshoeshoe's father was a very undistinguished petty chief, cattle-raiding was really the only way to achieve distinction. Again, like many Sotho before him, he set himself up as chief on a very small scale, endeavouring to acquire a large following by means of generosity and fairness to his subjects. Traditionally, a Sotho chief was supposed to be like a milch-cow, providing a living for his followers: the raided cattle therefore became the economic basis for a political career. Motlumi, a man famous for his wide travelling, extensive knowledge, and judgement of men, predicted that Moshoeshoe would become a great chief: but it was the unique circumstances of the Difaqane which brought Moshoeshoe's talents before a wider public.

Even then, he approached the new problems with traditional ideas. When Hlubi, Ngwane and especially Tlokwa refugees poured over the mountains and threatened the established Sotho communities, Moshoeshoe like many of his contemporaries chose to establish strongholds on flat-topped mountains which were impregnable to attack. After some years of this defensive fighting, he selected a particularly good mountain – Thaba Bosiu – as his headquarters: on top of the mountain were reliable water and a small but good pasture for cattle in case of emergency. Only in 1827, after successfully resisting the attack of Matiwane's Ngwane refugees, did he acquire a wide reputation. By this time the southern Sotho generally were in a desperate condition. Having been raided by the various refugees from the mountains, they badly needed security, food, cattle and – above all – hope. Moshoeshoe was indeed a generous chief, prepared (and able) to provide food and cattle for the destitute. By Sotho custom, the cattle remained his own possession, on loan to his subjects, who were thereby bound to him by ties of gratitude, economic dependence and political loyalty. Like other chiefs before him, Moshoeshoe could use his wealth to build a political following: unlike his predecessors, he could benefit from the unusually large number of impoverished people seeking that kind of clientage relationship. Not only Sotho, but some Nguni refugees as well, found in Moshoeshoe a refuge from the pillage of the plateau.

Another traditional method of building a state among the Sotho was through polygamy, whereby alliances could be cemented with numerous powerful communities and factions. Polygamy was an accepted form of political action, but it is doubtful whether any previous ruler had been quite as polygamous as Moshoeshoe eventually became, having probably more than 100 wives. Inevitably, a large number of sons were born to him, all of whom had to have some administrative post in the political system, and in course of time that proved a severe strain upon the system itself. That was in the future however, and in the short run polygamy was a successful technique for consolidating political power.

Finally, while Shaka and Dingane were striving to build communities in which political power was concentrated in the person of the monarch himself, Moshoeshoe remained in the mainstream of the political culture of his people. When whole communities arrived to seek refuge from him, he permitted them to settle in their existing organisation, retaining their existing chiefs and methods of government. Moshoeshoe became the head of a confederation, not the monarch of a united state: some groups near the headquarters were directly ruled by the central government; other groups further away conducted their own internal administration; and some groups on the periphery of the state were independent in all but name (and sometimes independent in name as well, when it suited their purpose to be so). Political and economic allegiance were, in an important sense, voluntary. If sections of the new community chose to go away, there was nothing to prevent them from doing so. Moshoeshoe had no standing army worth mentioning, and the defence of the community depended upon the ability of the people to defend positions rather than destroy enemies. The Basotho therefore never achieved (nor did they attempt to achieve) anything like the unity and uniformity of the Zulu state. Dialects continued unstandardised, customs remained peculiar to the particular community within the state; and the identification of the people as Basotho was a very slow process indeed. All of these characteristics of Moshoeshoe's rule marked him out as a bearer of the old standards: not only a refuge in the political storm, but also an outpost of traditional chiefly generosity and hospitality and traditional good sense. Even though the state system was a patchwork of variable and voluntary relationships, Moshoeshoe was an attractive focus of the dispossessed Sotho peoples.

Yet it must be stressed that in all these respects Moshoeshoe was not unique. His following in 1833 was probably only about 25,000; and as late as 1848, 80,000 altogether. NaNthatisi's Tlokwa people were also settling around defensible hills in the upper reaches of the Orange and Caledon valleys: Matiwane's Ngwane people, and Mpangazita's Hlubi had done the same. Smaller communities also tended to settle in the foothills west of the mountains. It is Moshoeshoe's great achievement that he conducted foreign relations in such a way as to establish himself as the predominant power in an area contested by many other chiefs. In his domestic policies there is great good sense; but in his foreign policies greatness itself. During 1825, Matiwane's Ngwane and Mpangazita's Hlubi, who had settled close together and close to Moshoeshoe, turned against each other. While Moshoeshoe adopted the policy of sending tribute to any potential aggressor, and thereby avoiding unnecessary conflict, these two rivals forgot the fact that they faced common dangers from both Zulu and Ndebele. In a massive set-piece battle in open country, each side suffered severe losses, Mpangazita was killed, and his followers dispersed. They lost their coherence and their identity, becoming either refugees in other communities, or allowing themselves to be subjected by the victorious Ngwane.

Though Matiwane had apparently won the battle, he had seriously weakened his powers of resistance and continued to over-estimate his military strength. Moshoeshoe quietly continued sending tribute to Shaka and others, thereby turning their animosity in other directions. In 1827, however, Matiwane was attacked in quick succession first by the Zulu and then by the Ndebele. These attacks dislodged him from his mountain refuge, and he was obliged to retreat from the area altogether. The only remaining direction for him and his followers was south, and they duly moved into the territory of the southern Nguni, creating so much havoc that the forces of the Cape Colony were dispatched against him. In 1828 the colonial forces defeated and dispersed his army: Matiwane himself was obliged to return to Zululand where Dingane had no hesitation in putting him to death; his followers found what refuge they could by breaking up and throwing themselves on the mercy of the Xhosa and Thembu who had recently been victims of their raiding. Moshoeshoe, who had played no positive part in these affairs, was immensely strengthened by the removal of these uncomfortable neighbours, and by the addition of many of their people to his expanding community. All that had been necessary was to avoid giving offence to stronger communities, and to repel a feeble attack by Matiwane between the Ndebele campaign and his flight into the border lands of the Cape Colony.

The Tlokwa, however, represented a more serious problem. NaNthatisi was at least as astute as Moshoeshoe himself, and avoided the pitfalls of Matiwane and Mpangazita. Unfortunately for the Tlokwa, her son Sekonyela came of age during the 1820s, claimed his father's political authority, and terminated his mother's regency. In 1829, while Moshoeshoe and many of his followers were absent on a cattle-raid to the east, Sekonyela attacked Thaba Bosiu, and although he failed to take the fortress he did capture some booty. Sporadic warfare between the two communities continued for the next twenty years, during which time Moshoeshoe's people generally prospered more than Sekonyela's, and thereby attracted more followers. The dispute was further complicated by the arrival of missionaries and of white governments in the vicinity and it was not until 1853 that Moshoeshoe found the opportunity to destroy the power of his antagonist, most of whose followers now joined the Sotho. One story relating to the early days of that long duel, which can not be true but which is now widely believed, explains how Moshoeshoe contrived to turn Shaka's attention against Sekonyela. Having sent regular tribute to the Zulu monarch for some time, Moshoeshoe abruptly suspended payment and accused Sekonyela of intercepting the cattle on their way to Zululand. Shaka is supposed to have sent yet another impi against Sekonyela as a result. A story which certainly is true, is that Moshoeshoe sent a present of cattle to the Ndebele after they had failed to storm his headquarters, explaining that they must be raiding through hunger: and this episode may well explain his relative immunity from further trouble in that quarter.

In addition to the problems created by the Difaqane, however, the new community was harried by Griqua and other Coloured parties migrating away from the Cape Colony and attempting to establish themselves in what had been Sotho territory. These groups were equipped with firearms, horses, and often with missionaries as well, and they brought a wider experience of warfare and modern military techniques than the Sotho possessed. On the other hand, Moshoeshoe was quick to perceive the advantages which these groups enjoyed, and adopted a policy of acquiring riding horses, firearms and even missionaries. As a result, although he was unable entirely to dislodge these new immigrants from the Caledon valley, and although he failed to assert his political supremacy over them, he was at least able to contain them and prevent them from expanding into the heartland of the new Basotho community.

Against the white communities, however, Moshoeshoe enjoyed far less success. His construction of a great new state in the interior had been accomplished mainly by means of traditional policies. These policies provided little information or suggestion as to the new situation. The white farmers refused to become absorbed into Sotho society, nor would they restrict themselves to limited areas of open country. Imperial British policy, too, was somewhat erratic, as it affected events north of the Orange river.

28

Traditional Sotho wisdom provided no insight into the motives and methods of these new factors in the situation. Moshoeshoe realising this, immediately decided to recruit some of the whites into his own ranks, the better to study them and if possible to win some to his own side. In the early 1830s French Protestant missionaries were 'recruited' by Moshoeshoe to come to Lesotho. They saw themselves as evangelists, but Moshoeshoe's ideas differed. They were, for example, positioned on the outskirts of the community, where their presence might help to discourage attacks. Furthermore, though he took great interest in their religious beliefs, and permitted (indeed encouraged) his sons to receive instruction, he did not permit himself to be converted. If any of his wives were converted, he granted them divorce: but if he himself had been converted the value of polygamy as an instrument of diplomacy would have been destroyed. J. M. Orpen was also recruited from the farmers' republic, and occasionally deserters from the British army were admitted to the community, to provide instruction in armaments and in military tactics. By the 1850s Moshoeshoe was probably better informed about the ways of the white communities than any contemporary African ruler. In the long run, however, that was of little value.

At the same time as having to deal with the problems of white settlement around and within his borders, Moshoeshoe had to begin to tackle a problem inherent in his style of government. Unlike the Zulu, his people were not a united community, nor was the political system centralised. It depended largely upon a network of differing obligations between Moshoeshoe and a multitude of local chiefs. The pitso, or assembly, was a crucial decision-making body throughout Moshoeshoe's reign. The network of alliances was a personal creation, depending to a great extent upon the personality of the paramount chief: the term king does not apply to Moshoeshoe in the way that it applies to some of his contemporaries. As Moshoeshoe advanced in age so the system became harder to operate. Further, a consequence of polygamy was a multitude of sons, all of whom felt entitled to chiefly positions and prestige. In pre-colonial times, many of these sons would probably have broken away and formed independent chiefdoms: but in the 1850s there was nowhere for them to go. Nor was there any way – in Sotho tradition – of ensuring that the succession passed to one son. As the years passed, so more and more of Moshoeshoe's sons clamoured for some of their father's power. Some could be appointed over people who accepted Moshoeshoe's authority completely: but very often such a group of people resented the imposition of an 'alien' chief in place of a kinsman. Inevitably also, following Sotho tradition, these sons were anxious to acquire fame for their courage and raiding ability. Whatever policy Moshoeshoe might adopt towards his neighbours, there was little chance of his sons behaving in a peaceful manner. The high spirits of these sons immensely complicated the task of conducting foreign relations.

By the 1840s, Moshoeshoe had achieved a traditional Sotho ambition through the application of traditional Sotho wisdom, in a situation of unprecedented difficulty for the people who gathered around him. It was very much a personal achievement and it is possible that, in the event of his death, it might have fragmented like other charismatic states. The durability of his creation was largely a consequence of events in the last twenty years of his life. If he had died in the 1840s at the end of a sufficiently remarkable career, it would not be necessary to say any more about him. However, he lived on into the 1860s, through an even more difficult period for his people, and with increasing domestic problems to contend with. How he dealt with the white threat to his creation will be discussed in Chapter 6.

In what became the Swazi nation, the core comprised the ruling Dlamini clan and some ten other subordinate clans. This small community lived north-eastward of present Swaziland, until a conflict with the Ndwandwe – another Nguni-speaking group – obliged them to move southward to their present location towards the close of the eighteenth century. Under Ndungunya (?1780–1815) the community closely resembled its neighbours, both in size and in the nature of political authority. Decision-making was shared between the ruler, a council of chiefs (*liqoqo*) and a national council (*libandla*) and the ruler never became an autocrat in the manner of the Zulu kings. The balance of power between these bodies changed over time, but essentially the Swazi people survived the Mfecane by means of altering, rather than overthrowing, their traditional political system.

Sobhuza I, who became king in 1815, steered the community through a series of crises until his death in 1836. During the Mfecane it was clearly necessary to provide for the stream of refugees from broken communities, and if possible to build up the size of one's own following. During Sobhuza's reign a further eight clans accepted the authority of the Dlamini. Unlike most of the earlier clans, these were Sotho-speaking, with rather different social and political traditions. Sobhuza's followers therefore classified themselves in three groups: the 'true Swazi', those 'found ahead' in Swaziland by the Dlamini, and those who were absorbed later into the nation, as a result of conquest or seeking refuge. Such a division within the nation was obviously dangerous. Unlike Shaka, but in the Dlamini tradition, Sobhuza permitted the new-comers to retain any chiefs they might have possessed, and to retain a distinct culture if they so wished. Political authority, in other words, was very loose. So long as the Zulu continued to menace the area, the clans were happy to remain part of the Dlamini following.

Realistically, Sobhuza I appreciated that his following was not strong enough to challenge the military power of the Zulu, nor of the Ndebele, and therefore that the community must retain friendly relations with its neighbours as far as possible. Partly, that objective could be achieved by living in difficult country: the hills and caves of Swaziland posed great difficulties for invading armies. In addition, however, Sobhuza applied the traditional remedy of marriage-relations. After the clashes with the Ndwandwe, for instance, he married the daughter of Zwide, their ruler. He further sent a number of Swazi girls to Shaka, including princesses of the Dlamini clan. Even when Shaka ordered the killing of some of these girls once they had become pregnant, Sobhuza refused to be provoked into warfare. With a measure of peace abroad, the internal process of national integration could continue unchecked.

His successor, Mswati, enjoys a more aggressive reputation among the Swazi, who have taken his name as their own, discarding the earlier identity of Ngwane. Unlike his father, Mswati had matured during the revolutionary years of the Mfecane, and was less interested in traditions, and more interested in military organisation, than any of his predecessors. His succession to the throne was followed by two successive Zulu attacks – in 1836 and 1837 – which underlined the importance of creating a reliable military machine. At that time, military power depended upon the clan leaders and chiefs who would mobilise their immediate followers. That system was cumbersome and not entirely reliable, since it depended upon a series of decisions by a series of military authorities without centralised command. Mswati set about adapting the Zulu military organisation to his people. Age-set regiments were introduced, and quartered in barracks throughout the country: officers became directly responsible to the central command. While the national councils remained effective, district authorities were now more closely controlled in the exercise of administration. Female relatives of the king could be used as informers in the provinces, reporting on any potentially subversive activity – in much the same way as Shaka's female relatives served him. The new regiments needed practice, since the encounters with the Zulu had normally involved retiring into the caves, rather than venturing open battles which would almost certainly be lost. Concentrating on weaker communities, the Swazi regiments began to raid throughout a large area to the north. The Sutu, to the north-west, were raided and robbed of their fine herds of cattle. An ambitious attack was also launched against the Pedi further north, but the Pedi in their hill defences were able to repel the invaders. An attack was also sent against the Shangane kingdom in southern Mozambique, but also unsuccessfully. Only when the founder of that kingdom – Soshangane – died in 1859, were the Swazi able to intervene safely in that direction. Even then the Swazi were less than effective, and despite their support Mawewe lost the succession war against his brother Mzila. Nevertheless the training was useful, and if the Swazi were not entirely successful, they did at least keep warfare at a safe distance from their own borders. More important, as in Zululand, national service proved a powerful instrument of nation-building, and it is no accident that the Swazi accepted Mswati's name as their new national identity.

Mswati was, in fact, much more successful internally than in his foreign military adventures. A polygamist himself, he encouraged polygamy among his followers as well: partly to provide homes for female captives, but partly also for a greater social purpose. Mswati's wives were drawn from a wide range of society; and his female relatives were similarly distributed as wives throughout the clans and lineages of the community. When his followers accepted and imitated this practice, a great change was initiated: intermarriage had the effect of destroying the old divisions between the clans of the nation, and the effect was felt very swiftly. Though the Swazi continued to suffer occasional raids from Zulu regiments (especially in the 1840s and

1850s when the Zulu felt unable to raid in other directions), and although these attacks could not be defeated militarily, the Swazi nation nevertheless preserved its unity. Again, the regiments may not have been impressive by comparison with other armies, but they served an economic purpose as well. In addition to military activities, the regiments performed construction work, and each military camp was economically self-sufficient. In this way the soldiers were prevented from becoming a superior, powerful but unpopular caste in the society. Altogether, a collection of friendly clans was transformed during Sobhuza's and Mswati's reigns into a coherent and centralised kingdom, well able to survive even so close to the centre of Zulu military power. That ability, in turn, resulted much more from internal unity than from the indifferent success of the Swazi regiments in warfare. Though the development of the Sotho and Swazi nations followed very different procedures, they do illustrate the fact that an intelligent adaptation of traditional political attitudes and practices could assist particular communities to survive the crisis. It is also clear that the rulers found it necessary to expand the scale of their rule, beyond any previous size; and they were assisted in this development by the existence of large numbers of refugees anxious to attach themselves to some powerful patron. The expansion of the size of the political system naturally imposed some strain, and it became necessary at least to modify the old political structure. The desirability of having a reliable standing army also involved some changes in the balance of power within the community. The king, as commander-in-chief, was inevitably more powerful than his predecessors. The authority of Mswati was that of a monarch advised by national councils: Ndungunya's authority had rested very largely upon the consent of clans which preserved a sense of separateness. In Lesotho, Moshoeshoe's authority resembled that of a chairman at a meeting of chiefs; but even so, his power was greater than that of any Sotho leader before him, and he can fairly be described as the first Sotho paramount chief.

These changes influenced not only the chiefs and officials at the top of the administrative hierarchy: ordinary people were also profoundly affected. In varying degrees throughout the new communities, the politics and economics of kinship were supplemented (and sometimes replaced) by the politics and economics of nation-states. There was a difference in kind between being a subject of Ndungunya and being a subject of Mswati, since many decisions previously made by a family or by a group of kinsmen were now influenced by policy and power emanating from a central government. In that kind of decision-making, the freedom of local clans was severely restricted; but on the other hand the survival of the new communities depended directly upon the loyalty of its citizens, and the importance (if not the power) of the local groups was thereby enhanced. One of the things that was happening in Swaziland and to a lesser extent in Lesotho, was the mobilisation of the ordinary people into a new political identity and a new feeling of community with the other people in the nation. It is possible in the mid-nineteenth century to speak of Zulu, Swazi and Sotho nationalism in a manner which was impossible half a century earlier.

Space does not allow a discussion of comparable changes taking place in other communities at much the same time. It might, however, be worthwhile to notice changes taking place among the Pedi in north-central Transvaal, the Mfengu refugees in the eastern Cape, and the ravaged Tswana communities along the border of the Kalahari desert. All of these peoples were deeply affected by the events of the Mfecane, and all of them were obliged to overhaul their traditional political habits. Whether the same process of centralisation and nationalism took place amongst them is not clear: but certainly some changes occurred. It is dangerous to assume anything in history, but it is a reasonable guess that the success of the Swazi and Sotho in their policy of defensive nation-building was imitated by other communities facing similar dangers.

Chapter 4

African imperialism

In describing the development of the Ndebele state, the Kololo conquerors in Barotseland, and other political systems which date their origin to the troubled times of the Mfecane, imperialism seems an appropriate term to use. It has however certain difficulties. Today, the use of the word implies not only a political system based upon military strength but also an economic system based upon the behaviour of capital. The economic system of the Ndebele conquerors bears some but not much resemblance to the economic systems involved in European imperialism of the nineteenth century; nevertheless the word imperialism can be used if we are careful to exclude the economic aspect of the definition. More seriously, the problem of military strength poses difficulties. Every political system depends to at least a limited extent upon possession of military power, either to suppress internal disorders, or to control crime, or to withstand external attacks. What can be said is that a state becomes imperialist when its control depends to a very great extent upon the military powers used to subordinate people who would not voluntarily accept the system. Hence we have not described the Zulu state as an empire, since it appears that, very shortly after the conquest and incorporation of each of the conquered peoples, most accepted their new identity without much resentment. Further, when the Zulu army was disbanded (first in the late 1830s and second in the 1880s) the political community and the people's identity survived. Nevertheless, the expanding Zulu kingdom contributed to the creation of empires elsewhere in Southern Africa and it is these new political systems which we should now examine.

The classic example of African imperialism is perhaps that of Mzilikazi. He was the son of a pre-Mfecane chief, but was young enough to adapt to the requirements of the new era. Although he was by nature a good-humoured and affectionate young man, he entered military and administrative service under Shaka. He became one of Shaka's generals, and eventually fled from Zululand in 1823, at the head of two or three hundred soldiers and their dependents. Other refugee groups joined them, and Sotho communities which they conquered were absorbed into the new political and social unit. First these refugees settled near where Pretoria now stands and the indigenous Sotho people described them as Ndebele – the Sotho name for the Nguni – a title which was accepted. The new community was defeated in battle by white emigrants from the Cape, and in 1838 moved northwards into what is now western Rhodesia. There Mzilikazi built up the new Ndebele nation until his death in 1868, when he was succeeded by his son Lobengula. Decades earlier, other Nguni groups had migrated inland and been described as Ndebele; but Mzilikazi's Ndebele differed from these earlier communities in almost every important respect. This was a new creation, and it is worth asking how it was created.

Because of their Zulu background, Mzilikazi and his followers derived much of their ideas and policies from the Shakan model. Chiefs were responsible to the monarch, who could and did dismiss them when he felt it necessary. The new nation was geared to war, and the basis of political power was the regimental system. As in Zululand, the economy was as centralised as the polity. Mzilikazi controlled not only the herds of the community, but also a substantial number of captured girls, who were (in one sense) an important form of wealth. Royal cattle could be used to reward loyal servants and soldiers, or to underpin the political loyalty of whole communities. The girls could be given as brides, and Mzilikazi himself sometimes provided the bride-price if the bridegroom were too poor to do so. Also following Nguni tradition, the female relatives of the monarch performed a useful role in supervising the administration of other chiefs in areas far removed from the king's court. However, it was not simply Nguni tradition, but more precisely Zulu tradition, on which the new state tended to draw for experience. At first the state was more like an army of occupation than a civil organisation. When civil administration became necessary however, it was the regimental system which provided it. However the essential problem facing the Ndeble was more complex than that facing the Zulu. Unlike the Zulu, Mzilikazi's subjects were not homogeneous in origin. Nguni, Sotho, Rozwi and Tswana, all comprised his following. The regimental system was not, by itself, sufficient to create a new and durable nation.

To the problem of assuring the loyalty of distinct groups of subjects was added the problem that the Ndebele quickly developed into a caste society. The original Nguni members regarded themselves as the proper ruling caste – the Zansi – with monopoly rights over responsible positions. The Sotho who had been absorbed in the 1820s and 1830s – the Enhla caste – were steadily working towards their own acceptance into the aristocracy. Those conquered from the Shona states – the Rozwi or Holi caste – were very recent additions and had no status within the community. What made that problem particularly dangerous was that most of the original Shona communities of the Rozwi confederacy, and even the Rozwi Mambo himself, remained unconquered and hostile to the intruding Ndebele. Any alliance between the independent external Shona and the internal Holi caste would make the survival of the Ndebele state extremely hazardous. Though many Shona communities agreed to pay regular tribute to the Ndebele, these theoretically subordinate communities were more likely to be hostile than friendly towards the interlopers. Finally, as we shall see, the risk of external attacks from the south was never far from Mzilikazi's mind; and to resist these, it was obviously sensible to bring about as great a degree of unity within the state as humanly possible.

Zulu experience offered a partial remedy, in the form of the age-regiments. Promising young men from the lower castes and volunteers from neighbouring communities were enlisted into these organisations, which served to assimilate all the servicemen into Ndebele customs, the Sindebele language and loyalty to the regime of Mzilikazi. Promotion and honour within the army were available to any serviceman of whatever ethnic origin; and so the regiments provided a nation-building – as well as a nation-protecting – function. Since civil administration was normally conducted by ex-soldiers, success in the army opened out even greater prospects after a man's retirement, if he proved competent first as a soldier and then as an administrator. In this way ethnic differences were quickly minimised as sources of internal weakness. The great test of the assimilation policy came in 1868, when Mzilikazi died and Lobengula succeeded him after a disputed succession and a civil war. At this point, the lower castes could have rebelled against Ndebele authority altogether, and perhaps have overthrown the state. They did not, and the state and the society survived intact. By that time the Ndebele were a nation-state rather than an empire, and the army could concentrate on external affairs rather than internal order.

External dangers were always a lively possibility. Attack from the Zulu quarter was an obvious risk; but so, too, was attack from the south. Most of the mixed communities of Griqua and Kora, as we have seen, settled quite peacefully along the Orange river banks; but the borders of white settlement also attracted more energetic and less peaceful elements. In 1829, for example, an alliance was formed specifically to attack the Ndebele. In the alliance were Jan Bloem – a half-caste outlaw – several Kora and Griqua individuals bored by agriculture and several groups of Tswana. Armed with muskets, and taking the Ndebele by surprise, the allies had an easy victory, but were then pursued and ambushed at dawn by Ndebele regiments which had been absent during the initial attack. In this case, only the overconfidence of the allies and their failure to post sentries, saved the Ndebele from great loss. Shortly afterwards a similar alliance was formed by Barend-Barends, another half-caste, who achieved exactly the same temporary success, and met exactly the same fate. Though the Ndebele were successful, their position was clearly perilous, and even before the fatal encounter with the white trekkers in the 1830s, Mzilikazi was thinking of a further retreat beyond the range of the armed and mounted Coloured communities. This constant risk during the formative years of the Ndebele state doubtless contributed to Mzilikazi's sense of urgency in welding together the separate groups within his nation.

The fate of the Gaza Empire north-east of the Swazi is an illustration of the perils of empire-building, when the monarch was less sensible and thoughtful than Mzilikazi and Lobengula. Soshangane, the head of the Gaza clan of the Ndwandwe people, fled before Shaka's attacks in 1821. Like Mzilikazi, his followers numbered only a hundred or so soldiers and their dependents. These people became known as the Shangane, derived from the name of their leader. At first they raided throughout the Thonga country, and into the easternmost chieftaincies of the Shona, but then settled down to dominate the Thonga on a more systematic basis. Unfortunately, the territory they chose was extremely unhealthy, and the new rulers had no resistance to the diseases which were endemic. While they could consistently control the disunited Thonga they had no defence against malaria or cattle diseases. Furthermore, they gained few followers from Zululand, and were destined to remain a very small minority within their sphere of power. Nor was it possible to absorb the Thonga piece-meal, by making some of them honorary Nguni. Their sense of insecurity may perhaps explain why they felt it necessary to demonstrate their power so frequently. Other Nguni refugees were driven off; the Portuguese settlements on the coast were destroyed; and there was little respite for the Thonga during Soshangane's reign. As a consequence, the Shangane people made unnecessary enemies for themselves, and helped contribute to the final destruction of the Gaza empire. On the other hand, the empire at its height was a very considerable power. In 1828 they defeated a Zulu army shortly before the assassination of Shaka, when it was still extremely difficult to resist Zulu military power. The decline and collapse of the Gaza empire cannot be explained in terms of military incompetence. On the contrary, military efficiency may have contributed to over-confidence and a failure to attend to the political problems of nation-building.

Essentially the failure is attributable to the Shangane's failure to resolve the problem facing all conquest states: how is the loyalty (or at least the acquiescence) of the conquered people to be assured? Assimilation failed, either because it was not attempted or because the numbers involved made it impossible. The Thonga did not learn to speak Nguni, and therefore language remained as a mark of differentiation between conquerors and conquered. More seriously, the age regiments did not contribute to a sense of single identity. Some Thonga were enrolled into the armies, but they were confined to their own regiments and did not serve alongside the descendents of the conquerors. Further, they were put under the authority of officers drawn exclusively from the ruling caste. It was even believed that, in time of battle, the most dangerous positions were given to the Thonga regiments. It followed that Thonga could not be promoted to important positions within either the army or the administration; and indeed the only eminent Thonga were chiefs who, by submitting easily, were permitted to remain in charge of their old areas. The conquered people were not only despised by their conquerors, but realised that they were despised. Gaza remained an empire; unlike the Ndebele state it did not develop into a nation. As a result, the conquerors behaved as if they were still an occupying army. And to make matters worse, in his old age Soshangane believed that he was bewitched by Thonga, and accordingly massacred a few of them. When he died, he bequeathed to his heirs a large variety of enemies – Portuguese, Swazi, Pedi, Zulu, Shona and especially Thonga.

If there had been only one claimant to the throne, the succession might have proceeded smoothly, and the state might have survived in reasonably good order. As it was, one son (Mzila) was supported by the Portuguese, and another (Mawewe) by the Swazi, and the succession war was greatly protracted to the advantage of the external allies of each contestant. Mzila's victory also gave the Portuguese a foothold in the country which they had previously lacked. The Gaza empire survived Mzila's reign, and even that of his successor Gungunyana, but its power steadily declined until there was a serious Thonga uprising towards the end of the century. The empire quickly collapsed into the hands of the Portuguese during the 1890s, leaving the Thonga (by now known as Shangane) disrupted but otherwise unaffected by their unwelcome masters. Unlike the Ndebele state, the Gaza organisation was unable to survive colonial conquest.

A similar case is to be found in the Makololo conquest of the Barotse in upper Zambesi. The conquest itself was undertaken by a group of Sotho, displaced by the Mfecane, and led by Sebitwane. Moving northwards in search of security, they skirted the Kalahari desert and, avoiding the Ndebele, arrived at the Zambesi river during the early 1830s. So long as the Lozi state remained intact, it was impossible for the Kololo to move further north. However, a serious civil war broke out among the Lozi in 1833, and Sebitwane took the opportunity to invade the country and establish Kololo rule over all the warring factions. Immediately the problem of relations with conquered people came to the fore. Sebitwane realised that his minority of conquerors would have to come to some sort of compromise, and he resolved to allow equal status and opportunity to the aristocracy of the Lozi community. The aristocrats responded warmly to these opportunities, and in so doing they permanently adopted the language and customs and attitudes of the conquering Sotho people. Like the Shangane, the Kololo had moved from a healthy to a very unhealthy climate, which affected them very forcibly since they were without immunity. With the passage of time, therefore, the power of the conquerors was bound to diminish, and although they did not realise this, it would have been expedient for them to come to terms while their numbers and strength were still sufficient for them to have a bargaining position. Age-regiments and equality of opportunity for the old aristocracy seemed a very promising way of dealing with this dangerous situation.

Unfortunately for the Kololo, Sebitwane was succeeded by Sekeletu in the 1850s, who lost sight of his father's political objectives. The founder of the conquest state enjoyed a charismatic aura which his successor could not inherit. As a leper, living in self-imposed isolation, he was unable to arouse any personal loyalties. Perhaps because of panic at the continued toll of diseases, which affected immigrants much more than indigenous groups, Sekeletu determined to recapture all power for the Kololo conquerors. In consequence, his rule was much harsher and less tolerable than Sebitwane's, and discontent grew very quickly. Outside the area of Kololo control malcontents gathered around Sepopa, as representative of the pre-Kololo rulers. In 1864 Sepopa's army defeated Sekeletu's and all

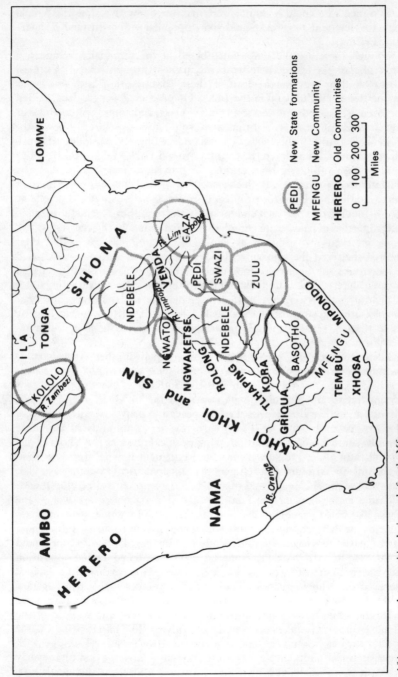

African states and communities during and after the Mfecane

Kololo men who could be found were massacred: by that time the Kololo were too few and too weak – and too unpopular – to withstand a determined rising.

Though these are the best remembered of the imperialist refugees, a series of more or less destructive bands passed through central Southern Africa on their way north. Two of these communities, both known as Ngoni, fled from Zululand in the 1820s. One, led by Zwangendaba, raided northwards, clashed with the Shangane in Gaza, and continued northwards across the Zambesi in 1835. From there splinter groups spread into south-western Tanzania in the 1840s. The second, led by Nxaba, followed much the same route, but entered the country around Lake Malawi. Both groups lived by their military power, raiding for provisions at first from necessity and later from preference. Both absorbed conquered communities into their ranks; and both delayed the problem of relations with conquered people by simply moving on after each conquest. By the time they reached Tanzania, the proportion of true Nguni among these Ngoni must have been very small. However, their major historical significance in this context is that their passage shattered the surviving kingdom of Mwene Matupa, and caused havoc among the Shona paramount chieftaincies, which were ill-prepared to resist determined and efficient military attacks. As a result, the states of central Southern Africa were left vulnerable to later intrusions, not only by other groups of Africans dislodged by the Mfecane, but also by white traders, settlers and administrators who arrived later in the nineteenth century.

These empires and marauding bands compelled other African communities, over a large area, to reconsider their systems of government and defence. Just as the Zulu obliged the Sotho and Swazi to devise new administrative and defensive techniques, so the Ndebele, Ngoni, Gaza, Mfengu and other groups disturbed the peace and provoked reorganisation. Perhaps the most vulnerable and hard-pressed community at this time were the southern-most Nguni-speaking people, known as the Xhosa. They were already under pressure from white settlement flowing from the west, by the time the Mfecane sent refugees to press upon them from the east. Half a century of racial contacts and quarrels on the frontier had produced considerable congestion on the land already. To make matters worse, the Xhosa had failed to achieve any kind of internal unity amongst themselves. None of the distinct political units which collectively comprised the Xhosa was prepared to sacrifice its independence. Increased pressure upon land seems even to have intensified internal feuds, and no concerted opposition could be presented to white or black intrusion. One further circumstance confused the Xhosa situation. Traditionally, younger sons setting up new political systems had moved westwards in order to do so. As a result, the migrating white farmers first encountered the smallest and weakest of the Xhosa groups – Gunukwebe, Ntinde and others. The latter, being unable to offer serious resistance, tended to flow eastwards to seek refuge with larger political units. Refugees were therefore arriving simultaneously from the west (dislodged by white pressure) and from the north-east.

In the early nineteenth century the most powerful Xhosa chief was probably Hintsa, of the Galeka, whose following exceeded 10,000, and whose seniority was recognised by numerous other chiefs including the Gaika. However, although many chiefs acknowledged Hintsa's seniority as representative of the most distinguished family, few were willing to accept his orders or advice. Colonial officials and farmers across the border were often hostile towards Hintsa, and may have encouraged Xhosa chiefs to oppose him, though that should not have influenced Xhosa opinion. An interesting attempt was made by Maqoma, perhaps the most astute strategist among the Xhosa, to bring all the chiefs into a military alliance. He recognised that political unity was impossible in the face of the jealousy and pride of numerous leaders, but believed that military association should nevertheless be possible. However, he was not himself a substantive chief, but the regent until a child grew up to inherit the chieftaincy. Despite his military and diplomatic skill, therefore, he could never command but could only recommend. Significantly, in his old age he gave up hope and settled on the colonial side of the border, despairing of Xhosa unity even in adversity. Xhosa unity was not attained by military or political means, and the Xhosa were therefore buffetted by a series of external difficulties. And if Xhosa unity were impossible, unity between them and their Thembu, Mpondo and Mpondomise neighbours was quite inconceivable.

Greater success was enjoyed by the Pedi people in what is now the eastern Transvaal. To the east they were marauded by the Gaza, to the north-west by the Ndebele, and to the south-east by the Swazi. When the Ndebele moved out of Zululand, their first victims were the Pedi, who were at that time divided by a succession dispute. All but one of the claimants were killed, but one claimant to the leadership – Sekwati – fled northwards and survived. When the Ndebele passed on to the west, Sekwati re-emerged and established himself as the Pedi leader. By the middle of the 1820s he had sufficiently restored the coherence of the Pedi to be able to repel further raids by Ndebele regiments, by the Swazi, and even by the Zulu themselves. Defence was facilitated by control over the Lulu mountains, which could be used as a refuge in case of attack, much as Moshoeshoe and Mswati also employed mountain fortresses. How Sekwati accomplished that feat of political and military reconstruction is not clear; but by the time he died in 1861 his people were still independent. His son and successor, Sekhukhune, remained a thorn in the flesh of the white settlers in the region until the fourth quarter of the nineteenth century, when he was defeated by a combined force of British, Swazi and Afrikaner troops. Even after that disaster, the Pedi remained a potential source of danger to the white farmers, on account of their internal unity and their defensive positions in the mountains.

Individual Tswana chiefs also contrived to re-form their followers and to re-establish a political organisation after the disruption caused by Ndebele, MaNthatisi and Ngoni armies. The BamaNgwato were fortunate in possessing a series of remarkable leaders in Sekgoma, Macheng and Khama, who organised the broken communities into a new political system. Sensibly preferring safety to dignity, they accepted the nominal overlordship of the Ndebele to the north-east, and paid tribute in exchange for being left alone. In peace they could build up the herds of cattle upon which they depended for a living. Similarly, the Kwena under Sechele, and the Ngwaketse under Gaseitsiwe, re-grouped themselves. Along the fringe of the Kalahari desert the process of reconstruction was assisted by the fact that the refugees had literally nowhere to go if they resisted the centralising ambitions of the new generation of chiefs. They could not move eastwards, on account of the Ndebele and then the white farmers; the desert prevented them from moving westwards; to the south lay the borders of the Cape Colony; and to the north lay desert and swamp and eventually the Ndebele as well. The only hope for the refugees lay in accepting the chiefs who were attempting to re-establish authority.

Imperialism was neither the only, nor the most promising, way of life for refugee groups. Many became clients of patrons who had the military power to provide protection. Many clans and families fled in this manner to Moshoeshoe, Sobhuza and Sekonyela. An interesting variation of the clientage theme was devised by remnants of the Hlubi, Zizi and Bhele communities when the Zulu dispersed them from what is now central Natal. Moving south, some conquered land from Xhosa groups, but most attached themselves to Xhosa patrons. Being refugees, they were described by the Xhosa term for refugees – Mfengu (sometimes corrupted into Fingo). Their new situation was little better than what they had left behind. The Xhosa had neither the resources, nor perhaps the interest to assist large numbers of landless and impoverished immigrants. A series of frontier wars against the Colony further weakened the Xhosa. In 1836, after a particularly disastrous border war, several thousand Mfengu abandoned their Xhosa patrons, crossed the frontier and joined forces with the colonists. There they received land of their own, conquered from the Xhosa. In effect the Mfengu had become corporate clients of the Colonial government, instead of family clients of Xhosa family-heads. The Xhosa, naturally, were furious, and the resulting Xhosa–Mfengu feud weakened the capacity of both communities to offer any resistance to colonial pressures.

If imperialism were not the only alternative, but a very dangerous policy involving constant alert and perpetual risk of internal revolt, nevertheless it was an attractive option. Where empires were established, they had a local effect similar to that of the Zulu state. Neighbours were first attacked and if possible destroyed, but then attempted to reorganise themselves in order to resist further raiding. Small groups were dislodged, to roam the interior either as potential clients or as sub-imperialists on their own account. The dislocation and re-grouping affected – to differing degrees – every community from the Lozi state to the Cape frontiers, and from lake Malawi to the Kalahari desert. These movements and hostilities, in turn, profoundly affected the attitude of the communities involved towards the white farmers when they, in turn, flowed on to the interior plateau and spilled over into the eastern lowlands.

Chapter 5

Afrikaner republicanism

It is arguable that there were three main influences at work forming the characteristics of the people who later described themselves as Afrikaners. These were their western European origins, inter-action with administration in Cape Town, and inter-action with Africans. These influences were, of course, liable to change, and during the early nineteenth century they did so. As a result, the aims, character and aspiration of the frontier farmers underwent substantial change as well. Since they were to play a leading role in future events in Southern Africa, some comment on their development may not be out of place.

Their contacts with western Europe – the Netherlands, Belgium and western Germany – steadily diminished. The western Europe from which they had migrated no longer existed: nationalism had replaced religion as the main focus of political interest, Britain had replaced the Netherlands as the leading naval power, and the whole intellectual climate changed during the eighteenth and early nineteenth centuries. In addition, circumstances in the Cape were unlike those of western Europe: large-scale grazing was the way to make a living, not small-scale peasant cultivation as in Europe; and the ideas of liberty, fraternity, and equality were not suitable for a racial aristocracy. The Dutch East India Company was pushed out of the Cape by the British in 1795, never to return; and that important link between the farmers and their countries of origin was severed. That link had been like an umbilical cord, which would have had to be severed sooner or later: and shortly before the British expelled the company, the white farmers had risen in revolt, feeling themselves strong enough to stand alone without European assistance.

If Europe had changed, so had the farmers themselves, since they were obliged to adapt themselves to African rather than European circumstances. They were frontiersmen rather than townsmen; their economy was based upon pastoralism; their religion based upon their own laborious reading of the Dutch Bible; their survival based upon each man's ability with a musket; and their society based upon companionship with their own kind. As pastoralists they had to travel light, having fewer material comforts than the townsmen; but they also travelled light intellectually, since schools and colleges and universities were not available for them. The grandsons of the first white settlers differed markedly from the original Dutch farmers: they were more efficient militarily, less tolerant of government, less well educated, and much more self-reliant. To that extent they became much less European, and in the tough conditions of the Cape they began to develop a new identity altogether. White settlers in Kenya remained very British in most of their attitudes, since there was constant communication between themselves and their stay-at-home relations: in the Cape it was different.

Imperial British interests in the Cape, though restricted almost entirely to the strategic naval base of the Cape peninsula, nevertheless brought the British officials into sharp contact with the interior farmers. The farmers had grown accustomed to the casual, ineffective and sometimes corruptible authority of a trading company: the methods of the British officials were rather different in style and in intention. Throughout most of the nineteenth century, British military officers were appointed to the Governorship of the Cape; and in every case the particular Governor was intolerant of the almost anarchic attitudes of the frontiersmen which affronted the nineteenth-century British passion for good order. To a great extent friction arose because the new government tried to govern, not because they attempted to govern in a particular manner. Matters which had been ruled by unwritten convention now became subject to legislation, and to regular court procedures. The British of the early nineteenth century were certainly not democrats, but they did insist upon due legal process and governmental control. Regular circuit courts were introduced in 1811, and their sittings made public in 1813. Legislation in 1809 and 1812 regulated the position, status and rights of Coloured workers, entrenching some of the existing racial discrimination against the Coloured community, but at least bringing them within the view of the courts of justice. The implication that Coloured people could take their white employers to court and possibly win a suit there, provoked considerable annoyance among the white farmers, and provoked a minor rebellion at Slagter's Nek in 1815. It must be kept in mind, however, that the social and political system was a long way from racial equality, and that it was the extension of the law, rather than the liberalism of the law, which aroused such hostility. Even Ordinance 50, passed in 1828, and causing a great outcry among the white farming community, brought about a less than equal situation. White and Coloured people had equal access to the courts, but their legal and civil rights remained different.

A more direct challenge to the racialism of the community was embodied in the legislation against slavery. The industrialisation of Britain had made slavery obsolete in the eyes of Imperial legislators: and in the eyes of the humanitarians it was positively evil. In 1807 the slave trade was abolished throughout British possessions, and in 1833 the institution was also abolished. Slave-owners were compensated by payments of, at most, a third of the slaves' market value. Naturally, this legislation outraged the slave-owners, but it should be noticed that the white farmers depended more on the employment of cheap and 'free' labour than upon slaves, and that it was the principle of slavery rather than its cash value which caused most annoyance. Nevertheless all the legislation mentioned so far had the effect of improving the conditions of free and unfree labour, and to that extent hurt the interests of the employers, who had previously been able to behave much as they wished towards their employees and slaves. Every colonist family was directly, and adversely, affected by this change in status.

A further cause of tension between British authorities and local white settlers stemmed from the British desire to Anglicise the local white population. Rather ineffectually, the Government attempted to encourage the use of English language for all public purposes. It was encouraged in the schools, made compulsory in courts of law, and even pressed upon the Church congregations by the recruitment of Scottish ministers in the absence of Dutch applicants for these positions. In practice, the effect of this policy was very slight indeed, though the use of English in courts was a serious nuisance to those who could not speak it fluently (or speak it at all, in some cases). Few Dutch-speaking children went to school at all; and the Scottish ministers tended to speak Dutch and marry local wives. Considered in conjunction with the assisted immigration of English settlers, however, the Anglicisation policy began to seem very sinister from the farmer's point of view. A more determined Anglicisation policy might have succeeded; a policy of leaving the language issue alone might have avoided friction; but the timid policy actually attempted annoyed the local whites without changing their linguistic habits.

The new officials tried to regulate the frontier, as they tried to regulate everything else. Clearly, one cause of frontier trouble was the trend for white pastoralists to hold vast tracts of land: scattered settlement complicated the tasks of administration, and also increased the pressure upon the frontier itself. In 1813, therefore, the Government offered to lease land within the Colony at very low rentals – but in a regulated manner which would restrict the size of land-holdings. The land-holders (who were seldom legally land-owners) rejected this policy; and if land became scarce within the Colony, they were content to migrate seasonally beyond the border to the north, where grazing land was more plentiful. A more promising policy was adopted in 1820 in order to bring some kind of order to the frontier by means of a close settlement of British immigrants. The conception was that British farmers, on small holdings, would form a barrier between the white pastoralists and the Xhosa peasantry, and would be numerous enough to act unofficially as a garrison as well. However, when the policy was implemented and some 5,000 settlers arrived in 1820, it was found that small-holdings would not support the immigrant families in anything like comfort. Many drifted into the small towns, others expanded their land-holdings, and in any case most of them sympathised with the white pastoralists as against the Xhosa on the other side of the border. The immigration policy therefore intensified the pressure on the land, without bringing any security to the frontier areas.

More frequently, governors tended to believe that if a little more land were annexed, as far as the next river, a defensible frontier could be created.

Since the rivers, and their wooded banks, offered perfect cover for cattle-raiders in both directions, the policy never worked, even when 'neutral' belts were imposed between Xhosa and white farmers. The best known of these attempts, however, was historically very important. In 1834, Governor D'Urban resolved to expel the Xhosa from yet another frontier area, and in their place to settle Mfengu and white farmers. The Imperial Government in London, however, realised that such a policy was not a solution, but an aggravation of the frontier problem, and demanded that the area be handed back. In 1835 therefore the Cape Government abandoned the policy. The effect upon white opinion was electric. The Government had not only complicated the problem of the farmers as employers of labour, but had failed to find them new land, and was even snatching away from them the newly-conquered land which they had expected to occupy. On top of the extension of law, the emancipating legislation, and various other grievances, this was the last straw which broke the farmers' tolerance of the British administration. In 1836 large numbers began to trek out of the Colony, leaving the Government behind them. In doing so, they were encouraged by the recent opening and development of Port Elizabeth near the frontier. While Cape Town had been the sole port, and therefore the sole market, they had been obliged to remain within a few hundred miles of the Cape peninsula; the opening of Port Elizabeth increased their range as pastoralists by several hundred miles. It was also known that Port Natal (now Durban) could be developed into a substantial market and trading outlet for pastoral products.

The third set of influences, those emanating from the African communities, is often overlooked and is less easy to grasp. Most obviously, the farming community defined themselves as non-African: they were Christian while the Africans were usually not; they were European as distinct from African; and they were white. Essentially it was a racial distinction, especially as increasing numbers of Coloured and African families became Christian, and adopted some of the customs and culture of the white community. Their sense of having a separate identity was quickly cultivated by the existence of a large and 'alien' community amongst them. When the extension of British Colonial law threatened to blur the distinction between the races, that also encouraged the farmers to assert the distinction, and to assert it more boldly and articulately than had previously been necessary. Yet however loudly the frontier farmers proclaimed their non-Africanness, they were steadily becoming 'Africanised' as they became less 'European'. At first they described themselves in terms of their economic activity – boer being the Dutch term for farmer – and in this way avoided the question whether they were European or African. However, to make profits from pastoralism they necessarily adopted pastoral habits not unlike those of their African neighbours. A man's value was established by the extent of his herds and his ability to protect them from cattle-thieves, or as a last resort to capture them from wealthier pastoralists. Further, the advance eastwards from Cape Town was also a retreat from the cash economy. Travelling traders did much of their business in kind, whenever there was business to be done. Partially outside a cash economy therefore, economic and social relations tended to resemble those of the non-monetary Xhosa. The position of farm-workers on white farms was sometimes very similar to that of clients to Xhosa family-heads. In each case, the economic relationship was an exchange rather than employment – the labourer being provided with goods and permission to cultivate a bit of land and keep a few head of cattle. Also in each case the social result was a patriarchal community: the patron and his family socially superior to the others, but accepting responsibility for the actions of the labourers even outside working hours (if these were defined), and meting out punishment as sole judge, jury and warder for the whole farm community.

In such a situation, the people who mattered in the white community were the land-holders, who comprised all adult and able-bodied white men. Being several hundred miles away from the protection (as well as the annoyances) of the government in Cape Town, it was this local community which had to provide for most of its military needs. What developed was a military system described as the commando, which was initially a voluntary organisation of all able-bodied males, who would assemble in a crisis, elect leaders for the occasion, and act together until the crisis passed away. Here again, there was a close resemblance between the white farmers and the Xhosa, though the Xhosa being an independent people had a more regularly available leadership. It would be misleading to assert that the white farmers copied the Xhosa: but what is certainly true is that they developed similar social and military institutions, to deal with problems which were frequently identical. By the 1830s the only reliable and important distinctions between white and black on the frontier were that the white farmers had a different language, were normally better armed for military conflict, and were racially distinct. With the passage of time, only race remained as a reliable distinction between the two communities.

When they began to move out of the Colony in 1836, therefore, the frontier farmers had developed a substantial and separate tradition of their own, distinct from that of the British and the farmers in the immediate vicinity of Cape Town. The British insisted upon describing them as 'emigrant farmers' and treating them as reluctant British subjects; but the term Africander (later Afrikander, and eventually Afrikaner) was beginning to be employed and was a much more accurate description. The term implied a European community adapted to an African environment, which was precisely what the 'emigrant farmers' had by this time become. Their attitudes towards Africans were already well-entrenched, their resentment of the British (or indeed any) government was pronounced and a distinctive economic, social and military system had already been created. They were not yet conscious of being a separate nationality (and their numbers were still too small for that to be possible), and they had yet to tackle the problems of state-formation, which immediately pressed upon them when they cast off the authority of Britain.

In order to move into the interior, the emigrants formed themselves into trekking parties; and as in earlier crises they elected leaders of these parties.

Since kinsmen tended to stick together in each party, election was often a matter of family connection and military reputation in the locality. In this manner four considerable leaders emerged to lead the parties: Hendrik Potgieter, Gerrit Maritz, Piet Uys and Pieter Retief, all frontier farmers with military reputations. Three major considerations governed the choice of direction once the parties moved beyond the Colonial boundary: to find grazing country within reach of one of the ports on the east coast, to avoid the more powerful of the African communities and yet to settle close to a plentiful supply of African labour. Nevertheless the possibilities were considerable, and a variety of healthy spots could be found within range of either Lourenço Marques or Port Natal. The trekking parties therefore moved in different directions, weakening their numbers to a dangerous extent. Two parties set off for Lourenço Marques in 1836, for example, and moved down to the lowlands of the Limpopo valley; one party was annihilated by Thonga, and the other by malaria. Climatic difficulties thereafter encouraged the trekkers to restrict their area of settlement to the high veld and to the Natal midlands.

These early parties had taken pains to avoid Mzilikazi's country in what was later the central Transvaal. Other groups were less cautious and in late 1836 Mzilikazi despatched patrols to restrict the movement of the trekkers into his territory. At this point the military superiority of the trekkers came into play. In October 1836, at Vegkop, they formed themselves into a laager – a defensive ring of wagons defending the community – and although they lost their live-stock, they successfully routed a determined attack. In January 1837 they followed up that victory with the aid of the Rolong, launched a mounted attack against the Ndebele and took them completely by surprise. Horses, guns and wagons turned the military scales, and Mzilikazi took his people north of the Limpopo river, out of harm's way. In the course of this contest, Potgieter emerged as a successful military leader, and claimed possession of all Mzilikazi's territory by right of conquest. That claim was unacceptable to other trekker leaders, and complicated relationships between the parties. During 1836 and early 1837 a series of meetings of the leaders had taken place, during which Retief and Maritz had been given office as Governor and President of the whole trekking community, but Potgieter and Uys had been given no positions whatever. Since those offices did not fairly represent the balance of political and military power, the arrangement was unstable, and unity between the trekking parties was not achieved.

Late in 1837 Retief led a party of his followers eastwards, to the passes over the Drakensberg mountains, while he and a small band crossed the mountains to negotiate with the traders in Port Natal and Dingane in Zululand for permission to settle. The traders proved friendly, but Dingane was distinctly alarmed at the proposal to bring white settlers so close to his territory. In order to have time to plan, he sent the Retief party to recover some stolen cattle and other property from Sekonyela. Retief duly tricked Sekonyela into returning the property, and returned to Dingane's court to receive a grant of land in exchange. By that time, however, the trekkers

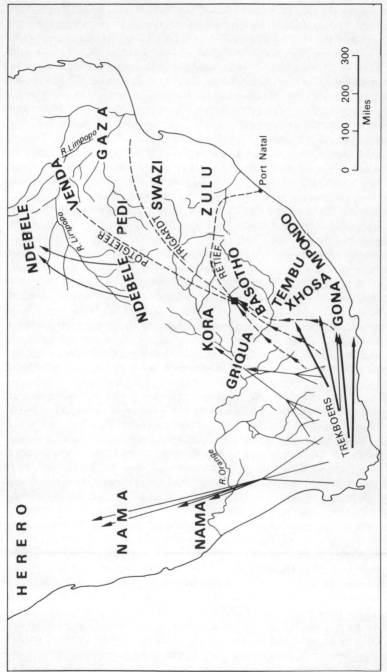

Migration from the Cape c. 1800–c. 1840: Trekboers moving east from the Cape peninsula; Nama, Griqua and Kora moving north from the Cape Colony; Trekkers moving north from the Eastern Cape.

49

had begun to flow over the passes and to enter the land which had not yet been granted to them. Dingane and his advisors naturally regarded such behaviour as a demonstration that the settlers would not accept Zulu authority. It was also clear (after Mzilikazi's defeats) that the trekkers would be formidable enemies. Dingane therefore determined to tackle them by surprise and to destroy them before they were organised. He signed the land-lease which Retief presented to him, but at the following celebrations when the Retief party were without their arms, had them arrested and killed. Regiments were sent off to attack the trekking parties as well. For several months it appeared as if Dingane might have calculated correctly. One trekker encampment was destroyed, though another resisted the attack; and a relieving force of trekkers from the west was ambushed and defeated in April 1838, when an important leader – Uys – was killed. Without the leadership of Retief, Uys and Maritz (who died), the trekkers were in a difficult position. In this crisis, however, a powerful military and political leader emerged in the person of Andries Pretorius, who brought reinforcements from the Cape. In a classic laager battle in December 1838 he destroyed the Zulu army at the battle of Blood river. In that battle three trekkers were injured, and some 3,000 Zulu were killed. When the trekkers could dictate tactics, they were nearly invulnerable.

Following the tradition built up in the Cape, the commandos disbanded as soon as the crisis was over, and spread throughout Natal as the new owners of the land, establishing patriarchal communities almost identical to those on the old frontier. However, as the distinguished historian Walker puts it, to settle in Natal was like Moses and the Hebrews settling in the Red Sea. The waves of Africans south and north of them would not part for long, and Pharaoh (in this case the British) was approaching from the east. An independent white state with access to the coast was a danger to British strategic interests and an obvious threat to peace and order in the Cape's hinterland. A British detachment occupied Port Natal, and after one or two skirmishes in 1842 the trekker republic was annexed as the Colony of Natal. Immediately, most of the trekkers began to move out of Natal to rejoin their independent comrades west of the Drakensberg. But even before they evacuated the colony, they noticed that the waves of Africans were beginning to return. For many African refugees from the Mfecane, white settlement and the defeat of the Zulu state represented an opportunity to return to their old places of residence. Without a permanent military force, and scattered on their vast new estates, the trekkers were unable to prevent this constant trickle of returning refugees, who threatened to engulf them.

The return of most of the Natal party to the interior brought the issues of leadership and form of government to the fore, since Pretorius and Potgieter both claimed supreme authority. In effect, difficulties of communication and the general trekker distrust of organised government ensured that each localised trekker community organised its own affairs without much reference to anyone else, unless a serious crisis arose. Even in a crisis, co-operation could not be guaranteed – Potgieter had failed to

The laager method of defence

support Uys in his attempt to rescue the Natal trekkers during the Zulu war. Religious disputes also divided them, as did attitudes towards the British, since some trekkers regarded themselves merely as economic pioneers while others (especially in the far north) regarded themselves as political refugees. The disputes between Potgieter and Pretorius, autocrats against white democrats, republicans against simple farmers, had not been resolved by 1848, when a fresh challenge was presented to the trekkers, and found them without a stable or strong government.

The challenge was presented by an impetuous military man, Sir Harry Smith, who was Governor of the Cape, and who argued that the only way to prevent trouble from spreading into the Cape from the turbulent trekker states was to annex the area between the Orange and the Vaal rivers. This he did in 1848, describing the new colony as the Orange River Sovereignty; and at the same time annexing a fresh area of Xhosa country as British Kaffraria. The creation of the Orange River Sovereignty enraged the more militant of the trekkers who, under Pretorius, invaded the Sovereignty and attempted to expel the British administration. The Battle of Boomplaats, however, went against them, and the militants retired beyond the Vaal river. Trekker opinion then increasingly polarised into the republic militants of the north and the non-political trekkers of the south who were prepared to tolerate any kind of government so long as it looked after their economic interests. In the event, the Sovereignty proved very difficult to govern, and the Imperial Government reluctant to rule an area of no strategic significance nor visible economic potential. In 1852, by the Sand River Convention, the British formally denied any interest in the Transvaal, and in 1854, by the Bloemfontein Convention, restored the Sovereignty to the trekkers, leaving the boundary between them and Moshoeshoe undecided.

The Orange River Sovereignty, or the Orange Free State as it was re-christened, contrived to hold together as a single trekker republic. Its citizens were less scattered than in the Transvaal, and the ever-present risk of war against Moshoeshoe served to hold the factions together, especially as most burghers lived within 100 miles of the undefined borders of Lesotho. As early as 1854 they agreed upon a constitution modelled upon the United States but modified so as to enfranchise white citizens only, and they ratified the position of President Hoffman. Hoffman happened to be a friend and admirer of Moshoeshoe, and in 1855 the white citizens deposed him for supplying some gunpowder to the Sotho leader. Nevertheless the community survived the difficulties of a constitutional crisis, and elected Boshof in Hoffman's place. Both the Cape Colony and the Transvaal were anxious to annex the little republic, and when it lost a war against Moshoeshoe in 1858 it looked as if it would have to abandon its separate identity in exchange for assistance from one of these neighbours. From 1858 until 1864 it was in fact ruled by President Pretorius of the Transvaal who was attempting to become President of both republics at the same time. Nevertheless the trekkers in the Free State held on to their separate identity and when Pretorius had to resign in 1864, Free State autonomy was restored, and for the next 24 years was ruled by President Brand. A successful war against Moshoeshoe in 1865 onwards consolidated the trekkers into a durable political system.

In the Transvaal, formal independence was followed by many years of intermittent civil war, similar in many respects to the Congo crisis from 1960 onwards. In the early 1850s there were four separate communities north of the Vaal, each with its own military-political leader. None of these communities was anxious to surrender its separate identity. The two most prominent leaders were Pretorius (in the central area) and Potgieter (in the far north); and although both were dead by 1854, each was succeeded by an equally ambitious heir – Pretorius by his son, and Potgieter by Stephanus Schoeman who later married Potgieter's widow. Though a single constitution for all these communities was adopted in 1855, no one paid it much attention. Only in 1858, after modifications to the constitution in order to satisfy the northerners, was the document accepted by three out of four communities, and only in 1860 did the last of the communities join in the united republic. The son of the first President Pretorius, Pretorius the younger, became President of this unwieldy republic. Since he was simultaneously serving as President of the Orange Free State, however, the Transvaalers insisted that he limit his great ambition and satisfy himself with one presidency at a time. When he ignored this instruction civil war broke out, which ended only in 1864 when he abandoned the Orange Free State and returned to the presidency of the Transvaal.

This account of faction-fighting among the trekkers does not provide much idea as to the normal way of life of the republics. Their economic, social and military organisation, developed in the Colony before the migration, remained substantially unaltered. What was necessary was to develop political institutions and organisation as well. Constitutions derived from America and Europe do not adequately describe this political organisation, since laws do not necessarily reflect what actually happens. What distinguishes the Afrikaners in the diaspora from those who remained in the Cape was precisely the question of political systems, since those who stayed at home remained within the governmental forms of a British Colony. Two striking features of political organisation in the diaspora are worth some consideration. First, it was small in scale, and until much later in the nineteenth century the largest was the Orange Free State with a white population of at most 20,000, while the little communities in the Transvaal were very much smaller. Second, and more significant, the political system depended to a great extent upon clan and kinship ties. An extended family tended to live in one area, and to a great extent to rely upon its own military and economic resources; weaker families tended to attach themselves to the great families. In this, the communities began closely to resemble the political organisation of African segmentary communities, perhaps because each faced similar problems of political authority. Each of these clan communities had a leader (or, on the African analogy, a chief) who could represent them in the political affairs of larger units. And to an extraordinary extent, political authority was a matter of descent. The younger

Pretorius inherited his father's ambition, his position and his political followers. The younger Potgieter also inherited his father's position, though he did not live to enjoy it. After his death, Schoeman inherited the elder Potgieter's position and even his widow. It is not over-stating the position to describe the Transvaalers and even the Free Staters as a white segmentary society. The communities were poor, and were largely outside the cash economy based upon the Cape. Economically the communities were not integrated and therefore economics provided no basis for political institutions or political life. A president could issue an instruction, or a meeting of the assembly pass a law, but there was no bureaucracy and no police force to compel obedience among unwilling citizens. The only way of ensuring cohesion and order was to trust one's clients and one's kinsmen. The struggle for the presidency of the Transvaal was therefore less serious than it may have seemed, since the presidency itself carried little authority and much frustration.

One institution hardly mentioned so far was to develop into an important focus of power: that was the volksraad, or people's assembly. Within the racial aristocracy, the adult males were egalitarian – which reflected the fact that each family head was in a sense sovereign over his own estate. In a constitutional sense, the volksraad was the parliament of a republic; in a more realistic sense it was a body representing the various clans and lineages of the white community. Especially after the disastrous experience of ambitious presidents, interest turned increasingly to the volksraad of each state as the expression of the white people's will. Nevertheless, so strong was the experience of commando organisation, that the presidency itself (the political counterpart of the military leadership) retained great powers, especially in an emergency when it was difficult to assemble the volksraad in time to discuss matters. In effect, relations between president and volksraad became those between a king and his council of clan elders. President Brand in the O.F.S. and President Pretorius the younger in the Transvaal, were effectively rulers for life, although the ritual election was carried out every four years. In other words, living in conditions similar to those of the African communities – without money or liquid assets, tied to the land, and obliged to be vigilant in order to be safe – they developed very similar methods of dealing with their situation.

In the diaspora, then, many of the characteristics of Afrikanerdom came to light; but the people themselves were not yet conscious of being a nationality, or of having a separate and distinct destiny. The diaspora represented only a minority of Afrikaners, the majority remaining British colonial subjects; and even the diaspora was disunited politically, and in religious organisation. Several important experiences and developments remained, before Transvaal trekkers, Cape wine-farmers and Orange River wheat-growers came to regard themselves as part of a distinct nationality, pursuing distinctively nationalist ambitions. Afrikaner nationalism developed first in the republican diaspora, which in the 1860s was still too feeble to impose its ideas, its culture and its organisation upon conquered African communities, let alone the relatively affluent and self-confident colonial subjects.

Chapter 6

Southern Africa on the eve of the mineral revolution

The mineral revolution, beginning in the 1860s, and accelerating during the 1870s and 1880s, is the most far-reaching change to have taken place in Southern Africa since 1800; more revolutionary than the Mfecane, and more influential than the trekking of the white colonists. To grasp the full implications of this revolution, it is essential to form a clear impression of conditions in Southern Africa before the revolution took place. The most startling feature of that situation, seen from the perspective of today, is that the Africans and their communities were stronger than most of their white competitors outside the Cape Colony. It is even plausible to suggest that, had there been no mineral revolution, the powerful white states of Southern Africa today could not have developed. It is convenient to assess the pre-revolutionary situation by examining first the military power of the white and African states, then their respective economic power, and finally to look at their prospects immediately before diamonds were discovered in Griqualand.

Militarily, the Zulu remained the key to south-east African power in the 1860s, despite the humiliating defeats of the late 1830s. Much of the credit for their remarkable recovery belongs to Mpande, a man whose merits are frequently underestimated. A half-brother of Shaka and Dingane, he had escaped assassination by appearing to lack ambition. He first became prominent as the leader of a regiment which scored a victory over Port Natal traders during the Boer–Zulu war of 1838. After the battle of Blood River, when the Zulu state seemed to be falling apart, Mpande allied himself with the trekkers in order to seize the kingship. Mpande's own army of invasion was accompanied by a trekker detachment, which took no part in the fighting, but which herded thousands of cattle from the kingdom after Mpande's generals had defeated Dingane and sent him to exile and death in Mswati's kingdom in 1840. The trekkers confirmed Mpande as king of the Zulu but in exchange insisted upon the subordination of the kingdom to themselves and the surrender of a large area of land in the south of the remaining state. At the outset of his reign, therefore, Mpande was open to criticism of having succeeded by means of a humiliating alliance, even though it was his own following which actually won the battles for him. It was an unpromising beginning to a new administration.

Mpande's personality seemed even less promising for the task of ruling a proud and military-minded people. He was patient, realistic, and tolerant of attacks on his dignity. Appreciating that the state might be destroyed in the event of war with the white communities, he firmly resisted the desire of some of the regimental leaders to win back their prestige and land and cattle. When the desire to launch military campaigns became very great, he ensured that the campaigns were fought in the north, against the Thonga and Swazi, rather than south and west against British and trekker groups. His foreign policy of co-existence with the white states and the avoidance of all pretexts for war with them over-rode all other considerations. Internally, this meant that government became steadily more civilian, and less regimental in style. Though the age-regiments did not disappear, they were less emphasised than before, and inevitably their nation-building role was minimised. The army was quietly strengthened by the purhase of arms from white traders, but Mpande's intention was to keep the peace and to ensure that the white communities appreciated his peaceful intentions. From 1840 until his death in 1872, Mpande succeeded in preserving most of his people's independence (the trekker claim to authority lapsed in 1843 with the annexation of their Natal republic), most of their land, and most of their internal unity: he also enabled the people to recover from the destruction and excitement of the turbulent 1820s and 1830s. His policies and personality were unexciting, but he was one of the very few African leaders of his generation who could boast of such an achievement.

Precisely because of the lack of excitement, when a new generation of Zulu grew up, hearing about Shaka but not experiencing the ill effects of war, they hankered after a more ambition administration. The militant young men formed themselves into factions around two of Mpande's sons, Mbulazi and Cetywayo. That development may be seen as the spilling over of aggression in internal conflict, having been prevented from expressing itself externally. At any rate it was potentially a very dangerous development for the Zulu, since their main source of strength in the mid-nineteenth century was their internal unity rather than their possession of modern armaments. It was also, obviously, an insult to Mpande himself, since the conflict amounted to a succession dispute during the life-time of the monarch himself. In the event Cetywayo routed his opponents, and was recognised as heir apparent not only by the Zulu but also by Shepstone on behalf of the Natal government, in an attempt to establish good relations with the emerging leader. The nature of the conflict also suggested that Cetywayo would be more likely to emulate Shaka than Mpande, and that a renewed Zulu expansion was at hand as soon as Mpande should die. Cetywayo, however, was much shrewder than observers assumed, and had apparently used the support of the militants only in order to secure his own guarantee of the kingship. Once installed as king in 1872, he continued his father's foreign and domestic policies unchanged. His difficulty was not in the policy, but in the aggressive manner in which he had secured power: he might genuinely attempt to pursue a policy of peaceful coexistence, but no outsider was likely to believe that his intentions were peaceful. In consequence, the Natal settlers and through them the Imperial Government became convinced that the Zulu would eventually precipitate a war, and during the 1870s they deliberately began to prepare for the war which they assumed was inevitable. Nevertheless the Zulu still had it in them to inflict a resounding and humiliating defeat on the British army when the war eventually did break out in 1879; and at that point they demonstrated that their military capacity had not, in fact, been exaggerated during the previous thirty years when they formed the key to military control over southeastern Africa.

Although the Basotho also remained a formidable military force, and although they succeeded in the end in preserving a separate identity for themselves during the partition years in Southern Africa, their power as against their trekker neighbours was dangerously declining immediately prior to the mineral revolution. Their major difficulty was that, despite being able to acquire horses, and despite having the money with which to purchase firearms, the British authorities in the Cape made it easier for the trekkers to acquire firearms than for the Basotho. The British and trekkers understood each other, after all, and they had parted on friendly terms. Against that background, assistance to the trekkers seemed both sensible and natural. At the same time it must be said that British policy was based upon racialist assumptions. Though the Basotho were still able to obtain arms illegally, the supply was expensive and unreliable. The longer they waited, therefore, the weaker they became in comparison with their better-equipped white neighbours. Also, Moshoeshoe in old age, as we have seen, was beset by the problem of numerous and ambitious sons and grandsons. Finally, the British had evacuated the Sovereignty without making a clear and workable boundary. Trouble with the trekkers was almost inevitable, and the Basotho were not very well equipped to deal with it.

The first crisis came in 1858, when the trekkers decided to punish Moshoeshoe for the land encroachment of his border chiefs. The border chiefs regarded themselves as recovering land which was legitimately theirs, but the trekkers naturally saw matters in a different light. The war of 1858 – *ntoa ea Senekale* – resulted in a Basotho victory; but Moshoeshoe was anxious for a peaceful settlement rather than a humiliating defeat which would force the trekkers to fight again later. Both sides appealed to the British for arbitration, and the British Governor of the Cape awarded the Basotho a small part of the land which they claimed. Trekker disunity, the remaining military strength of the Basotho, and Moshoeshoe's defensive genius in warfare had made this modest success possible. The civil wars among the trekkers ensured that there was a peace for the next few years along the frontier. Moshoeshoe, appreciating that war would begin again soon, and that the Basotho might not be able to defend themselves for ever, tried desperately hard to gain an alliance, or a protectorate from the British. Seeking the status of 'fleas in the blanket' of Queen Victoria, they humiliated themselves in pursuit of her protection. However, by this time the Imperial Government was reluctant to assume any further expensive responsibilities, and did not intervene. In 1865 war broke out once more, soon after peace had been restored within the white trekker communities. This time matters went badly for the Basotho; so badly that refugees began to flow over the colonial border into the Cape, causing further disturbances on that sensitive frontier. Largely in order to reduce the risk of such disturbance, the British Governor annexed Lesotho to the Crown in 1868. When Moshoeshoe died in 1870, his state was no longer independent, his people still not united, and much of their land lost to the trekkers. Nevertheless they cannot be dismissed: as late as 1880, they fought a successful war against the Cape Government in defence of their arms and their status as an imperial, rather than a colonial possession. Formally, by the late 1860s, Sotho power was at an end, but in real terms the Basotho remained an independent-minded community, capable of causing immense problems to any white administrator who tried to transform the protectorate into direct administration.

Of the other major African communities, the Mfecane states generally retained their powers at least until the 1860s: the Gaza empire, the Ndebele kingdom, the Swazi kingdom, and Sekhukkune's people were all formidable in military terms, even when surrounded by communities of white farmers. The Swazi, for instance, entered a military alliance with the trekkers against the Zulu, in which each side guaranteed to assist the other in a crisis. So long as the Zulu remained a serious military threat, the alliance was relatively equal: it was only in the 1870s and especially in the 1880s that the trekkers began to behave more as overlords of the Swazi than equal partners. The Swazi retained sufficient military power to make that alliance useful and valuable to the white states. The Pedi, under Sekwati, signed an agreement with the trekkers whereby each side observed a border; and the Pedi had sufficient strength to ensure that that border was retained. When Sekhukhune came to the throne, he expelled the missionaries (whom he regarded as spies for the trekkers) and began to build up arms for a future war with the trekkers. Until he was defeated in the late 1870s, his strength was sufficient for that purpose. In general it may be said that the trekker communities were able – when united – to defeat any single one of the African states; but that the balance of military power was not reliable nor clear, and there was always a substantial risk of defeat. In the Cape, of course, matters were different: here an Imperial British army could confront the Xhosa chieftaincies, and count upon victory. Even there, however, the sheer density of Xhosa population and the complexity of Xhosa politics tended to prevent the whites from encroaching upon their land or establishing permanent administration over them.

If the African states beyond the Cape frontier were vulnerable militarily, so too were the trekker republics. Their military superiority depended upon their use of horses (which gave them great mobility), their possession of wagons for defensive battles, and their firearms. In all these respects their advantage was precarious. Moshoeshoe encouraged his people to acquire ponies and to learn to breed and ride them. It was possible for the African generals to acquire familiarity with the strategy of the laager (though this does not seem to have happened), and most of the African states were trying hard to acquire firearms, either legally or through renegade white traders. When African regiments had the advantage of surprise, they could neutralise most of the advantages possessed by the trekkers. The latter, realising that their advantages were not always decisive, were wary of provoking unnecessary and hazardous warfare. On the other hand it is unlikely that the African generals realised quite how vulnerable the trekkers must have been.

The other immense risk facing the trekkers was their inability to achieve internal unity. During the 1860s they were divided into two Churches and into a varying number of political units – sometimes two but often as many as five or six little republics. In addition, civil war within these republics was almost endemic, and the wars of the 1850s and 1860s terminated largely because of the continuing inability of any central authority to exercise much power. British officials in the Cape contributed to that lack of trekker unity but it was largely a result of weaknesses inherent in their style of life and of administration. The struggle over presidencies came to an end largely because the presidency itself in a non-monetary community had very little meaning. By comparison, most of the African states already mentioned had stable, regular governments over populations which accepted the legitimacy of those governments. During the war of 1865 no African states came to the defence of Moshoeshoe; but on the other hand the Transvaal allies of the Free State deserted the alliance once they had captured cattle and before the fighting became dangerous. If the African states were disunited, the trekkers were little better off.

However, the crucial point of comparison is between the economic viability of the African states, as against the poverty of the trekker governments. The viability of the Zulu and Gaza states, let alone the Ndebele and Shona, has already been mentioned. These states were internally prosperous and also able to produce goods for export – hides, skins, ivory, occasionally slaves, sometimes copper and gold. With the profits of this trade they were able to acquire military equipment for defence against the trekking groups. By comparison, the trekking states were chronically bankrupt. They were attempting to run European-style government without European-style resources. Lacking schools, export crops or other export commodities except beef and hides, and lacking reliable governmental revenue, their governments tended to be paralysed. After the granting of political independence in 1852 and 1854, the republics stood in a neo-colonial relationship with the prosperous Cape. When the Cape banks withdrew banking facilities from Bloemfontein (there were none at all further north, since there was no money worth banking) the Free State was obliged to print its own paper money; and since no one believed the republic to have any resources, the paper money soon became worthless. The Transvaal in the 1870s failed to raise a loan in Europe with which to build a railway. Arms, ammunition, clothes and wagons had all to be bought from the Cape, where pastoral products from the interior commanded a relatively poor price. Lacking schools, the republics lacked trained man-power, and were obliged to import their presidents from elsewhere – particularly Brand, the Free State President, who came from the Cape, and Burgers, the Transvaal President who had been educated in Europe as a minister of religion. The Cape, controlling the trade routes, was further able to charge duties on goods bound for the interior, and thereby established a stranglehold over the feeble economies of the interior states. The failure of the trekkers to obtain a harbour perpetuated that dependency.

Much more seriously, though not quite so obviously, the trekkers were failing to establish themselves upon the land. They were of course well able to obtain land, either by conquest or by purchase or by misrepresentation, but they were unequipped to make good use of it once acquired. Outside the Cape Colony, white settlers had to be able to make a living off the land, as there was simply no other way to make a living. The relative inability of the white settlers to succeed in this venture was therefore of overwhelming significance. Within the Cape, there was a much lesser problem. Wine and grain producers near Cape Town and wheat producers and sheep and cattle farmers near Port Elizabeth were all close to reliable and usually profitable markets. Further, the Cape with a white population of some 200,000 was large enough to provide its own markets, and to sustain a fairly diverse and modestly prosperous economy. It was beyond the Cape's area of fairly dense white settlement that the settlers were in danger. The extent of that danger may be seen in each of the communities involved.

White settlement in Natal began with traders at Port Natal harbour, early in the nineteenth century, trading with the Nguni and the Zulu state. The brief Natal trekker republic in the late 1830s left very few white settlers on the land; and despite efforts by the British administration in Natal there were fewer than 10,000 white residents in the Colony during the 1850s. A major difficulty was the absence of suitable export crops, and in the late 1850s sugar was introduced as a means of establishing an export staple. Then the difficulty arose that the Zulu and other neighbouring Nguni people were not prepared to labour on the sugar estates at the wages offered to them. The white Natal economy could not afford to pay attractive wages; and the Africans were sufficiently well established on the land to resist the temptation of poor remuneration. To solve this difficulty, the Government imported indentured labourers from India, who were obliged to work for a contract period at a very low wage rate. With this supply of cheap labour, the sugar estates flourished during the 1860s, and by the middle of the 1870s the white population was approaching 20,000, mainly English-speaking. However, at this point a further economic weakness appeared: namely the superior industry of the Indian labourers, many of whom stayed in the country after the expiry of their contracts. As merchants, semi-skilled labourers, clerks and small farmers, they proved very efficient and hard-working – and cheaper and more efficient than their white competitors. There was a considerable risk that jobs being held by whites would steadily come to be held by Indian immigrants instead. The Government could legislate against this development; but the cheapness and efficiency of the new community was bound to enable them to establish themselves, and was bound to restrict the ability of the country to support a large number of white residents.

At the same time, land companies began to buy up large areas of land vacated by the trekkers. Since the companies wanted profits from the land, and since African peasants were more efficient and productive than white farmers, the companies tended to rent the land to Africans rather than whites. As a result, most of the country was reverting to African occupation, except along the coastal belt where sugar farmers were flourishing; and in the towns, many grades of urban employment were passing into Indian hands. The Government could attempt to slow down this process, but it was not strong enough to reverse it. The essential difficulty was that the white settlers were simply not efficient, and their prospects were accordingly very bleak. Their future appeared to be in the realms of plantation-ownership and wholesale trade, and it is impossible to build a strong community around those two categories of employment, since they involve dependency upon the productive capacity of other communities. The feebleness of the Portuguese settlements further north was largely the result of the Portuguese limitation to plantation ownership and wholesale trade, and it looked as if Natal might follow in the same direction. Military and technical superiority were not enough for the creation of a strong white community.

In the trekker republics, the economic prospects of the burghers were even worse, since they were further from export markets, had no export staple like sugar, and had no wholesale trade enterprises. They were not cultivators at all, except on a very few acres in each farm, where grain could be produced for domestic consumption. In areas where irrigable cultivation was possible – along the Orange and Caledon rivers near the Cape border – the cultivators were Griqua, Sotho and Rolong. The Griqua were one of a series of coloured communities which had moved beyond the orbit of white settlement in the Cape, and had established themselves reasonably securely along the Orange river. Economically they were self-contained, militarily they enjoyed the advantage of familiarity with commando techniques and the possession of firearms. As a result, it had not been possible for the trekkers to expel them from the valuable arable land which they had acquired. Sometimes with missionary advice, and sometimes without it, these little communities seemed relatively prosperous and secure even as late as the early 1860s. The trekker republics treated them with reluctant respect and the Imperial officers regarded them as valuable buffers between the Cape's white population and the Bantu further north.

The trekkers, then, were largely confined to open country, which had been vacated (because it offered no shelter) during the Mfecane, and which permitted large-scale pastoralism. And within that country they were further obliged to settle near reliable sources of African agricultural labour. However, pastoralism could support only a very sparse white population, whereas African peasant production could support a relatively dense rural community. The obvious deduction from this state of affairs is that trekker pastoralism was economically inefficient. It produced very little exportable beef or hides, while the sheep produced mutton and fat but no wool. The way to measure productivity, therefore, is to measure the number of people who were supported by a given number of acres. On that count the trekkers were clearly less efficient than the Africans. One of the penalties of this inefficiency was sparse settlement which made the trekkers vulnerable in the face of African resistance. Admittedly trekker standards of living were more expensive than peasant standards, but it is still true that five thousand acres would support one trekker family and its labourers in comfort, or several dozen African families nearer to subsistence level. It is hardly surprising therefore that trekkers found it profitable to lease large acreages to African peasants, in exchange for rent in kind; and to allow their farm labourers to become labour-tenants. That was the sensible and economical way to use conquered land; but here again there was a penalty, namely the fact that white prejudice against manual labour, and white absentee landlordism prevented the white farmers from improving their knowledge of agricultural production. The trekkers were becoming, quite literally, a community of planters and land-owners. This economic incompetence restricted both their numbers and their productivity. Here again, white settlement was based upon the dangerous foundation of military strength but economic inefficiency. So long as they could move northwards to fresh conquests, that was not desperately important, but as soon as the frontier was closed the problems would become acute.

In the 1860s it was still true to say that the great source of power and influence in the sub-continent was the British naval and military presence. Though British policy was occasionally confused and involved by local events, especially on and beyond the frontiers, nevertheless British officials retained great initiative, and British interests could be implemented without much risk of opposition. British attempts to 'solve' the problem of the frontier so as to reduce military expenditure consistently failed; nevertheless it was the British who were free to decide what policy to adopt, and therefore it was the British who held the power to initiate great changes. That power was infrequently used, but it was always available. During the late 1830s, for example, they decided to keep frontier peace by means of alliances with border rulers, whether African or coloured. Treaties were made with the west Griqua leader Waterboer (1834), another Griqua chief Adam Kok (1843) and with Moshoeshoe himself (1843). Despite settler and trekker annoyance, the British recognised the sovereign authority of these rulers, paid them a small gratuity, and attempted to pull them into a peace-keeping alliance. When that policy failed to provide security, Smith annexed the whole country between the Orange and Vaal river (1848) and easily suppressed trekker resistance at the battle of Boomplaats. Conversely when the Imperial Government decided to abandon these new territories, there was nothing to prevent them from doing so. However, the important criterion of Imperial policy was whether or not British strategic interests were affected. Though they marginally preferred to collaborate with white rulers, that preference did not lead them to ignore their own strategic objectives. Whoever proved most capable of serving those interests could be pulled into an alliance, no matter what colour that ruler might be. Apart from restricting the sale of arms to African societies from 1854 onwards, the British did not seriously interfere in the interior, and remained almost neutral in the

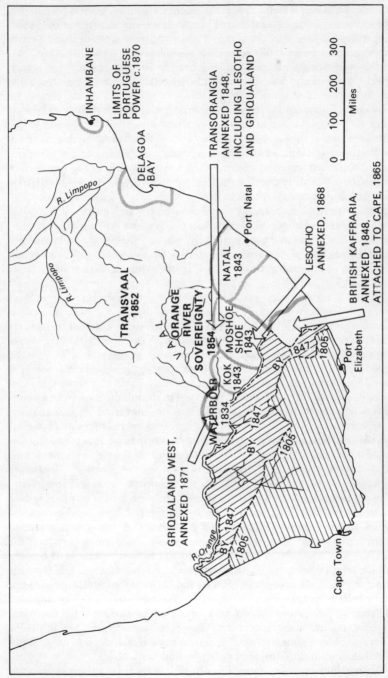

British and Portuguese Imperial frontiers 1800–1870. Treaty relations established between Britain and Waterboer, Kok and Moshoeshoe on the dates shown.

struggles for power which were taking place beyond the colonial boundaries. The last demonstrations of this unchallengable power occurred in the 1860s; first, when Moshoeshoe was annexed and his people were declared British protected persons in 1868; second, when diamonds were discovered and British officials annexed the diamond-bearing country and its inhabitants. That easy supremacy was soon to be challenged; but in the 1860s there was still no challenger in sight.

By comparison, the Portuguese Imperial power was in trouble. The slow death of the slave trade in the mid-nineteenth century left Mozambique without much economic justification. Soshangane had been able to brush the Portuguese aside, and even his son Mzila was able to contain them and control their economic and political activity. It was only in the last third of the nineteenth century that the Portuguese discovered a use for Portuguese East Africa, and recovered some of their strength in the area. Until then, they were steadily declining as a source of power and historical initiative. In the whole region north of the Cape Colony, the African communities seemed likely to control and contain the white penetration of the interior, and there was even some possibility that the extent of white settlement might have to be retrenched until such time as the white settlers became more productive.

No reference has been made so far to the 'missionary factor' in pre-industrial Southern Africa. That omission is deliberate, since discussion of missionary activity was much more widespread than actual missionary effects upon the Southern African situation. Nevertheless their presence and activities did have some interesting consequences, which must be considered. The missionary impact, with some early exceptions, was very late. The Portuguese had encouraged mission work in Portuguese East Africa as early as the sixteenth century, and in the middle of the seventeenth century the Mwene Matupa had even been converted to Christianity. However, mission work was closely connected to Portuguese authority, and the ineffective control exercised by the Portuguese involved a corresponding failure on the part of the missionaries they sponsored. Sustained mission work really dates from the arrival of the London Missionary Society's missionaries in 1799, led by Dr Vanderkemp. Dr Vanderkemp followed the example of an earlier German mission effort, in working first among the growing Coloured community within the Colony, and in organising his converts into a self-contained community. A policy which tended to attract Coloured labourers away from their white employers, and his marriage to a freed slave, both infuriated the colonists. The L.M.S. then sent Dr John Philip to the Cape, to superintend mission work; and from his arrival in 1820, the colonists regarded him as being completely hostile to their interests, and extremely influential in Westminster. Retief's manifesto, referring to the reasons for the trek, specified missionary influence upon Imperial policy. Recent research, however, particularly by Professor Galbraith, has demonstrated that missionary influence was very slight indeed in determining Imperial policy in Southern Africa.

Mission influence was more important in two fields: the missionaries annoyed the colonists who therefore severely discouraged mission work in the Afrikaner republics once they had the power to do so; and they were used by both colonial and African authorities for non-religious purposes. Missionaries were frequently employed as negotiators between colonial and African authorities, as diplomats rather than evangelists. As diplomats they represented interests other than their own, and cannot be said to have represented a 'missionary factor'. Moshoeshoe as we have seen employed them also as guardians of the border regions of his state, and as educators of his young men. Philip's policy of trying to build Christian communities amongst the Griqua on the colonial border was perfectly compatible with the colonial authorities' interest in bringing stability to that sensitive region. More generally, African leaders perceived the missionaries as bringers of a revolutionary and divisive doctrine, which would undermine the allegiance of converts to the traditional political authorities. Among the Xhosa people therefore, it was not until after the 'National Suicide' and the collapse of existing authority, that the missionaries made much headway, although mission stations had been planted in that area from the 1820s onwards by a variety of Protestant organisations. Conversely, the Mfengu, whose traditional authorities were already overthrown, were much more amenable to missionary and general western influence. Whether the missionaries realised it or not (and at first they seem not to have realised it) they came as evangelists but were regarded as diplomats and educators and westernisers. Though the colonists regarded them as dangerously pro-African, many African leaders (with greater justification) regarded them as dangerously pro-settler and pro-Imperialist.

In the long run, mission activity in Southern Africa (just as elsewhere in the continent) had the effect of dividing African communities into the 'red' and the 'school' men. In the short run, however, by the time of the mineral revolution that effect had scarcely been felt except in the border African societies and among the Coloured communities.

Chapter 7

White penetration of the interior

In the mid-nineteenth century, African states of the interior could reasonably have expected to be able to control the expansion and activities of the new settlers. Their prospects were diminished drastically from the moment that diamonds were discovered near the confluence of the Orange and Vaal Rivers in 1867. It was a disastrous coincidence that the mineral revolution should have started in an area where the African societies were unusually weak, since the disputes over possession of the diamonds created the precedent that African claims could always be ignored. The area in which diamonds could be exploited was claimed by a variety of different societies: the Cape Colony, the Orange Free State and the South African Republic all laid claim to part or whole of the area; as did those with stronger claims based on residence and actual control, namely Nicholas Waterboer's Griquas and the southern Tswana Ba-Thlaping. Waterboer, having a reasonable legal case, let it be conducted by an astute but not very scrupulous lawyer, David Arnot. At one time Arnot was also representing the interests of Mahura of the Ba-Thlaping: his only consistency lay in that he was anxious to extend British authority over the Missionary Road, if necessary by extending that authority over his clients.

These claims were all made to look unreal by the influx of diamond diggers who declined to acknowledge the sovereignty of any of the local powers, set up an independent republic of their own in 1870, and elected Stafford Parker – an ex-sailor – President. A meeting of Tswana chiefs, Waterboer and the two Afrikaner presidents failed to reach agreement, and the issue had therefore to be submitted to Britain for arbitration. The arbitrator was Keate, Lieutenant-Governor of Natal, and his selection underlined the political reality that no agreement disposing of the diamond fields could be effective unless Her Majesty's Government endorsed it. Unfortunately for all the claimants, Britain had interests of her own, in an area which straddled the road to the interior. Keate's decision pinned back the two Afrikaner republics to the east of the diamond diggings, awarded a substantial tract of land to the Tswana chiefs and acknowledged the full extent of Waterboer's claim: but within a few days the legal victory of Waterboer was shown to be meaningless, when the High Commissioner and Governor of the Cape annexed the diamond fields to the British Crown.

Waterboer's independent Griqua republic of 1867 became, by the end of 1871, the British colony of Griqualand West. The British had moved back into the interior once more: not – as in Lesotho – at the request of an independent ruler; but to control the economic and political power of the diamond fields.

The benefits from the diamond fields were unequally distributed; not in proportion to what people needed, nor in proportion to legal claims upon that wealth, but entirely in proportion to the power of the various parties concerned. For that reason, and because their presence near the fields made them most vulnerable, the Griqua lost the most. Dispossessed not only of the diamonds but also of the land itself, they found themselves excluded from skilled employment, from the scramble for claims, and from the government. All these areas were rapidly monopolised by the diamond diggers, using the Diggers Committee and able to influence (if not to coerce) the local representatives of the Imperial Government.

The circumstances of the Tswana societies was marginally better, since they could retire beyond the reach of the new administration, but the loss of the springs and waters of the Vaal and Orange rivers was a serious blow. The Afrikaner republics, though they lost their claims to the diamond fields, were otherwise little affected. President Brand of the Orange Free State was even able to obtain financial compensation from the Imperial Government when it was discovered that the British claim to Griqualand West was founded on questionable legal bases. Since the republics had not actually controlled or used Griqualand West, its loss did not alter their economic state. Within the diamond mining community, inequality also flourished. White miners first ousted Coloured and African claim-holders, and were then absorbed into the monopolistic De Beers company which bought out the individual claim-holders.

Economic control was not enough: diamonds have no intrinsic value, and are only expensive because they are scarce. Any wise diamond magnate must therefore ensure that he controls all the available diamond supplies, otherwise competition will ruin the market. To ensure that De Beers' monopoly was secure, and to ensure that a docile labour force was made available, De Beers moved into the political arena. When Griqualand West was amalgamated with the Cape in 1880, De Beers – as the political bosses of Griqualand West – were able to use the government and facilities of the largest South African state for their economic purposes. Rhodes, as the political strategist of the De Beers Company, at the head of a solid little group of Kimberley representatives, was able to form alliances with Cape politicians and eventually to become Prime Minister of the Colony.

The Cape Government, and the colonists generally, prospered greatly as a result of the industry though it was at first beyond the border. The diggers had to be fed (which created a market for agricultural produce), supplied with brandy and clothes (which created a boom in the Cape wine industry and increased the volume of traffic going inland), and provided with machinery (which encouraged the Cape to build railway lines so as to profit from the heavy traffic to Kimberley). The mines had also to be supplied with

Mining in Kimberley in the early 1870s: sifting the earth for diamonds

unskilled labour, which enabled African labourers to enter the cash economy and to purchase firearms in case of future need. In 1872 the Cape was strong enough economically to be granted responsible government by Britain, and increasingly over the next dozen years Cape ministries were able to determine the course of events throughout the sub-continent. For the first time, and as a direct result of the prosperity created by the diamond industry, white colonists were able to take charge of events: they had the money with which to pay for military campaigns against the African societies within and beyond the Colony, and they acquired the resources to ensure that laws passed in Cape Town should be obeyed on the frontier itself. Equally important, the Cape could afford to defy the Imperial Government, on which it no longer relied for defence or for economic aid. There came into being a 'colonial' power, distinct from, and sometimes hostile to, 'Imperial' power; and at the head of the 'colonial' party appeared two remarkable colonists – Cecil John Rhodes of De Beers at Kimberley, and Jan Hendrik Hofmeyr of the Afrikander Bond. Their alliance was a powerful one, combining the electoral power of the Afrikaners with the economic power of De Beers itself. For several years they largely controlled the destinies of the white colonies.

The British Government regarded this development with mixed feelings. While it was gratifying to observe that the Cape might henceforth pay for its own border wars and – through its own government – accept responsibility for its own actions, it was irritating to have to deal with colonists who did not need to obey imperial instruction or heed imperial desires. In any case, the continued Balkanisation of the white communities into three colonies and two republics was obviously wasteful and a potential source of friction. On one hand the Imperial Government was anxious to see the Cape absorb the other little white states and thereby take over the imperial role of protecting them; on the other hand the Cape was understandably reluctant to assume responsibility for other colonists who seemed always to be in danger from African insurrections, and whose economies were chronically in deficit. Because of its wealth, the Cape could no longer be coerced by the Imperial Government, and yet some means had to be discovered to bring about the confederation of the white societies. The Secretary of State for Colonies, the Earl of Carnarvon, resolved to press ahead with the other white societies, and deal with the Cape later. Accordingly, a detachment of police marched into the Transvaal in 1877 led by Theophilus Shepstone, who persuaded the Republican Government not to resist annexation, and who then ran up the Union Jack and annexed the Transvaal to the British Crown. The Natal colonists, who enjoyed a measure of self-government without the money and the arms required to defend themselves against their African neighbours, were persuaded to surrender their limited political rights in exchange for a promise of imperial protection. The Orange Free State was surrounded by British territory and could therefore be coerced without the formality of annexation. Of the white communities, only the Cape now stood in the way of confederation imposed by imperial dictation: but the Cape resolutely refused to acquiesce, and the result was an embarrassing dead-lock. The other colonies could not be attached to the Cape, nor could they easily be disannexed, since that would be an open admission of imperial failure. The deadlock lasted for almost four years until 1881.

The Cape was not the only obstacle to imperial confederation, otherwise that confederation might still have been achieved. The major reason for white reluctance to accept self-government and thereby relieve the Imperial Government of expense was a very sensible fear that the colonists would be unable to defend themselves against African resistance to white control. Natal was alarmed by the presence of the Zulu state and by the military revival which Cetywayo seemed to be achieving – the Zulu regiments were known to be anxious for action and able to arm themselves with fire-arms. The Transvaal was equally alarmed by the Zulu state and in addition it had recently lost a small war against Sekhukhune's Ba-Pedi in the north-east. The Orange Free State was in a condition of armed peace as against its Basotho neighbours. All the white states had been alarmed by the Natal Government's failure (in 1873) to disarm Langalibalele on the Basutoland border, and by the military mess made during the ensuing campaign against that very minor chief. It was clear that the colonists (whether British or Afrikaner made little difference) had accepted imperial rule because it involved imperial protection; and that they would not accept responsibility for government unless the military situation was changed in their favour.

Accordingly, the Imperial Government obliged by permitting two military campaigns to be conducted by imperial troops: one to destroy the Zulu state, and another to remove the menace of the Pedi. The Pedi campaign of 1879 was simple: a month was sufficient to capture Sekhukhune and to send him to exile in Cape Town. The Zulu campaign was a different matter. Cetywayo, though determined to keep the peace, was well prepared

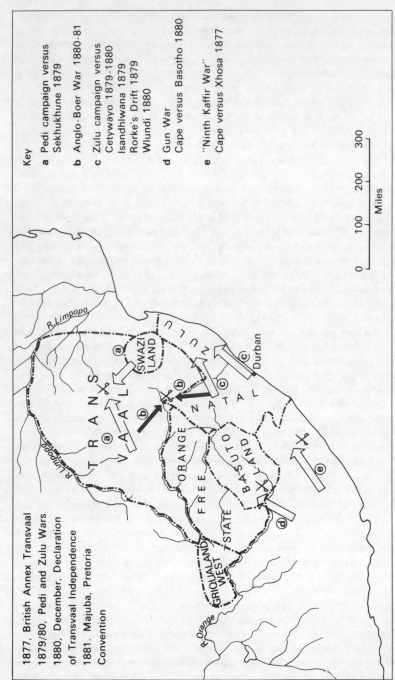

Key

a Pedi campaign versus
   Sekhukhune 1879

b Anglo-Boer War 1880-81

c Zulu campaign versus
   Cetywayo 1879-1880
   Isandhlwana 1879
   Rorke's Drift 1879
   Wlundi 1880

d Gun War
   Cape versus Basotho 1880

e "Ninth Kaffir War"
   Cape versus Xhosa 1877

0   100   200   300

Miles

1877, British Annex Transvaal
1879/80, Pedi and Zulu Wars
1880, December, Declaration
of Transvaal Independence
1881. Majuba, Pretoria
Convention

Confederation and conflagration, 1877–1884

for war. His determination to keep the peace is illustrated by the fact that his armies were instructed not to cross the border, even during the war itself. That strategy had the important consequence that the campaign took place in country which the Zulus knew much better than the imperial and colonial troops. That strategic advantage was well exploited: at the battle of Isandhlwana on 22nd January, 1879 the Zulu regiments ambushed and cut to pieces the invading British army, whose remnants fled back across the border to Natal. Paradoxically, that victory sealed the fate of the Zulu kingdom which, by proving itself militarily efficient, also proved itself too strong to be allowed to remain independent. Reinforcements were brought up, and by the end of 1879 Zululand had been divided into 13 chieftaincies, Cetywayo deported to Cape Town (with Langalibalele and Sekhukhune) and the proud Zulu state dismembered. In death, as in life, that state placed its trust in its strength, and earned such glory in resisting imperial rule that its own imperialism has been overshadowed.

By a further paradox, the British victory in Zululand sealed the fate of the British confederation policy. The Transvaal Afrikaners, relieved of their fears, saw no further advantage in the British presence. At the end of 1880 they rebelled, defeated the British troops in a series of engagements culminating at Majuba Hill (February 1881), and thereby presented their demand for independence in unmistakeable form. It is difficult to avoid the impression that the new Afrikaner militancy was a direct consequence of Cetywayo's and Sekhukhune's defeat. The British authorities surveyed the ruins of confederation: the Cape was still unwilling to participate, the Transvaal was (at least temporarily) beyond control, the Unionist Government at Westminster had been replaced by Gladstone's Liberals who were less enthusiastic about Imperial adventures anyway, and there seemed no good reason to persevere with a policy which no local group seemed to welcome. By the Pretoria Convention of 1881 (amplified and amended by the London Convention of 1884), the Transvaal Afrikaners were given republican independence limited only by an undefined British 'suzerainty', and the confederation policy was formally scuttled. Responsibility for the failure of the Imperial Government's policy must be shared by the Cape (whose economic power enabled it to resist Imperial pressure) by the Pedi and by the Zulu, whose victory undermined British confidence, and whose defeat led to the militancy of the colonists. From 1881 onwards, the British would have to worry far less about African power, and far more about the power of the Afrikaner republics and the Cape Colonists.

The extinction of Zulu and British Imperial power left the Cape (and Griqualand West which it annexed in 1880) in a position of great strength, from which it might perhaps have achieved a colonial federation instead of Carnarvon's Imperial alternative. Within the next few years, however, the balance of economic and political power was altered dramatically by yet another mineral discovery: the Witwatersrand. The gold-bearing reef had long been known in the Transvaal, and it seems likely that some pre-colonial African societies actually mined the gold in the same way as the Zimbabweans. The irruption of first the Zulu and then the Afrikaners onto the high

Paul Kruger, President of the Transvaal Republic, 1883–1902

veld dispersed whatever industry had been going on, and the producition of gold was only a memory. Payable gold was discovered in small quantities in several places during the 1860s and 1870s, but the major reef (now known as the Witwatersrand) was discovered only in 1886. Now the technology of the Afrikaners was no more relevant than the technology of the Africans as a means of exploiting the gold deposits: but the crucial difference was that the Afrikaners controlled the political system of the gold-fields and could thereby tap some of the profits of the industry which rapidly blossomed around Johannesburg. Just as the benefits of Kimberley diamond mining were unequally distributed, so were the profits of Johannesburg gold mining – but this time the economic benefits were immensely greater and as a result the political consequences much further-reaching.

Within a matter of months the Transvaal Afrikaners made a reality of their previously unreal state: the state now had money with which to pay salaries of a bureaucracy, resources with which to arm its burghers beyond the scale which the African societies could emulate, a vast market in which to sell their agricultural and pastoral products, and the wherewithal to support schools, newspapers, a judiciary, a police force, and any other European amenity which seemed desirable to have. They could, at last, afford to live a distinctively nineteenth-century European life. President Kruger, one of the original trekkers and a survivor of the civil wars of the 1860s, had achieved the presidency after the renewed independence of the Transvaal in 1881. Until the late 1880s the presidency had meant very little, and the tasks attached to it had not strained his very limited educational resources: nor had the presidency seriously interrupted his daily and prolonged reading of the Bible. Even in the new circumstances of the Transvaal his style of life was substantially unaltered, except that this leathery survivor of an earlier epoch was now the object of courteous interest on the part of governors and commissioners, industrialists and financiers, prospectors and speculators and concessionaires. That relationship was profoundly symbolic of the real tribute which the new industry paid to the old political order of Afrikanerdom.

It was never an easy relationship. The industrialists tended to mistake Kruger's unsophisticated manner for stupidity, and his religious references for lack of realism – though they soon realised the error of this assessment. More seriously, the representatives of nineteenth-century industry found it hard to tolerate the pace and methods of a predominantly pastoral society. On the other hand, the Transvaal Government had not the resources to levy severe taxes, and seemed content with a modest share of the proceeds of industry; it was capable of keeping some sort of order, and of supplying a reasonable volume of migrant African labour; and if the laws proved inconvenient, the law-makers could always be bought – the Transvaal Government was no less corrupt than any society accustomed to a life-time of poverty followed by a glimpse of immense wealth. If the new immigrants – the *Uitlanders* or foreigners – thought the Government absurd, at least they concealed their amusement and tolerated the existing order. By tolerating it and paying their taxes, they steadily strengthened the old political system until it was too late to attempt to overthrow it. There was to be no digger republic.

The power of the republic in inter-state relations was also immensely enhanced, since it could play off the maritime states one against the other. On the west coast, Germany had annexed South-West Africa during the early days of the scramble for Africa, in 1884. The Portuguese were still (more or less) in control on the east coast around Lourenço Marques. To the south, three railway systems reached for the Rand from the Cape, and one railway system stretched from Natal. It became the Republic's objective to link up with the Germans as well as the Portuguese, the better to resist British neo-colonial control from the south. To divide the British amongst themselves it was sufficient merely to hint to Natal that railway traffic could best come from the Cape, and to the Cape that it could best come from Natal. Upon Kruger's decision depended which of the two British colonies would have a balanced budget. Conversely, it became the object of the Cape Government to surround the Transvaal with British (or preferably Rhodesian) territory, so as to limit Kruger's international contacts and tactical options. For that reason the Cape and Britain resisted Transvaal attempts to expand into Botswana, and indeed annexed Botswana during 1885 in order to prevent a junction between Kruger and the Germans in the west coast. Similarly, Rhodes's expansion into Mashonaland cut off Kruger from northward expansion, and Rhodes's ambitious attempt to get the British to purchase Lourenço Marques had the same object in view. Nevertheless the continued presence of the Portuguese on the eastern border, and the continuing rivalry between Natal and the Cape, meant that the encirclement was never complete and the initiative remained with the Republic.

When we speak of the scramble for Africa, we generally mean the European division of African territory and sovereignty. In South Africa there was another aspect to the phenomenon – the scramble for African resources. Diamonds and gold were amongst these, but perhaps the most valuable resource, and that for which the colonial authorities scrambled passionately, was African labour. Just as the old European and Arab traders had bought slaves elsewhere in Africa, so the new labour recruiting agencies scrambled for unskilled labour to work in the mining fields. Whereas the old slavers had taken people away permanently, the new labour recruiters hired them for periods of six to twelve months at a time, and paid the labourers for their work. The techniques of obtaining·labour were often very similar to those of the slave-trade, even though a pretence was made of freedom of contract. The Portuguese authorities, for instance, assisted in rounding up 'recruits' and handing them over to the recruiting agents on payment of a fee which was paid not to the labourer but to the government. In Angola and Zambesi and Katanga (by the turn of the century) recruiting agents from the mines of the south were competing with agents from the Portuguese forced labour plantations in the Bight of Benin. Often the new recruiters (like the old) resorted to bribing chiefs and kings to provide 'voluntary' labour for them.

This new phenomenon of migrant labour steadily altered the whole nature of South African life. The 'reserves' to which Africans were often restricted were unable to support the growing population: able-bodied young men were compelled (in order to make a living and in order to pay the new taxes) to enter employment outside the reserves. They had almost no control over the new economic situation, and had therefore to join the mute stream of labour flowing to Kimberley and Johannesburg, working there for several months at wages determined by the employers, living meanwhile in compounds, and returning eventually with cash, guns or consumer goods. Because they were migrants, they did not acquire skills in industry, and furthermore they lost their fathers' earlier expertise in agriculture. They

Contrasting ways of life: making mats in Zululand and historical Kimberley

steadily became what the industrialists wanted them to be – a reservoir of unskilled labour, working in the mines, recovering their strength with their families in the reserves, and increasingly dependent upon migrant labour for their livelihood.

On the other hand – as we will consider in Chapter 14 – white workers in the new industries were able to obtain much better terms and conditions. They were drawn from industrial countries where workers had already appreciated the importance of organising themselves. Regarding the Coloured and African workers as a threat (since they would accept miserable working conditions) the white workers immediately began to organise themselves against the managements and also against their unskilled competitors.

As we have seen, the mineral revolution, from about 1870, altered the balance of power and the quality of South African life decisively. It brought large numbers of Europeans to the interior, where they reinforced the Afrikaners who were there already: it provided the white political systems with the money, the technology, and the resources required to conquer the African states; and it transformed many African societies from independence and self-sufficiency into a rural reservoir of industrial labour.

Chapter 8

African reactions

With the introduction of industry and the strengthening of the local white communities, the initiative passed out of the hands of the African states: as the chapter heading implies, they were now obliged to react to European initiatives rather than to initiate events themselves. We should not exaggerate the degree or the speed of this change, however, for the decline of African power was usually gradual rather than abrupt, and uneven in its effect. Many small goups in the northern Transvaal remained unconquered until the end of the century; the Basotho were never conquered (or at least they were never conquered as completely as their white neighbours would have liked): and even the conquered Zulu were regarded as a potential threat to the new political order. The reaction of the African leaders, then, was a matter of considerable historical importance; and they also provide some useful indications of the astuteness and determination of at least some of the societies involved.

·Logically, one of the obvious reactions was to move out of the danger zone altogether, abandoning the field to the intruder. Mzilikazi, as we have seen (Chapter Four), was obliged to flee first from Shaka and later from the trekkers, to set up a new Ndebele kingdom beyond the Limpopo. It was somewhat unfortunate for him that he selected a refuge in what later became Rhodesia, but at the time of the decision it seemed a sensible course of action. The trek of Adam Kok and his Griqua followers from Griqualand to Griqualand East was a similar reaction, which might best be described as flight by invitation, since the British authorities offered them security on the east coast in place of turbulence where they were. These two societies were unusual in deciding upon flight: Mzilikazi was disposed to flee since he had not settled into a permanent home anyway, and the same was true of Adam Kok's Griquas. Most of the other societies preferred to stay where they were and defend what they held, rather than pack up and try their luck elsewhere.

If there were good precedents for flight, the precedents for outright resistance were discouraging. Dingane had attempted it, but the Zulu were not sufficiently united nor well enough armed to make that policy effective. The repeated and determined (and sometimes united) resistance of the Xhosa had eventually to yield to the repeated and determined pressures from the white side of the frontier. Although many individual African societies achieved individual victories over British and Afrikaner forces, it was becoming increasingly clear that military valour was inadequate to the purpose, and that other techniques must be developed. The glamour of outright resistance was ultimately misleading and dangerous, since the Afrikaners or the British (or even both) could and would unite in a crisis and bring up more troops than the African armies could muster, and deploy greater weapon-strength than the Africans could purchase.

One policy which seemed promising at the time, but which in retrospect produced unfortunate results, was to attempt peaceful co-existence. The leading protagonist of that policy was perhaps Mpande, who overthrew Dingane with token Afrikaner assistance, and was installed as king with Afrikaner approval. Becoming king as a puppet, he nevertheless attempted to regain freedom of initiative and to protect Zulu independence in the substantial area still left to him. The departure of most of the pastoralist trekkers out of Natal on to the Transvaal high-veld facilitated that policy, since it removed the most dangerous potential enemy from the immediate neighbourhood. It was essential to prevent the regiments from taking any action whatever which might incur the wrath of the Natal British or the Transvaal Afrikaners; and as the Swazi state became an ally of the Afrikaners, it was even necessary to impose some restraint upon the regiments' desire to harry the Swazi. Considered purely as a foreign policy, co-existence was effective: throughout Mpande's thirty-year reign, when a whole series of other African states were over-run, Zululand was preserved from external aggression.

The trouble was that Mpande's vision of external affairs was not shared by the young men of the regiments, whose courage was great even if their political awareness was limited. A nation geared to war and depending upon expansion is not easily transformed into a nation of agriculturalists. The young bloods could see no reason for the restraint imposed upon them – especially those who were too young to recollect Blood River – and quite naturally blamed Mpande for excessive timidity. Since external raids were severely restricted, the young men had to make do with internal warfare, and so the price of external peace included internal turbulence. Mpande seems to have accepted this as a necessary and acceptable price to pay for independence, and perhaps he was justified. At any rate he took no action to suppress the growing militancy of the internal factions. These factions focused their attention and their loyalty upon two sons of Mpande, of whom one was almost certain to succeed him – Cetywayo who had once been Mpande's favourite son, and Mbulazi, a younger son by a later favourite wife. Order disintegrated to the point where Cetywayo and Mbulazi were in open conflict, from which Cetywayo emerged victorious and became something like the heir apparent in 1856. His status was confirmed when Shepstone, the Native Affairs Secretary in Natal, acknowledged him as heir. From then onwards, all the eager young soldiers rallied to Cetywayo, hoping that his reign would approximate more to Shaka's than to Mpande's. Mpande must have been an anxious and unhappy man when he died, leaving the state to a son who seemed unlikely to carry on the existing foreign policy, and who might well engulf the people in one final, cata-strophic encounter with one of the neighbouring white societies.

Once in power, however, Cetywayo's attitude to public affairs swung full circle. It seems likely that his aggressive political activity during Mpande's lifetime was intended consciously to outbid his rivals in popular estimation, in case of a disputed succession. Once installed, that requirement was no longer valid, and he perceived international affairs in the same terms as did his father. Nevertheless expectations had been aroused: the young men wanted to see the regiments back in action; and the colonists feared exactly that development. Unlike his father, Cetywayo could not afford to encourage internal divisions, and an opponent had to be found for the un-blooded regiments. Once again the Zulu looked to their northern neighbours, the Swazi and Thonga, and limited actions were launched against them. Con-versely, the encroachments of the Afrikaners from the north-west were studiously ignored lest they lead to an outbreak of violence which would imperil the state as a whole. The territory around Blood River was claimed by both the Zulu and the Afrikaners: the details need not detain us, but it is worth noticing that a British arbitration on the question reported and vindi-cated much of the Zulu claim. Since it seemed necessary to the British High Commissioner of the day (Sir Bartle Frere) to bring the Zulu issue to a head, the arbitration report was suppressed and Zululand invaded. The ensuing destruction and division of Zululand was a resounding defeat for – among other things – the co-existence policy which Cetywayo had pursued since his accession. Why did that approach fail? For one thing, the Zulu had a reputation among the white communities, who believed them to be preter-naturally aggressive and efficient warriors: the colonists were therefore incapable of believing that the Zulu could possibly want peace. On the other hand, even by purchasing as many arms as were available, Cetywayo could not create an army strong enough to hold out for long. His soldiers could win a battle, but not a war against the whites. Zululand was too strong to be ignored, but not strong enough to withstand a determined British invasion.

Elsewhere in South Africa, though less dramatically, outright resistance proved equally vain in the long run. As the Cape became increasingly capable of financing its own border wars, so the authority of Cape Town began to be felt among the Xhosa tribes beyond the border – Pondo, Tembu, Bomvana and the rest – and in 1879 the Government felt strong enough to attempt to disarm the Basotho themselves. In the Transvaal, Sekhukhune's resistance was suppressed when the British threw their weight behind the Afrikaners; and from then on the African societies of the Northern Transvaal were able only to mount a rearguard action. That action was successful until the end of the century (when the British, once again, threw their weight behind the Afrikaner farmers) but it was extremely marginal in its effect upon the other societies and upon the white societies themselves. If the Zulu were not strong enough to resist effectively by military means alone, what hope was there for smaller and less militarist peoples?

Not surprisingly many of the weaker states had evolved considerable

Laing's Nek Tunnel, South Africa 1889

skill in inter-state diplomacy, which they attempted to apply in the new circumstances. Two of the foremost diplomats of their generation were Montshiwa (1814–1896) of the Tshidi Ba-Rolong and Khama of the Ba-maNgwato, both small Tswana states on the western border of the Transvaal. Montshiwa's skill was acquired in the troubled days of the Mfecane, when refugees from the east had poured onto and over the Tswana peoples on the southern high-veld. He had proved one of the most capable of a series of small-scale rulers who helped to re-assemble remnants of Tswana peoples. More recently, he had been oppressed by Afrikaners moving westward from the Transvaal, and by Tswana and Griqua groups who were being dispersed from the diamond-bearing lands of the Vaal–Orange confluence. Recognising that the Transvaalers were the strongest and least amiable of his enemies, he determined to bring in the British as a counter-balance to Afrikaner power in Tswana country. Like Moshoeshoe, who had employed the French Protestant missionaries, Arbousset and Casalis, as diplomats and secretaries, Montshiwa employed a series of Wesleyan missionaries. By 1870 Montshiwa and his advisers were conducting a firm and persuasive correspondence with governors of the Cape, trying to induce them to extend a protectorate over the Tswana on the Transvaal border, while expostulating with the republican authorities in Pretoria as well. It was many years before the British were prepared to do more than send friendly but non-committal replies, and even then it was the German intervention in South-West Africa, and the implied Afrikaner–German threat to the Missionary Road, which induced a change of heart in official circles. The British annexation came just in time to save the Tshidi Ba-Rolong from incorporation in the Transvaal, in 1884. Montshiwa ultimately achieved his purpose of bringing in the British to counter-balance the Afrikaners. Too late he realised that he had been moved into the Cape Colonial orbit instead of achieving a separate Imperial protectorate as Moshoeshoe had done.

In the long run, greater success was achieved by Khama, who became chief of the Ba-maNgwato in 1875. The succession of Khama put an end to a long period of internal strife, which had been exacerbated by the difficulties imposed by foreign affairs. Khama himself first rose to eminence as a result of his personal courage during the Ndebele attack on the Ba-ma-Ngwato in 1863, and the continued presence of the Ndebele as neighbours created considerable tension within the society. It was necessary for the chief to exercise unchallengeable authority, and Khama was prepared to be so arbitrary that at various times he alienated all his close relations, including his father Sekgoma I and his son Sekgoma II. His passionate conversion to Christianity also created tension between himself and some of his non-Christian followers. However, the struggles of the 1850s and 1860s were a very relevant training for the days of the Scramble, since the small Tswana groups were compelled, in their weakness, to develop a high degree of diplomatic skill.

The two immediate dangers were Afrikaner expansion (and some Afrikaner trekkers had actually passed through Khama's country on their way to South-West Africa, which underlined the danger) and Ndebele conquest. The beginnings of the Scramble, in 1884, also brought the British into the area, and it was the British whom Khama and others determined to manipulate. At a meeting in 1885 with the British authorities from the Cape, Khama designed the tactics which were pursued by himself and by two other Tswana chiefs, Gaseitsiwe of the Ba-Ngwaketse and Sechele of the Ba-Kwena. In requesting British protection, they stipulated that they would prefer a continuation of existing laws, particularly those prohibiting the sale of alcohol (Khama's determined policy) and the sale of land. However, they realised that the British Government would almost certainly require land for white settlement, so they offered land for that purpose as well. Significantly, they offered land which was of no value to themselves in any case. Khama granted land which was actually controlled by Lobengula and the Ndebele; Gaseitsiwe offered a vast stretch of the Kalahari desert; and Sechele offered another stretch of desert. Through a combination of diplomacy and fortuitous external factors, the chiefs obtained an Imperial protectorate which was extremely favourable to them. The British were more concerned to keep European rivals out than to intervene in detail, with the result that for several years the only effect of the protectorate was to protect against the Afrikaners. Again southern Tswana country was transferred to the Cape (much to Montshiwa's disgust) while the north (apparently by accident and lack of interest) remained a separate political entity.

The severest test of Khama's diplomacy began in 1889. Rhodes's British South African Chartered Company had been formed for the purpose of settling and exploiting the area which became Rhodesia and the company was anxious to secure rights and privileges in Bechuanaland Protectorate

Cecil Rhodes founder of Rhodesia, De Beers, Consolidated Goldfields and Prime Minister of the Cape 1890–6

as well. The Imperial Government was apparently willing to allow the company to do so. From Rhodes's point of view it was desirable to secure non-imperial control over the Protectorate, so as to facilitate communications between his base in the Cape and his extension into Rhodesia, and in order to reduce the risk of imperial interference in his rather dubious activities. First a telegraph line was run through the Protectorate (1890) and then a railway line began to approach the Protectorate's southern border from Cape Town (1894). Rhodes's conquest of the Ndebele (1893) with some assistance from Khama's people was also a portent for the future. The Tswana chiefs had not invited the British in merely to make room for Rhodes's colonisation schemes, though they had no objection to Rhodes as an ally against the Ndebele. In 1894 Rhodes submitted a formal request to the Imperial Government for the right to administer the Bechuanaland Protectorate; and it looked as if the Imperial Government might acquiesce in his suggestion. On the other hand a substantial body of missionaries, and the surviving humanitarians in Britain, were sufficiently impressed by Khama's religious attitudes and by his claims upon the Imperial Government, to protest against Rhodes's proposal.

In 1895, Khama set off to London, accompanied by Sechele of the Ba-Kwena and Bathoen of the Ba-Ngwaketse, and reinforced by a letter signed by themselves and by Lentswe of the Ba-Kgatla. In London the new Unionist Colonial Secretary, Joseph Chamberlain, was apparently willing to hand over the whole protectorate to the company, on the same terms as it administered and controlled Rhodesia itself. In the face of the protests from the chiefs, however, he agreed to compromise: each chief and his people would have a demarcated reserve, while the remaining area (of which the most important was a thin strip of country running parallel with the Transvaal border) was handed over to the chartered company. It was not a perfect arrangement, but it did preserve the *status quo* in most of the protectorate and it did obviate direct company control over most of the Tswana. It was clearly an advantage to the chiefs that so little of their land was suitable for white pastoralism, and that all of the country was so important in colonial strategic terms: nevertheless their own contribution was considerable and it seems reasonable to suppose that their diplomatic skill was a crucial factor which preserved their people from rule by colonists. One further point should be noted. The company might eventually have succeeded; but immediately after the compromise described above, it was discredited and humiliated by its participation in the Jameson Raid. In disgrace, the company did not re-assert its claims. If we now ask how the Tswana chiefs contrived to become British Protected persons on relatively good terms, part of the answer must be that external circumstances were favourable to such a decision; but much of the reason is the diplomatic skill of the chiefs, in seizing their opportunities.

If the Tswana leaders were fortunate in the external circumstances which furthered their interests, the Shangane were very unfortunate in finding external circumstances unfavourable. Mzila, who had become king in 1860 by means of Portuguese assistance, had no intention of behaving like a Portuguese puppet; and like so many other African rulers of his generation he appealed to the British for support. Until 1879 certainly, and to a certain extent even later, British Imperial rule was preferred to colonist control, on the grounds that it permitted communities to retain their social integrity and most of their land. It was also believed that trading opportunities were better with the British than with the Portuguese. In 1870 therefore, Mzila sent his first embassy to Shepstone the Natal Secretary for Native Affairs: to resolve a dispute with the Swazi, to establish diplomatic contact and to enquire about trading possibilities. Then, and consistently thereafter, Shepstone and the British declined to interfere in what they regarded as Portugal's sphere of interest.

During the 1880s Portuguese interest in the interior intensified, partly because one of the 'rules' of the Scramble for Africa required proof of effective occupation. Gungunyana, who had succeeded his father Mzila in the early 1880s, was anxious to avoid any surrender of power and sovereignty, and revived the old policy of bringing in the British to counterbalance the Portuguese claimants. In 1887, therefore, a further delegation was sent to Natal, but with the same negative result as before. British Imperial authorities were simply not prepared to annoy the Portuguese for the sake of the Shangane. Rhodes, on the other hand, showed as much interest in the Gaza kingdom as he did in the Ndebele: through Gaza he might arrange access to the sea for his projected settlement in Mashonaland. In 1890 therefore, one of Rhodes's agents signed a treaty with Gungunyana, along similar lines to those of the Lobengula treaty. What is significant about this treaty is not its commercial content, but its style, which is that of an international treaty involving the British Imperial Government. Rhodes had no authority to involve the Imperial officials, but Gungunyana was anxious for British involvement, and Rhodes's agent falsely promised that the British Government would be involved. In the same year, the crucial treaty was signed between the Portuguese and British Governments, whereby most of the Gaza state was recognised as being Portuguese territory. Not understanding international realities, Gungunyana had been involved in a side-show while real decisions were taken elsewhere. As a result, during the war of 1895, when the Portuguese eventually imposed direct control upon the Gaza state, Gungunyana was still sending emissaries to the British, without the slightest prospect of bringing them into Mozambique.

The Swazi state, though equally dependent upon diplomatic skills, had far less room for manoeuvre. The Zulu, from the 1820s onwards, were too close to ignore, and the Swazi were in no position to pick and choose among possible allies. The arrival of the Afrikaners into the immediate vicinity of the Swazi during the 1840s therefore represented a useful opportunity to form an alliance against Zulu threats. Until the British conquest of Zululand in 1880, the Swazi–Afrikaner alliance was reasonably equitable. The Afrikaners wanted land, and Mswati let them have the land of dependent non-Swazi people to the west and north of what is now Swaziland. In exchange, cattle were handed over to Mswati. These exchanges seem to have involved sovereignty over the ceded areas, since in 1864 Mswati assisted the Afrikaners to suppress the inhabitants of the region who declined to accept Afrikaner authority. As late as 1875, the Swazi saw no harm in the intervention of an Afrikaner commando to ensure the succession of Mbandzeni as king, in the face of rival claimants.

Also with a view to forming anti-Zulu alliances, Mswati sent representatives to Shepstone in Natal, and in the manner of traditional diplomatic alliances offered his sister to Shepstone himself – a gesture which Shepstone appreciated but felt unable to accept. With the British annexation of the Transvaal in 1877, it was obviously desirable for the Swazi to establish some formal alliance with their new neighbours. To ease the way towards such an understanding, and to demonstrate Swazi good will, Mbandzeni sent a regiment to assist in the defeat of the Pedi in 1879. For the British, however, Swazi affairs were definitely marginal, and the significance of Swaziland was represented mainly by its strategic position between the Transvaal and the sea. After the first Transvaal war of independence in 1880–1881, therefore, the British insisted upon Swaziland remaining outside the jurisdiction of the Transvaal, but were prepared to allow substantial parts of Swazi territory to be absorbed into the Afrikaner republic. Further, the removal of the Zulu threat by the sub-division of Zululand meant that the Swazi no longer possessed any great bargaining counter in negotiations with the Afrikaners, who no longer required the alliance which the Swazi offered.

During the 1880s numbers of concession-seekers crowded around Mbandzeni, and extensive concessions – for land, mining rights, grazing rights and even the right to collect revenue – were awarded. Mbandzeni's motives in granting these concessions are obscure. In the event, many concessions were duplicated, so that alien authority in Swaziland was vested in dozens of colonists and Afrikaners, whose concessions conflicted. In this way, many of the concessions neutralised each other, and the alien concessionaires were severely disunited. Conceivably that may have been Mbandzeni's intention; but it seems more likely that he could think of no alternative to yielding, since the Swazi possessed insufficient power to resist a determined attack. By 1887 Mbandzeni felt the need of a permanent white adviser to deal with the concessionaires, and rather unwisely selected Shepstone's son, Theophilus Shepstone junior, for that post. Throughout the 1880s, the economic partition of Swaziland continued, while its sovereign independence remained theoretically intact.

In 1890, however, the British and the Transvaalers proposed to hand over authority to the Transvaal. Mbandzeni had died the previous year, and was succeeded by the young Bunu who, being a minor, had his mother as Queen Regent. The Queen Regent and her councillors despatched an embassy to Britain, to request an Imperial protectorate instead of a Transvaal alternative but the plea was rejected, and in 1894 a Convention between Britain and the Transvaal established that the Transvaal would, indeed, exercise a protectorate over the Swazi. That protectorate was terminated only by the South African War, during which the Swazi remained neutral, awaiting the outcome of the war to discover their future status. The Queen Regent continued to exercise effective authority despite the death of Bunu in 1899 and the accession of his minor son, Sobhuza II. The fact that Swaziland remained a separate Imperial protectorate seems to be unrelated to Swazi efforts in the same direction. The Concessions Commission, established after the war to enquire into the propriety of the Swazi concessions, took a long time to sort out conflicting claims, and then to recommend that each concessionaire voluntarily surrender a third of his entitlement. By that time Swaziland had in practice been administered separately from the Transvaal for six or seven years, and remained separate largely through inertia. From then onwards, Swazi aspirations were devoted to recovering the land and other rights lost to the concessionaires, and to a series of legal battles against the protectorate authorities. Despite the military weakness of the state, despite its having no adult king for most of the crucial period and despite the alienation of many of its economic resources, Swaziland somehow managed to remain outside the sphere of direct colonist authority.

In many cases, however, societies were doomed to be conquered no matter what efforts were made by the political leaders. The kingdom of the Ndebele is a good case in point. Lobengula observed the steady advances of the Germans from the west, the Rhodes interest and the British from the south-west through Tswana country, the Transvaalers from the south-east and the Portuguese from the east, and he cannot have been surprised when emissaries of these powers began to appear at his court from about 1887 onwards. Like Mpande and Cetywayo, he arrived at a policy of avoiding all pretexts for white invasion, while attempting to build up the military strength of his state in case war should prove unavoidable. Like his neighbour Khama, he was also prepared to give away territory over which he had no actual control. In pursuance of this policy, he first signed a treaty with a Transvaal representative, whereby Afrikaners moving into his country would have special rights and be answerable to their own consul. That was in 1887, and in 1888 Lobengula signed a counter-agreement with Moffatt the missionary acting on behalf of the British Government. In terms of the Lobengula–Moffatt treaty, Lobengula undertook not to alienate any territory without the permission of the British High Commissioner – an undertaking which he was happy to provide. Later in the same year he signed a further agreement, this time with Rudd who represented the Rhodes interest. The Lobengula–Rudd agreement gave rise to the 'Rudd concession' whereby the Rhodes interest acquired a monopoly of all minerals within Lobengula's domain, and in exchange provided the king with 1,000 rifles, 100,000 rounds of ammunition, an annual pension of £1200, and a steam-boat for use on the Zambesi. That concession formed the economic basis of the British South Africa Company Charter. In these agreements Lobengula's purposes are clear: to avoid giving offence to foreigners who might take by force what they were refused by peace; to obtain armaments and money to service those armaments; to play off each white group against other white groups; and to divert European attention from his own Ndebele towards the neighbouring Shona (in whose territory many of the concessions were located).

At first the plan seemed to be working. During 1890 Rhodes despatched a column of 380 white pioneers (and their African and Coloured servants) to occupy Mashonaland. The column duly skirted Ndebele country and set up their headquarters – Salisbury – at a safe distance beyond Lobengula's impis. As in Natal/Zululand however, co-existence between a notably powerful African state and a white colony was not possible. In addition, the pioneers found that Mashonaland was less fertile and less abounding in gold than they had been led to expect: Matabeleland (the colonists' term for the Ndebele state) might well be more useful for minerals and was certainly more suitable for white agriculture. By the end of 1892 pretexts had been found, and in 1893 the company (preferring the extinction of the Ndebele state to its own bankruptcy) invaded Ndebele country, whence Lobengula had to flee. He was in no physical condition to withstand the hardships of fast movement, and early in 1894 the second and last king of the Ndebele died. The company's campaign was sufficiently swift and successful to forestall imperial intervention (which at one time seemed likely) and so the Ndebele, like the Shona, passed under direct company rule. Within the terms of the situation as Lobengula faced it, he had done all he could. His diplomacy was faultless in dealing with alien powers, and he had built up his military resources as impressively as was possible. It was scarcely his fault that his father had chosen to settle in an area where gold was expected to be found. The plain truth was that no single African state was strong enough to withstand a determined colonial or imperial attack.

Forces operating from the south found the Barotse state in a very delicate predicament. After the overthrow of the Kololo conquest dynasty in 1865, no claimant had been able to establish himself securely on the throne for more than a dozen years. In 1878, when Lewanika came to power, he could not rely upon retaining it. His policy of encouraging inter-marriage between the different castes and ethnic groups of his kingdom was sound, but would obviously pay off in the long run rather than the short. The avoidance of regional bases for administration, similarly, minimised the risk of regional rebellion but did not entirely rule it out. One major circumstance working in his favour was the fact that the state was economically viable (and therefore did not need to form alliances with slave-traders or other disruptive entrepreneurs) and economically integrated, such that each specialising group depended upon the others. Economic integration had contributed largely to holding the community together despite the chronic political instability of the post-Kololo years. Nevertheless Lewanika was in a dangerous position, being unable to count on internal unity in the face of the rising tide of white settlers and concession-hunters moving towards him from the south.

Khama was a near neighbour, who had successfully negotiated the troubles of the 1870s, and Lewanika was inclined to accept Khama's advice to seek an Imperial protectorate. Coillard, of the Paris Evangelical

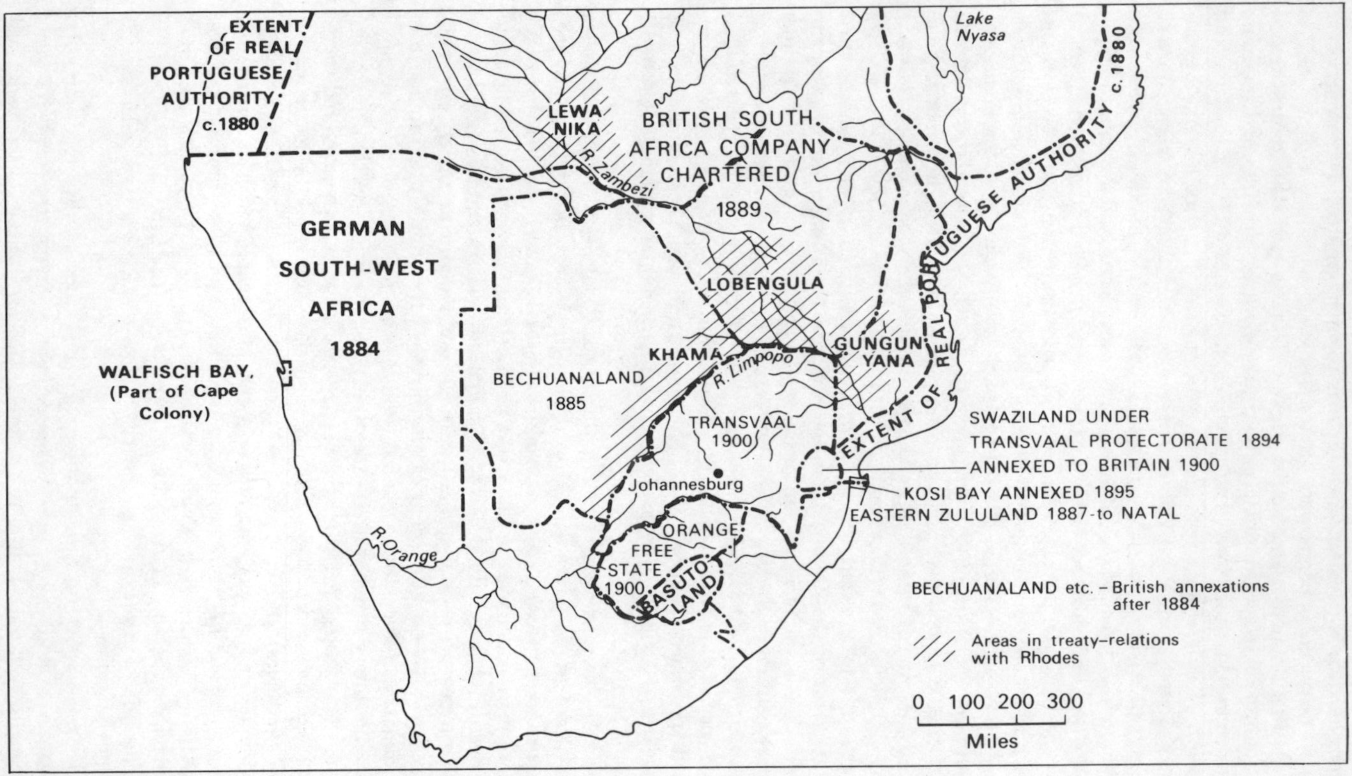
EXTENT OF REAL PORTUGUESE AUTHORITY c.1880
Lake Nyasa
LEWA NIKA
BRITISH SOUTH AFRICA COMPANY CHARTERED 1889
R. Zambezi
GERMAN SOUTH-WEST AFRICA 1884
WALFISCH BAY, (Part of Cape Colony)
LOBENGULA
KHAMA
R. Limpopo
GUNGUN YANA
EXTENT OF REAL PORTUGUESE AUTHORITY c.1880
BECHUANALAND 1885
TRANSVAAL 1900
Johannesburg
ORANGE FREE STATE 1900
BASUTO LAND
R. Orange
SWAZILAND UNDER TRANSVAAL PROTECTORATE 1894
ANNEXED TO BRITAIN 1900
KOSI BAY ANNEXED 1895
EASTERN ZULULAND 1887-to NATAL
BECHUANALAND etc. – British annexations after 1884
Areas in treaty-relations with Rhodes
0 100 200 300
Miles

White conquest in Southern Africa

Mission, who had served Moshoeshoe's diplomatic purposes, was stationed in Barotseland, and Lewanika was therefore able to call upon Sotho experience as well. Coillard's and Lewanika's interests coincided with those of Rhodes's chartered company, with which a treaty was signed in 1890. The company wished to retain the full extent of Barotseland, since they enjoyed mineral concessions wherever Lewanika's authority stretched; Coillard wished to secure the king through this external alliance, so as to minimise the anti-Lewanika and anti-Christian factions in Barotse politics; Lewanika needed external support to hold his throne and to preserve order within the community. In the absence of Imperial officials and white settlers, a reasonably favourable agreement could be reached between the company, the mission society and the central authority of the kingdom.

In general, an important contributary factor to the speed and relative completeness of the various white conquests was the willingness of African states to collaborate. It is important not to accuse these societies and their leaders of treachery. They saw the present in terms of the past, and could not forget old animosities even in the face of new menaces. Furthermore, it was clear that outright resistance and even clever negotiations were likely to be unsuccessful. Bearing these circumstances in mind, we can see a certain wisdom in the popular decision 'If you can't beat them, join them'. The collaboration of individual African groups did not *cause* the white conquest – it assisted and hastened a process which could probably not have been resisted. In any event, as we have seen, the Swazi assisted the Afrikaners in their contests with the Zulu: in the 1870s they even assisted the Transvaalers in the conquest of Sekhukhune. Khama sent military aid to the Chartered Company in the campaign against the Ndebele. In all the wars on the Cape frontier some tribe or group of clans would always be found taking the part of the white frontiersmen. In all Moshoeshoe's skirmishes against the Afrikaners in the Orange Free State he had to count on a certain number of Africans opposing him by force. In South-West Africa, Herero and Nama continued their pre-colonial feuds in the face of the German conquest, and the Nama were prepared (after their own defeat at German hands) to assist in the suppression of their old enemies as well. In the 1970s it may seem remarkable that there was so little sense of African unity, but it must be remembered that in 1870 'African' like 'Africa' were non-African concepts, and one society was not prepared to assist another simply because they shared the same colour. Furthermore, much as we might like to see in history a record of heroism and (if possible) success, we are much more likely to find leaders who estimated situations realistically, saw what was inevitable, and tried to come to terms with it before it was too late.

Chapter 9

Resistance from within

The extension of European authority over the African societies profoundly changed the tactical situation. Invariably, the nature of political leadership was altered, and often the old leaders were dismissed by the new white authorities. After Lobengula died, the B.S.A. Company prevented the Ndebele from selecting a successor as king, so that leadership devolved upon the indunas. Similarly, Cetywayo was never re-instated as king of Zululand, and the division of the country into thirteen principalities effectively prevented the Zulu from reuniting for more than a generation. The Transvaal Afrikaners in Swaziland, like the Cape Colonists in the Transkei and the Imperial representatives in Basutoland made sure that traditional leadership posts were filled by men who depended upon the white officials for their authority. Even when the leaders remained in office the nature of internal power was altered: Khama and Montshiwa as colonial chiefs were at once stronger internally and weaker externally than they had been before. Because of these wide-ranging changes in leadership within the African states resistance tended to be led by individuals who were from families which had not previously exercised power.

In another important way, the tactical situation was changed: after the conquest the African societies were much better acquainted with the white authorities, and their new knowledge was often applied to deal with the new situation. For one thing, it was widely appreciated that no single people could hope to succeed in a lone resistance, and that combination would increase the chances of success. Again, familiarity with the white-controlled society sometimes suggested points at which that society might be vulnerable. For these reasons it seems legitimate to distinguish between the pre-conquest and the post-conquest resistance movements, even though they all had the same purpose, namely to resist white and restore African authority.

A very clear example of this difference is to be found in the combined resistance of the Shona and Ndebele after they were incorporated in the new colony of Rhodesia. The Rhodesian colonists, like the Ndebele, were contemptous of Shona military weakness and political division: they failed to recognise (and therefore failed to replace) the old paramounts of the loose Shona federation. Again, having seen the last of Lobengula, they thought they had removed the only possible organiser of Ndebele resistance.

Above all, they could not conceive of Ndebele–Shona co-operation, since they knew the tradition of Ndebele overlordship. In that respect they were almost correct: the tradition of hostility between the two major African societies in Rhodesia did make co-operation extremely difficult, and neither group would accept the leadership of the other, even for the purpose of expelling the colonists.

In the event, the two societies were able partly to co-ordinate their efforts, by means of a communication system which comprised the old religious cult whose centre was in the hills of the south – the Matopos – and which pre-dated the Ndebele invasion. When Jameson invaded the Transvaal and was forced to surrender with a detachment of Rhodesian forces, the opportunity had come. The Ndebele rose early in 1896, and were quickly followed by the Shona. On no occasion did the two societies fight alongside, but the co-ordination of resistance doubled the effectiveness of the rebellion, and for several months Company authority was confined to the towns, while the countryside reverted to African rule. In the end the revolt was crushed by re-dividing it. Rhodes hurried up from Cape Town, anxious to suppress trouble before the Imperial authorities intervened and restored a different kind of order. He met the Ndebele indunas and persuaded them to conclude a separate peace, leaving the Shona to fight alone. Even then, the Shona continued to fight for several months, well into 1897, when the Company forces finally restored their authority throughout Rhodesia. The strength of the revolt lay in its co-operation: its weakness lay in the continuing inability of the two major societies to unite.

A very similar episode occurred in South-West Africa. Of the three major African societies, the Ovambo in the far north were unaffected at first by German rule, and played no part in the great uprising. The two other societies – Herero and Nama – had an unfortunate tradition of enmity, having struggled for control over the few areas of pastoral country surrounded by semi-desert. The leader of the Nama, Hendrik Witbooi, was a literate and thoughtful man. He had resisted the Germans successfully until 1894, when he concluded a peace treaty which permitted his people to keep their firearms. Though Witbooi deplored the tribal divisions of the African societies, he could not overcome them, and sensibly decided that he might as well collaborate with the Germans since he could not himself defeat them. From 1894 to 1904 therefore, he sent several detachments of troops to assist the Germans in various campaigns against other societies. The paramount of the Herero, Maharero, was also able to defend his country against the Germans until he died in 1890. At that point a succession dispute broke out, and the Germans were able to exploit the Herero divisions and impose a certain amount of control. In 1894, Samuel Maharero was recognised by the Germans as paramount, in exchange for allowing a small German garrison to be posted in his midst. He too was literate and he too assisted the Germans in their campaigns against minor tribal groups who resisted.

At first German rule seemed harmless, since it was largely ineffective and always indirect. The steadily increasing settler population, however,

A sketch depicting an engagement during the Shona–Ndebele Rising, 1896–7

changed the balance of power, and the Nama and Herero became increasingly nervous. During 1896 and 1897, small groups of the two societies combined in local resistance, though the political leaders disapproved of this development. Furthermore the rinderpest epidemic of 1897 had a disastrous effect on the pastoral economies, almost wiping out the herds. By 1903 the Herero were desperate: they were losing their land to the settlers and the railway companies, they had lost many of their cattle to rinderpest, they were losing what remained to the traders. In January 1904 they rose unanimously in revolt, and Samuel Maharero appealed to the Nama to assist him. In the middle of 1904 German re-inforcements arrived, commanded by General von Trotha, who made up his mind not only to defeat the Herero but to exterminate them by forcing them eastwards into the desert. So successful was that policy that something like 75–80 per cent of the Herero died, though Samuel himself and a few hundred followers crossed the desert and were given refuge by Tswana chiefs in the British Bechuanaland Protectorate.

Witbooi's Nama rose in October 1904. Samuel Maharero's letters of appeal had not reached him, otherwise he might have acted sooner. As it was, his rising was too late to derive maximum benefit from co-operation, since the Herero had already been defeated in August at the battle of Waterberg. The same tactics were applied against them as against the Herero, but the Nama were better skilled at guerilla tactics in the desert country, and were able to resist for much longer. Witbooi was fully aware of the consequences of rebellion and appreciated that there could be no compromise: the Germans must either be driven out or they would certainly attempt to wipe out the rebels. His resistance was astute and determined, but in October 1905 he was killed. Leadership then devolved upon one of the most astonishing personalities to appear in African history – Jakob Morenga, half-Nama and half-Herero, a man educated both at home and in Europe, and who had great skill as a guerilla leader. His followers came from a variety of different tribes, and his own resistance had started in 1903, even earlier than the Herero revolt. He regarded the chiefs as collaborators with the Germans – which indeed they had been until 1904 – and shared Witbooi's opinion that a compromise peace was impossible. Significantly, the Germans offered 20,000 marks for his head, whereas Samuel Maharero's head had been valued at only 5,000. As the guerilla war continued it spread beyond the colony and it was a bullet fired by British police, in the Bechuanaland Protectorate, which killed Morenga in September 1907. The last leader of the Nama was Simon Cooper, one of the original chiefs under Hendrik Witbooi, who continued the war until 1909, when he agreed to stay out of South-West Africa in return for a cash payment. The rising ended, as it had begun, as a sectional campaign: the co-operation had died with Jakob Morenga.

Meanwhile, on the other side of the sub-continent, another rebellion had broken out, which was equally an illustration of the need for a larger unity, though in a different form. In 1897, the Imperial Government had at last permitted the Natal Colonial Government to annex Zululand, thereby placing the Zulu under direct control of the colonists. The South African War of 1899–1902 had prevented the Natal Government (comprising Colonists, since the grant of responsible government to them in 1893) from giving much attention to its new subjects. Thereafter, the Government encouraged the alienation of Zulu country for white settlement, the imposition of increased rents and taxes to encourage the Zulu to work on white farms and in white industry, and the stiffening of labour laws to ensure greater control over the African working population. In an important sense the Natal Government drove the Zulu to rebel, by ignoring the warnings of the civil service against increasing the burden on the Africans under their authority. Early in 1906 there was a small rising in Natal itself. The Government 'over-reacted', declared martial law, sent in troops, sentenced a dozen leaders to death in a military court, and then – despite further warnings from the Imperial Government – carried out the executions. It was a series of events which was only too likely to happen when a white population of only about 50,000 was given control over upwards of a million Africans: the Colonists were almost certain to become panic stricken in the face of a political crisis.

The executions provoked a more widespread rising in Zululand, led by a minor induna called Bambatha, who gave his name to the rising itself. Once the Colonists had been reinforced by Imperial troops from elsewhere in South Africa, the idea of a general 'native war' appealed to them very strongly. The Colonists had been anxious for many years to find some reason to cow the pride of their over-mighty subjects; and when the war broke out they had no scruples about punitive measures. Little attempt was ever made to distinguish between those who had rebelled and those who had not, and the troops quartered Zululand destroying whatever and whomever they found. The Zulu campaign differed very little in terms of savagery from the South-West Africa campaign of the same period – even the British Colonial Secretary was disturbed by the savagery of the sentiments expressed by the Colonists and their Government. The campaign itself lasted only a few months, since the Zulu were in no condition to put up any great resistance. After the campaign the Government decided upon a show trial, which it was hoped would prove that the organiser of the rebellion was Dinizulu, a son of Cetywayo and a local chief under the Government. In view of Dinizulu's unambitious and pacific character, the accusation was extremely hard to believe, and was almost certainly untrue. The rebellion itself showed no signs of having been concerted at all, and Dinizulu's only 'crime' seems to have been his decision to give shelter to Bambatha. In other words, the traditional leadership was almost certainly unimportant in fomenting the rebellion: what was more important was a series of spontaneous reactions by a series of otherwise unimportant men. The Zulu were not united even among themselves.

Another instance of 'resistance from within' may be seen in the War of Disarmament in Basutoland. Like so many South African trends 'internal resistance' occurred earlier in Basutoland than in most other parts. In 1871, the Imperial Government – despite its agreement with Moshoeshoe –

handed over Basutoland to the Cape. The Cape Government was unaccustomed to dealing with such a powerful and defensible society, and before long it fell into the error of underestimating Sotho strength. In 1879 the Prime Minister Sprigg decided that all Basotho must surrender their arms by April 1880. His decision was influenced by the relative ease with which he had recently disarmed the Galeka and Fingo populations. Furthermore, since Moshoeshoe's death the internal divisions among the Basotho had become more pronounced: for example, the Paramount Chief (Letsie) was prepared to surrender his arms, and the hard core of resistance centred upon other chiefs. In September 1880 Sprigg sent in the police, and the war began in earnest. The Basotho leaders were severely divided, but on the other hand some of the Xhosa peoples in the Transkei and Griqualand East rose simultaneously, thereby compelling the Colonial forces to cover a much enlarged area of disaffection. The Colonial forces were strong enough to win individual battles, but could find no way of controlling the people themselves, and were therefore doomed to an expensive campaign whose end was never in sight. General Gordon, one of the ablest British soldiers of the time, refused to help the Government in what he considered to be an unjust aggression. In April 1881 the Imperial High Commissioner intervened in order to rescue the Cape from humiliation: an agreement was reached whereby Basutoland remained its old size (the Cape had been anxious to rob it of its last remaining arable areas) and the arms would be retained by most of those who possessed them. That still left the issue unresolved, and at last, in 1884, the Imperial Government agreed to resume direct control, since the Cape was incapable of dealing with the situation. The Transkei, it was thought, would create quite enough problems for one Colonial administration.

One thing which all these risings proved was that military resistance was not necessarily enough. In Rhodesia and in South-West Africa they failed in the end, leaving the rebels exposed to greater Colonial control. Even in Basutoland the resistance succeeded only because the objectives were limited and negative in scope. Furthermore, military resistance raised the issue of leadership, and that was a particularly difficult problem. Traditionally, the military campaigns were led by the political authorities. With the removal of some of the most able of the traditional leaders – Cetywayo, Lobengula, and Sekhukhune by war, Montshiwa and Moshoeshoe by old age and death, Khama by conversion – military leadership became scarce. The men appointed as 'traditional' chiefs by the Colonial officials were seldom willing or able to lead military risings. On the other hand, traditional political leaders, owing their power to traditions, were often very conservative when it came to forming inter-tribal alliances: even in Rhodesia, the Ndebele did not accept military orders from Shona chiefs, nor did the Shona from Ndebele officers. Quite apart from the inherent difficulty of persuading people that they could win a rising against white rule, the nature of leadership was such that military action was unlikely to be attempted and even less likely to be effective. A new way of dealing with the situation had to be evolved, preferably dispensing with the old leaders.

Paradoxically, religious leaders often filled the gap left by political leaders, and religious ideas filled the gap left by political ideologies. We have seen the importance of the religious officials in the Shona–Ndebele rising, where they acted primarily as a trusted means of communication between two suspicious societies. In the eastern Cape religious leadership was even more prominent. The Xhosa were in a desperate state of affairs. Constant white pressure on the frontier had only temporarily been abated by the Afrikaner Trek of 1834–1835. Each British Governor of the Cape had devised a new 'solution' to the frontier problem, with the result that the Xhosa had been subjected to a wide variety of different colonial policies. D'Urban (after the war of 1834) had determined to push the frontier tribes back and fill up the vacuum with white settlers: the British Government had vetoed his policy and attempted to undo its effects. Smith (after the 'War of the Axe' in 1847) found a system of treaties governing frontier relations, and decided to abandon treaties in general – which he did theatrically by blowing up a wagon in which the treaty forms had been transported to the frontier. The country was annexed piecemeal, sometimes by the Imperial Government and sometimes by the Cape Colony, but was consistently reduced in size and economic viability. To make matters worse, the British often adopted a policy of settling 'neutral' groups in Xhosa territory, in the hope of keeping the major forces apart. German ex-servicemen, Fingo refugees from the Shakan wars, Hottentots from the western province of the Colony, Griquas from Griqualand, were all at various times pushed into the country between the Cape eastern border and the Natal southern border. In short, the Xhosa were subjected to ever-increasing pressure from their neighbours, and were concentrated into ever-decreasing areas of the countryside. In 1850 the tribes rose once again, and this time they were assisted by Tembu people from further east, by Hottentots from within the Colony, and even by some African police and militia who deserted from the service of the Colonial Government. The suppression of this un- usually large-scale rebellion, however, was a terribly disheartening blow to the Xhosa: so much so, that it became exceedingly difficult to persuade anyone that it would ever be worth trying again. It was, in modern terms, a crisis of confidence. In this crisis, prophets arose among the Xhosa and Tembu, bringing new hope in the form of a strange message. The people must place complete confidence in the supernatural. To demonstrate that faith, they must abstain from witchcraft, refuse to plant crops, and kill their cattle. Having demonstrated their faith, they would be rewarded by the resurrection of the cattle, the crops, and the old warriors, while a wind would blow the Europeans into the sea. The people obeyed the instructions, but the reward never came, and as a result a large proportion of the people starved to death. As a demonstration of faith it was unsurpassed: as a measure of the people's desperation it was eloquent: as a serious means of resistance it was disastrous. After 1857 the Xhosa survivors lost much of their remaining land, many of them dispersed throughout the Colony and beyond its borders, and it was not for another twenty years that the Cape Government had to worry about their spirit of independence.

Though the national suicide of the Xhosa was in many ways an act of supreme folly, it may help us to understand later resistance movements. The merits of a religious approach included the fact that a religious leader – unlike a traditional chief – could appeal to the loyalty of more than one polity at a time. A religious movement could provide (what no other organisation could offer) an ideology which would cut across ethnic division. It did not matter whether the religion was an indigenous African one or a version of Christianity: all could be turned to account. While the Shona and Ndebele (who had generally rejected such Christian offers as were made to them before the conquest) applied a traditional religion to a political purpose, other groups made use of Christianity. They did not, of course, use the established missionary-controlled Churches, since the missionaries would on no account permit such 'applied religion'. The missionary Moffatt had indeed acted as one of Rhodes's messengers to Logengula, thereby abusing his old friendship with the king. But even the missionaries who resented the brutal methods often used by Colonial conquerors were in an ambiguous position. Much as they might deplore the methods of the Colonists and Colonialists, they did not object to Colonial rule itself, so they could not bring themselves to assist anti-Colonial movements. Coillard was very effective in advising Lewanika of the Barotse on how to obtain the best possible terms from the Colonial authorities; Colenso helped to soften the worst effects of Colonial rule among the Zulu; but all the missionaries seem to have believed that Colonial rule could be made humane and beneficial. For that reason they often devoted their lives to bringing about a reform within the Colonial system – but they were reforming, not overthrowing.

As happened elsewhere in Africa at much the same time, towards the end of the century Africans in South Africa increasingly resorted to the creation of independent Christian churches. African clergy grew tired of the refusal of the white clergy to trust them in responsible posts, and African congregations increasingly resented the failure of the white congregations to accept them as equal in the sight of man. One impetus towards independency was the discovery that Negroes had their own Church organisations – the African Methodist Episcopal Church, for example (an American Negro organisation) sent missionaries to South Africa in the late 1880s. Although the American Negroes, like the white missionaries, were human enough to want to keep power in their own hands, their presence caused a widespread sensation. Another impetus was the news, which soon spread to South Africa, that the Ethiopians had successfully defeated the Italians at the battle of Adowa (1896). All that was known of Ethiopia was that it was an African Empire, a Christian community, dignified with a long history, and a successful resister of European intrusion. This somewhat incomplete image of Ethiopia served as an inspiration to African Christians, and encouraged them to believe (what the missionaries denied) that Africans could run their own affairs. Throughout the 1890s then, there was a series of breakaways, in which Africans abandoned the parent organisations and set up independent Anglican, Presbyterian, Lutheran and other churches.

Congregations followed the separatist ministers, though their frustrations may well have been different from those of the leaders. Loss of land, absorption into a migrant labour economy and general loss of status and control over their own lives, may help to account for the immediate popularity of the separatist movements. One of the 'prophets' of this movement was active in South-West Africa some months before the outbreak of the Nama rising, and may have been influential in that predominantly Christian community. In general however, the independent Church movement provided the African societies with a peaceful means of acquiring Christianity, western education, organisational power and experience, and (as we will see later) a means of acquiring land. It was a means of acquiring certain advantages from the western world, without having to suffer the indignities of racial discrimination. Though the Colonists regarded 'Ethiopianism' as a dangerous political phenomenon it was more typically a safety-valve.

It was also typical of an increasing familiarity with westernism, and of an increasing ability to distinguish between useful and harmful aspects of the dominant culture. In the Cape, the inclusion of some African and Coloured citizens in the electorate provided opportunities for political action. As we shall see, two African newspapers attempted to marshal African voting strength so as to derive maximum benefit from political opportunity; and a trickle of African students was making its way to and from universities in Britain and America, bringing back skills and knowledge which were not available locally. Although effective political parties, in the western style, were most prominent in the twentieth century, they had their origins in the nineteenth.

These developments affected only a small minority. The overwhelming majority of Africans even at the end of the nineteenth century were rural, illiterate, and unskilled except in traditional techniques. While the literate élite thought they could see increasing opportunities in the future, the majority could not. In the Cape, for instance, Rhodes as Prime Minister had passed the 'Glen Grey Act', whose purpose was to divide Africans into prosperous landowners and landless industrial labourers, and whose method was to encourage the spread of individual tenure in the African areas. That legislation of 1894 was the logical culmination of steadily increasing restrictions upon Africans, whereby they were prohibited from drinking liquor and from moving freely around the Colony. Rhodes also restricted the number of African and Coloured voters by tying the franchise more strictly to individual property qualifications. The Governmental coalition of Rhodes and the Afrikaners was easily strong enough to overrule objections from the African élite and from the handful of white liberal parliamentarians. Similarly, further north, increased Afrikaner strength led to increased control over the lives and land and labour of the African subjects. In the 1890s, for example, the Transvaal gold mine owners were strong enough to extend the area of industrial recruiting so as to include Portuguese East Africa. Conversely, the African labour force, divided by ethnic and linguistic and historical differences, had not yet grasped the potential value of industrial strike action as a means of bringing about economic and even political change. They still, generally, regarded the British Imperial Government as the most promising instrument for improving their circumstances, and still hoped that the 'imperial factor' would remain strong enough to curb the excesses of the increasingly powerful 'colonial factor'.

In short, though none of the African reactions of the late nineteenth century had much direct success, they are evidence of a willingness to experiment with new forms of political and other action. Those experiments had not yet demonstrated any positive results, but they certainly illustrated the mood of the resisters. On the other hand, with the passage of time new and dangerous divisions were appearing, which made delay disastrous. In South-West Africa, as we have seen, the radicalism of Jakob Morenga the guerilla leader was at odds with the conservatism of the Nama chiefs: in Zululand and Basutoland resistance had been led by men who were not traditional leaders, while the appointed chiefs had been slow to act. Particularly in the Cape, a westernised élite felt itself increasingly distinct from the non-westernised majority, and a further division was being encouraged by the Government, between the landed and the landless. Action was required before these divisions grew too acute. Contrary to the opinion of members of the African élite, time was not necessarily on their side.

Chapter 10

White unity and white union

Many texts on South African history have laid great and misleading emphasis on the battles between different white groups in the sub-continent. Because the writers ignored the presence of an African majority, it was possible for them to write as if British had fought against Afrikaner in a political vacuum. More recent scholarship has tended to alter this emphasis, and it is now possible to see that the potential threat offered by the Africans (even when they were not in fact doing anything) altered the nature of the white quarrels. There were, of course, important battles between the white communities, but at the same time there was a wide measure of basic agreement between them, and that agreement included the assumption that Africans must not be given arms or rights.

Bearing this in mind, we may have another look at political developments from the 1890s until union in 1910. Let us consider the background briefly. In 1893 there was war between the B.S.A. Company and the Ndebele. In 1894 the Transvaal was at war with Malaboch, one of its reluctant African subjects; and there was a risk of war breaking out in Swaziland. Throughout the early 1890s the series of African secessions from the mission churches was in progress, and the white community did not know how much importance to attach to that phenomenon. In 1896 until 1897 the Ndebele and Shona were in revolt against the Company; and in South-West Africa the German conquest was by no means complete. During the South African War of 1899–1902 there were constant (and sometimes realistic) white fears of African intervention. In 1904 the Herero rebelled against the Germans, and there was a serious 'Black Peril' scare in the Transvaal. In 1905 the Nama joined the Herero in revolt, and the rebellion continued until 1908. In the same year serious fighting broke out as the Portuguese tried to assert their authority in Portuguese East Africa. In 1906 the Bambatha rebellion broke out. At any given time, there was either a resistance war going on somewhere or one had just finished, or there were rumours of another outbreak. Given this background, it is inconceivable that the white communities would commit all their forces, military or indeed emotional, to battle against each other.

The Jameson Raid at first sight destroys the above argument. Rhodes was not only Prime Minister of the Cape, Director of De Beers and the

The Jameson Raid: calling up volunteers at Pitsani on the Transvaal border

leading figure in the Chartered Company in the Rhodesias, but also a large investor in Transvaal gold mining. In 1895 he and other investors in Transvaal mining determined that the Transvaal Government must be overthrown. The early gold mining companies, which exploited the easiest gold desposits near the land surface, were making very substantial profits; but the latecomers (like Rhodes and Beit) who were extracting gold from very deep levels, were crippled by high working costs, and they blamed the Government for their predicament. Of course they could not simply say that they were overthrowing the Government for financial reasons, so an elaborate plot was devised whereby the white Uitlanders in the Transvaal would rise against the Afrikaner Government, and Rhodes would send in troops to rescue them from the Transvaal forces. For several months during 1895, Rhodes's newspapers gave great publicity to the 'grievances' of the Uitlanders, some of which were quite real, but none of which was sufficient to make the Uitlanders rebel. Towards the end of 1895 the Transvaal leaders of the plot (who formed themselves into the Reform Committee) decided that the Uitlanders were not going to rise, and they informed Rhodes to that effect. By that time, however, Rhodes had obtained a strip of Bechuanaland country from the Imperial Government and had set up an armed camp on the Transvaal border, and had put Dr Jameson in charge of it. Jameson was anxious to provoke troubles, in the hope of forcing the British Imperial Government to annex the Transvaal; and Rhodes's opinion was probably not very different. When the Reform Committee told Jameson that there would be no rising since the Uitlanders were not sufficiently angry to rebel, Jameson decided to force the issue by invading the Transvaal anyway. If he could not ride in as the saviour of the Uitlanders, he would ride in as provocateur, and perhaps then the Uitlanders would change their minds and rebel. The success of his maxim guns against the Ndebele made Jameson over-confident. His force was insufficient for the purpose, and on the fifth day of his invasion, 2nd January 1896, he had to surrender to the Afrikaner commando which encircled him at Doornkop on his way to Johannesburg.

That was the end of Rhodes's political career. Proved guilty of encouraging the overthrow of a friendly neighbouring state, he had to resign as Prime Minister and as director of the Chartered Company. Jameson and several leading Reform Committee men were sentenced to death by the Transvaal Government, but were then pardoned and released in exchange for a cash payment. The Shona and Ndebele took the opportunity to stage their own more genuine rebellion.

But how serious was it all? If Rhodes had succeeded in transforming the Transvaal into a British colony like the Cape, or into an Uitlander republic like the Digger Republic of Griqualand West, or into a republic on the old pattern but with a different economic approach to the gold mines, how would that have affected matters? In each case white rule would have continued, though the particular white rulers might have changed. The worst that could happen to the Transvaal Afrikaners was to become like the Cape Afrikaners (who normally formed part of the Government coalition): the best that could happen to the Uitlanders was to share political power (perhaps unequally) with the Afrikaners. The Africans would have continued to be vote-less, power-less and a source of unskilled migrant labour. The relative unimportance of the events is demonstrated by the fact that none of the plotters who was captured lost his life or his property: even in gaol they were attended by their African servants. Again, when the Ndebele–Shona rising broke out, no one prevented Rhodes from travelling from Cape Town to Rhodesia to deal with the crisis – white politics stopped while one of the participants took time off to deal with a more serious crisis.

Nevertheless, the Jameson Raid did poison relations between Afrikaner and British Colonists throughout South Africa. In the Cape the old alliance between some British and all the Afrikaner politicians broke down. In the Transvaal the Uitlanders began to be mobilised for political battle against the Kruger Government, and began to appeal (successfully) to the Imperial Government for support. The years from 1896 to 1899 were marked by a series of Imperial protests against Republican activities, and by a series of disputes between the Colonies and the Republics. One of the very few points of co-operation – but a significant one – was the flow of white volunteers from both language groups to assist the Chartered Company suppress the Rhodesian rebellion. Matters were further exacerbated by the new tough line taken by the Imperial Government, and personified by the new Imperialist High Commissioner, Sir Alfred Milner, who took charge of Imperial interests in South Africa in 1897. Imperial policy assumed that war was extremely likely, and therefore prepared for it: the Republicans, observing the new tough diplomacy and the preparations for war, also prepared themselves. The actions of each side helped convince the other that war would break out. The Imperial Government was the more willing to force a conflict, since it believed that the enfranchisement of the Transvaal Uitlanders would swamp the Afrikaners and place a reliable group of Imperial patriots in charge of the country. Firm in that belief, the Imperial Government demanded that the Transvaal give political rights to white non-Afrikaners. Kruger, believing that the Uitlanders would take over his country if given the chance, rejected the demand. In October 1899 they went to war – technically the Republics declared the war, but both sides had caused it. The war lasted two and a half years, caused great loss of life and destruction of property, and resulted in the British annexation of both the Transvaal and the Orange Free State as Crown Colonies administered by Imperial officials and with Milner as Governor.

But some curious features of the war should be observed. Some writers described it as the 'last of the gentlemen's wars', implying that each side had treated the other with considerable chivalry. In fact there was not much chivalry demonstrated, but it is true to say that it was not 'total war'. The British army was offered the chance to recruit Indian, Chinese and Hausa troops, but the offer was refused on the grounds that this was a 'white man's' business. For the same reason, the army refused to provide arms for the Zulu, some of the Xhosa, some of the Tswana and factions of the Basotho who offered to help defeat the Republics. Africans were employed as bearers, sometimes as scouts, and even as transport drivers, but not in a combatant capacity. On the other side, the Republics refused to arm the Swazi, some of the Basotho and the few Tswana chiefs who offered to assist. The early months of the war saw remarkable Afrikaner victories, after which they laid siege to the British garrisons at Kimberley (where Rhodes was living), Ladysmith (in Natal) and Mafeking (where Baden-Powell commanded the British troops). The British were forced back to the coastal areas, but even then they refused to enlarge the war by arming potential allies of the wrong colour. Early in 1900 the tide turned, the British captured Republican towns, and the Afrikaner commandos were forced back into the countryside where the guerilla war continued for two years. Even then, they too refused to arm their potential allies. Throughout the war, in fact, both sides devoted considerable efforts to preventing arms from falling into African hands, and to keeping the Africans neutral.

Nevertheless the Africans sometimes intervened. In the Northern Transvaal they had never fully acknowledged white conquest, and took the opportunity to settle old scores with the neighbouring farmers: in Swaziland, no provisions were given to the Afrikaners except on payment in exchange: the Zulu particularly harried the Afrikaner commandos, especially towards the end of the war. When the Afrikaners eventually surrendered in 1902, they mentioned that one major reason was the difficulty of dealing with African as well as British commando action. They referred particularly to the recent episode in which Zulu warriors had killed a party of Afrikaner troops, and to the increasing hostility demonstrated by the Transvaal tribes. It seems likely also that the Basotho would have taken part in the war, with factions fighting on both sides, if not for the discouragement of the British officials to whom they were responsible. As a result of official attitudes of both British and Afrikaners, the war remained predominantly, though not entirely, a white business.

It was therefore followed by a 'white man's peace', the Treaty of Vereeniging signed on 31st May 1902. Like the war, the peace attempted to preserve as much as possible of the traditional division between the white political community and the African work-force. The Afrikaners agreed to lay down their arms and become British citizens: the British agreed to restrict full citizenship (in other words, the franchise) to the white community – an agreement which they fully intended to honour. Many of the Afrikaner soldiers were allowed to keep their rifles for defence against their African neighbours: conversely the police force led by Baden-Powell set about disarming those Africans who had kept or acquired firearms during the war. Perhaps the most significant episode of the war occurred when the British troops reached Johannesburg in mid-1900. In the town were thousands of African mining workers who had been unable to go home when war broke out. When the British arrived, these labourers seem to have expected a substantial improvement in their status, and they burned the Pass books which symbolised their menial place in society and industry. The British were swift to disillusion the demonstrators, handed out severe punishments for breaking the (Republican) law, and set the labourers to work on road and railway building at arbitrarily low wages. When the war ended the workers were still there, and they rioted when they were still not allowed to go home. It is also worth noticing that the war-time suffering of the neutral Africans attracted far less attention than the suffering of the Afrikaners. To deal with guerilla warfare, the British decided to clear the country districts, burning houses and crops so as to deprive the Afrikaner commandos of food and lodging. The civilian population was rounded up into concentration camps where living conditions were wretched. When the conditions in these camps were brought to the attention of the Imperial Government, prompt action was taken to ensure that the death rate was reduced and the standard of living increased. But the conditions operating in African camps – where the mortality rate was equally high – never attracted attention. Though it was a white man's war, Africans were permitted to lose their lives and their property in the course of it.

British policy in the new colonies was based upon the assumption that the Uitlanders outnumbered the Afrikaners. During the war it was demonstrated that this assumption was inaccurate. The Imperial authorities were therefore obliged to set up Crown Colony Governments until such time as industrial expansion had attracted enough British working men to the Transvaal to ensure that they could win an election against the Afrikaners. Unfortunately for this plan, it depended for its success upon the willingness of Africans to come forward in increased numbers to do the unskilled work in the mines, so that there would be some justification in employing more white workers as skilled artisans and overseers. The mine-owners were confident that British rule would facilitate and cheapen the recruiting of African labour: for that reason they decided to cut the rate of wages by almost half – from over 50 shillings per month down to 30 shillings. In 1902 therefore, Transvaal and other Africans were in a sad plight. The British victory had not improved their political and social status, and had further reduced their power to resist. The war itself had involved the destruction of many lives and much property. Now the rate of wages in the most important sector of the economy was cut. Mining workers who had remained on the Rand during the war returned home bringing the bad news and discouraging their fellows from returning to the mining industry. Recruiting figures dropped sharply, and in 1904 there were still fewer workers available than had been employed in 1899. This large scale withholding of labour forced the mine-owners gradually to increase the rate of wages offered; but still the number of recruits remained disappointing. Further, the high mortality rate of tropical recruits, and the rebellion of potential recruits in Portuguese East Africa prevented the mines from finding alternative sources of industrial labour. In the end they imported indentured labour from China, and thereby broke the back of the African 'strike'. As soon as the Chinese began to arrive – in 1904 – wages paid to African workers began to decline once more. Also the white artisans refused to permit the importation of Chinese labour unless there were a legal guarantee that the Chinese would not be permitted to perform skilled or even semi-skilled work. The Government allowed that legislation to be enacted, and in course of time its application was extended to cover African workers as well. The net result of the 'strike' therefore was once again to reduce the rate of wages, and to hasten the creation of the industrial colour bar. As so often happens in southern African history, a white bargain was sealed by a black sacrifice: in this case a bargain between white employers and white employees, and a sacrifice on the part of African industrial labourers.

The South African War, then, failed to alter the essential nature of South African race relations. It also failed to alter the balance of power within the white community. The Imperial Government could not indefinitely deny political power to the white community without running a serious risk of rebellion, and without annoying the white Dominions and European and American opinion generally. Imperial power depended upon the collaboration of local British Colonists, and that collaboration would not last indefinitely under a Crown Colony system. In 1906 therefore the Imperial Government decided to allow elections and white self-government in the Transvaal in 1907 and in the Orange Free State (re-christened the Orange River Colony) in 1908. When the Transvaal election took place, the British voters were so divided that the Afrikaners won the election. The Afrikaners combined into Vereeniging Het Volk (the People's Union) led by the generals who had commanded them during the war – Louis Botha, J. C. Smuts, de la Rey and others. The British voters split their forces between three different parties which fought against each other more often than they fought against Het Volk. The Afrikaners therefore won a majority of seats although they had a minority of votes. In the Orange River Colony there were hardly any British voters anyway, and there was nothing to stop the Afrikaner party – Orangia Unie – led by Fischer and

General Hertzog from winning handsomely. Also in 1908 an election was held in the Cape, and Jameson's pro-Imperial Progressive Party was defeated by the South African Party, most of whose members were Afrikaner Bond men, though its Prime Minister was the English-speaking J. X. Merriman. Only in Natal were English-speaking whites still in power, and Natal was discredited by its mishandling of the Bambatha rebellion. Though the Union Jack flew over all the Colonists, within six years of the end of the South African War, three of the four most important Colonies were governed by Afrikaners. Further, the war had removed Kruger and his generation from power, and Afrikaners were thereafter led by a younger, more sophisticated group, whose political vision was larger and clearer. Instead of the old farmers, professional men (like Smuts and Hertzog) joined progressive farmers (like Botha) in leadership roles.

What the war did change was the 'flag' issue. All white South Africans had approved of some sort of federation or union of the white-ruled states, but they had previously been divided between those who favoured a republican constitution and those who preferred to seek dominion status within the Empire. The removal of the Republics removed a stumbling block to agreement, and within a few weeks of their coming into power, correspondence began between Merriman, Smuts and various other leading white politicians, on the desirability of closer association between the Colonies. The Bambatha rising underlined the lesson that the Colonies were really inter-dependent whether they liked it or not: all the Colonies had feared the spread of trouble from Zululand to their own black subjects, and the larger Colonies had sent re-inforcements to strengthen the Natal Government in its peril. The Colonists shared a common interest in uniting against any African rising, and that interest was a powerful incentive towards unification. Official negotiations among the Colonial Governments began in Durban in 1908, continued at Cape Town in 1909, were sanctioned by the Imperial Government in the same year, and came to fruition in 1910 when the Union of South Africa came into being on 31st May – the anniversary of peace in 1902.

One of the arguments which had been resolved in these discussions was the choice between Republican racial exclusiveness (as practised in elections in the Transvaal, O.F.S. and Natal) and the Cape's system of token political integration. In the event, the Colonies agreed to differ, and each Colony took into Union its existing franchise regulations, which would remain in effect until such time as a two-thirds majority of both houses of Parliament decided otherwise. The northerners hoped eventually to dis-enfranchise African and Coloured voters in the Cape: the Cape liberals hoped eventually to convert the northerners to their way of doing things. The compromise was therefore overwhelmingly accepted, and it was issues such as the location of the Union capital which created more trouble in negotiations.

There were some, however, who looked at the Draft Act of Union with alarm, and who travelled to London to try to persuade the Imperial Government to alter it before agreeing to enact it. One of these protestors was

W. P. Schreiner. He had been a very conservative Prime Minister before the war, concentrating more on keeping the Afrikaners and British together than on bringing African and Coloured citizens into the political community. During his period of office, however, he had been horrified at the poverty of the African areas of the Colony, and had converted to a more liberal attitude towards race relations. When the Cape Parliament voted on the draft Act of Union, he and Sprigg opposed its passage, but these two conservative ex-Prime Ministers were alone in the House. Schreiner had not been a member of the negotiating body, since he had suspended his political activity in order to defend Dinizulu at the treason trial in Natal, which took place simultaneously. He therefore felt free to oppose the compromise as an unsure means of protecting the rights of the Cape's non-white citizens. He was joined in London by a deputation of Cape Africans whose purpose was the same. Their appeal to the Imperial Government, however, was blunted by the unfortunate circumstances that the self-professed 'friends of the Africans' – Sauer and Merriman in the Cape – had already agreed to the compromise and were preparing to seek election under the new scheme. The British were also reluctant to interfere in a matter which concerned them very little, and thereby risk alienating all the important political groups in South Africa itself. Since all white groups in South Africa had agreed to the draft Bill, there was little the Imperial Government could or would do. In constitutional theory the Imperial Government, which had to enact the Act of Union, could have altered it: in reality, they would probably lose their remaining influence over South African affairs. Further they were anxious to create a strong local government so that it would no longer be necessary to send Imperial troops to suppress African risings. The only consistent theme in Imperial policy from 1896 onwards was, as Milner put it 'to make South Africa a source of strength, not weakness, to the Empire', and that theme was incompatible with intervention for African rights. The presence of a vast and potentially dangerous African majority not only encouraged the white communities to sink their internal differences but also tempted the Imperial Government to abandon direct responsibility for the internal affairs of the Colonies.

Chapter 11

Re-grouping

The unification of the four Colonies – Cape, Natal, Transvaal and Orange Free State – required that political life fit into a new and larger mould. No purely local party, with its power restricted to one province, could hope to influence (much less control) events in the Union. Conversely, the states which were left out of the Union – Portuguese East Africa, German South-West Africa, Bechuanaland, Basutoland, Swaziland and Rhodesia – had to come to terms with the new and immensely more powerful Government of the Union. Within the Union, re-organisation was fairly simple, since there, were already important and durable links between the political parties within each province. Outside the Union it was not so easy.

The most obvious and predictable regrouping was the amalgamation of the Afrikaner parties, Het Volk in the Transvaal, Orangia Unie in the O.F.S., the South African Party (which included the Afrikaner Bond) in the Cape, and the few Afrikaners in Natal. The leaders of the first two parties had fought together in the South African War, and had collaborated in the revival of Afrikaner nationalism thereafter. It was also frequently the case that individual Afrikaners had cousins and even closer relatives in other provinces than their own. It was these parties, united into the South African National Party, which formed the first Government of the Union in 1910, and it was the Transvaal leader, Louis Botha, who became first Prime Minister. From that position of power it was easy to bring about the formal amalgamation of the parties in 1911, and to add to them a few independent English-speaking Natal members as well. In 1910 and 1911, the S.A.N.P. offered the only available forum for Afrikaner nationalism in the political arena. However, it did also include English-speaking members. Botha's Transvaal Government of 1907–1910, for example, had had at least half-a-dozen English-speaking M.P.s and two English-speaking cabinet Ministers. His first Union Cabinet included three English-speaking members as well as the most conspicuous leaders of Afrikaner political life.

As against Afrikanerdom, the English-speaking white politicians were unable to muster a united party structure. The largest and most powerful local parties were the Progressives of the Cape and of the Transvaal. They shared not only the same name, but also the same kind of leadership:

Jameson was the leader of the Cape party, and two members of the late Reform Committee, Fitzpatrick and Farrar, were leading the Transvaal Party. These two parties had no difficulty in amalgamating to form the nucleus of the Unionist Party, but it was difficult to expand the membership. For one thing, Natal politicians had not operated in terms of political parties before Union. Individual M.P.s therefore felt free to join whichever party appealed to their immediate interests. There was also a strong Natal tradition of hostility against the Cape establishment, which discouraged them from amalgamating. In the event, two Natal men joined Botha's Cabinet, four joined the Unionists, and the majority retained a nominal Independent status. There was only one recruit from the O.F.S., most of whose members as Afrikaner nationalists fell in behind Botha and Hertzog. But the most serious source of division in the English-speaking white ranks was the emergence of the white Labour Party. Before Union it had been strongest in the Transvaal, where there was the largest concentration of white artisans, but even there the Party was weak, since so many artisans were migrants expecting to return to Britain, and since they had entered an informal alliance with the Afrikaners as against their own employers – the Progressives who now formed the Unionist Party. It was unthinkable for the white workers to combine with the white employers. On the other hand their alliance with Botha had been disappointing in terms of results and it was really only in 1910 that they formed a serious and separate political group. Led by Colonel Creswell, they won only three seats in a House of 121, but their proportion of the vote was almost 5 per cent, and the Party looked dangerous for the first time. The further source of weakness in English-speaking ranks was the fact that most of their supporters were urban and the Afrikaner framers of the Act of Union had taken the precaution of ensuring that rural Afrikaner voters were allowed rather more than their fair share of seats. A weighting factor of up to 15 per cent was permitted in either direction. In effect, this could often mean that it took 115 per cent of the norm to create an urban seat, and only 85 per cent to create a rural constituency. Consistently thereafter, rural voters have been over-weighed, and it has been possible for a party to win a majority of seats with a minority of electoral support.

African re-grouping was a much more difficult business, owing to the very uneven distribution of politically articulate leaders. A further disadvantage was the fact that most of the useful media of communication – radio, large-circulation newspapers, even transport itself – tended to be owned or controlled by the white community. It was that much more difficult for the aspirant African leaders to form themselves into a coherent body. Furthermore, the differences in approach between the urban, literate people and the rural chiefs made co-operation extremely hard. Most awkward of all, there had been little contact before and even after the war, between the different colonial associations. In the Cape, Jabavu lent his support to the liberal political leaders in the white community – Merriman and Sauer – who were now members of the ruling party: that experience was obviously very different from the experience of African leaders in other provinces who had never had any alliance with people in positions of authority. In the Transvaal there had been a series of protests from *ad hoc* organisations of both urban and chiefly Africans during the ten year interval from the war to Union, but the Transvaal Native Congress was created only in 1905, and even then displayed vitality on only one issue – the Imperial grant of Colonist self-government. In the O.F.S. and Natal there were comparable organisations, also élitist, and vocal only on occasions of crisis. Finally, the exclusion of Africans from political power had the important consequence that the political leaders were unfamiliar with the machinery of government. For that reason, they continued to look to Westminster for relief, long after Westminster's will and ability to intervene had disappeared. Nevertheless in 1912 a group of leaders came together to create the South African Native National Congress (which later changed its title to the African National Congress, which is rather better known). The moving spirit behind that move was Pixley Ka Izaka Seme, who had recently returned from studies in America: the leading opponent was Jabavu, who saw the Congress as a potential threat to his own eminence as spokesman for Africans to white politicians. The difficulties faced by the creators of Congress are illustrated by the fact that they proposed also to create an 'upper house' comprising traditional chiefs, in order to attract them into the organisation at all. And the initial meeting was punctuated by repeated calls for inter-tribal co-operation and an end to inter-tribal strife which divided African forces. Finally, the limited aims of the Congress are illustrated by the fact that the Government was invited to send a representative to open it.

The Coloured community, based predominantly in the Western Cape, and with considerable experience of the working of white politics and the existing political institutions, was rather better placed. In 1902 they had formed themselves into the African Peoples' Organisation, and by the time of Union the A.P.O. was led by Dr Abdurahman, who continued to lead it for thirty years. With the creation of Union, the A.P.O. simply expanded its focus to include Union politics as well as provincial and municipal affairs, without having to re-organise itself. The Indian communities, based largely in Natal with perhaps 15,000 in the Transvaal, were in the midst of Gandhi's experiments with satyagraha as a means of persuading governments to remove civil disabilities. Since they were already involved in an inter-colonial struggle, there was no great problem in adjusting to the new constitutional situation.

The Act of Union made provision for the future incorporation of Rhodesia, and of the High Commission territories of Basutoland, Bechuanaland and Swaziland. Although that incorporation has never taken place, it was clearly anticipated by the framers of the Act and by the Imperial Government which sanctioned it. The inclusion of Rhodesia would have strengthened the English-speaking electorate, while the inclusion of the High Commission territories would directly have boosted the labour force and the volume of land available for alienation to white farmers. The condition was mentioned that the consent of the inhabitants would be sought before any action was taken. In the event that consent was never available. Rhodesia remained an anomalous area governed by the Chartered Company, but with advice and great influence exerted by the settlers who, in 1911, elected a majority of the members of the legislature. The settlers, like the Company itself, feared the prospect of rule by Afrikaners, and in 1914 voted to extend the charter by a further ten years. At the same time, white and African areas were re-arranged in such a way that Africans tended to move over to the thin sandy soils while the settlers acquired more of the heavy and fertile loams. All was set for a political future separate from the strong southern neighbour.

Basutoland in 1911 had a population of just over 400,000 people, compressed into a land area of less than 12,000 square miles, most of which was extremely mountainous. As a result, as early as 1904, one in five of the total population was seeking work in the neighbouring Colonies each year. On the other hand, the overwhelming majority of inhabitants were Basotho, which gave the country some sense of unity, and hardly any of the land had been alienated. In 1903 a Basutoland National Council had been set up, most of whose members were chiefs and descendants of Moshoeshoe; and in 1910, as some rearrangement was necessary, that Council was constituted the political and administrative forum of the people. The economic vulnerability of the country, the inherent conservatism of the councillors, and the continuing succession disputes, all prevented the Basotho from playing any major role in South African affairs. They were not only Colonial subjects, but also depended upon the South African Government for the collection of customs duties, which composed a large part of revenue. Until the winds of change penetrated this remote and inaccessible enclave, it remained in a state of stagnation: the population grew every year, and soil erosion steadily decreased the area of arable land, so that the number of migrant labourers also rose steadily. Basutoland Protectorate was not a state, it was a dormitory for industrial labour.

Bechuanaland in 1910 differed in almost every respect from Basutoland. Its population of 120,000 was less than a third of that of Basutoland; its land area of some quarter of a million square miles was more than twenty times as large; its population was far less homogeneous. The figures are somewhat misleading however: most of the land area is effectively desert, and some of the remainder is swamp; the pressure upon arable and pastoral land was therefore felt (though less severely) quite early. Furthermore, the closely related Tswana societies formed a large majority of the population, and Khama of the Ba-ma-Ngwato was widely acknowledged as paramount even over senior branches of the Tswana. The chiefs, from 1908 onwards, when Union was being discussed, protested strongly against the impression that Bechuanaland would eventually have to join. Nevertheless the political exclusion of Bechuanaland from the Union should not lead us to overlook the fact that economically it was a dependency of the Union economy. While Basutoland provided labourers, Bechuanaland provided meat for the Johannesburg market. Being in any event a backwater in southern African affairs during the early twentieth century, no reorganisation had to take place to deal with the exclusion from Union.

Swaziland, like Basutoland, was predominantly a homogenous society; but like Bechuanaland it suffered from large scale land and resource alienation during the nineteenth century. In 1911 there were just over 100,000 Swazi inhabitants and about 1,000 settlers in an area of 6,700 square miles. Though the Swazi had ensured the survival of the kingdom and its exclusion first from the Transvaal and then from Union, they did so only at the cost of losing a major proportion of their resources. A concessions commission, set up to examine the propriety of the many concessions granted in the nineteenth century, reported in 1907, and although it was recommended that the concessionaires voluntarily return a third of their land concessions so as to make room for the Swazi themselves, the Swazi denied that the concessions deserved to be upheld at all. Since the Imperial Government would not insist on the expropriation of these concessions, Swaziland was to an astonishing extent controlled by non-Swazis throughout the Colonial years. Like the other territories, it received much of its revenue in the form of a proportion of total South African customs revenue, an arrangement which underlined the real dependence of the territories upon their stronger neighbour.

The Portuguese authorities in Portuguese East Africa, seeing the Union of the British Colonies coming, strengthened their grip while the Colonies remained separate. Relations between the Portuguese and the Transvaal were regulated by a *modus vivendi*, whereby the Portuguese guaranteed a flow of industrial labour 'volunteers' to the Rand, and the Transvaal guaranteed a flow of remunerative traffic over the Portuguese railway line which led to the port of Lourenço Marques. With the extinction of the Transvaal republic, the agreement had to be re-negociated in 1901, when the Portuguese insisted on more favourable terms: a monopoly of labour recruiting in Portuguese territories, so as to prevent labour recruiters from smuggling recruits across the border and evading the recruiting fee; and an increased proportion of the Transvaal's railway traffic for the Lourenço Marques line. Shortly before Union, that agreement was extended, thereby perpetuating the Portuguese hold over the Transvaal economy. Internally, however, matters were less satisfactory for the Portuguese. Failing to discover any other way of exploiting most of the country, they had given concessions to chartered companies (very similar to Rhodes's in Rhodesia) to rule and exploit three provinces of the north. In 1904, when these companies agreed to start recruiting their subjects for the Transvaal mines, revolts broke out which prevented the Portuguese or the companies from deriving any profit for two or three years. Though the Portuguese steadily increased their hold over the interior, they could not think of any use for it once it came into their hands.

The Germans had no such problem in South-West Africa. After the Herero–Nama rising there was no immediate possibility of further African resistance – nor were there many Africans left at all, except in the unexploited and largely unknown far north. The settlers steadily tightened their hold on the political system, and by 1914 had acquired as much power as any white settler community in Africa, with the exception of South Africa itself. That trend towards settler self-government was assisted by the fact that the German Government was handicapped in exerting strong control. The constitution of 1871 had been drafted before there were any colonies to deal with, and responsibility for Colonial administration was a matter of considerable argument. Furthermore, German Imperial authorities had been discredited by the publicity which surrounded von Trotha's war of extermination in South-West Africa and the simultaneous suppression of the Maji Maji rising in German East Africa. Since the Colonies were of very little economic importance the German Government was inclined to regard them as nuisances which could usefully be handed over to German Colonists to administer.

Ironically, the only territorial acquisition made by the Union was one which no one had anticipated in 1910, namely South-West Africa. When the First World War broke out in 1914, the South African defence force conquered South-West Africa for the British Empire; and in 1919 the South African Government resolved to keep it for South Africa. The League of Nations legitimised the conquest in the same year, by creating a system of mandates whereby ex-German colonies were ruled on behalf of the League by one of the member states, and South-West Africa was mandated to the Union Government.

Union, in other words, was the last step in a process whereby the 'Imperial factor' became a force of only secondary importance in the affairs of the sub-continent. It provided for the consolidation of 'Colonial power' and minimised the internal differences which divided Afrikaner from British settler, Colony from Colony and party from party. While the Imperial Government continued to be responsible for a vast land area and even for a considerable population in the Protectorates, economic and political power were now firmly in the hands of the Colonists. In a sense, too, Union provided an opportunity to the African inhabitants, since it provided a larger platform on which to act. That opportunity was somewhat unreal, however, since the white Government made sure that the opportunities for communication and for political action were severely curtailed. The cynicism of the new white Government in its relations with the Africans is best illustrated by the fact that Moor – who had been Prime Minister of

South African population statistics at the time of the Union, to the nearest thousand

State	White	African	Others	Total	
Cape	580	1,425	405	2,410	
Natal	97	904	108	1,109	1904
O.F.S.	143	225	19	387	
Transvaal	297	937	35	1,269	
Union	1,117	3,491	567	5,175	
Basutoland				400	1911
Bechuanaland				120	
Swaziland				100	

Natal during the Bambatha revolt – was made Minister for Native Affairs, and (because he lost his election contest) was given a seat in the Senate as a representative of Native interests. A man less likely to respond to African pressure could hardly have been found. It is also, paradoxically, the case that the decline of Imperial power was a blow to African aspirations, since there was no longer any serious counter-balance to the power of the local Colonists.

Chapter 12

The struggle for parliamentary power

A history of the South African parliament is clearly not a history of South Africa – indeed the history of any country is not the same as the history of its formal legislature and executive. In the South African case, the vast majority of the people have never been represented adequately in parliament and many have never been represented there at all. Nevertheless parliament is obviously an important aspect of a country's life, since it is there that power is contested and legitimised. For that reason, the events of the South African parliament, from its creation in 1910, until the electoral victory of Dr Malan's Nationalists in 1948, form an important theme in South African history. Parliamentary history has the further advantage of providing a skeleton of dates and information, upon which a body can afterwards be draped. In this case, it seems useful first to describe the formalities of parliamentary power, before turning our attention to events outside parliament. This chapter, then, must serve a dual purpose: to survey the fortunes of the formal political parties, and to provide a background for the other themes of modern South African affairs.

The Union constitution of 1910, like other constitutions which have been born in Africa more recently, was based largely upon British constitutional traditions, and was for that reason somewhat mysterious to many of the members of parliament. Except in its franchise features, the new governmental structure closely resembled other British Colonial constitutions of the nineteenth and early twentieth centuries. The edifice was topped by a Governor-General, representing the British Crown, but exercising as little authority as the monarch did in Britain. The legislature was composed of two houses: legislation was normally initiated by the lower house (the House of Assembly) and afterwards considered by the upper house (the Senate). Of these two houses, the House of Assembly had the power: its members were elected directly by the (predominantly white) electorate, whereas the Senate was elected indirectly by the Provincial Councils (except that the government itself nominated some to represent 'native interests'). Again, the lower house had the power of the purse, and its financial proposals could not be considered by the Senate. The theory was the same which lay behind the two houses in Britain – a democratic lower house, whose proposals should be considered and if necessary revised by a conservative upper house. In practice, in both cases, almost all decisions of any importance were taken in the Assembly and approved in the Senate. The government was carried out by a cabinet, all of whose members must have seats in parliament, and which must command the support of a majority of the members of the House of Assembly. To obtain power, then, the object was to ensure a reliable majority of members in the Assembly: the Senate, the weak provincial councils, and the Crown itself, were powerless to challenge decisions of the Assembly.

To the Afrikaners, especially from the two northern provinces, certain features of the constitution were puzzling. There had been similar constitutions in the Transvaal and Orange River Colony before Union – but only for three years in the Transvaal and two in the O.R.C. The absence of a President, and the continued presence of a Governor-General representing the British Crown, made it seem that the new Union was neither independent of Great Britain, nor following the constitutional traditions of the old Afrikaner republics. While unsophisticated farmers in the country districts might be puzzled, the politicians themselves were not unduly concerned. Despite the British trappings of the constitutions of the Transvaal and O.R.C., Afrikaner parties had successfully contested elections there and had effectively wielded power, unhampered by the strangeness of the formalities. More important than the British style of the constitution was its characteristic South African content: the loading of rural votes, and the racial limitation on the electorate. These familiar characteristics determined the nature of the parliamentary struggle for power, much more than the British form in which the constitution was cast.

Part of the compromise which brought the Union to life was the provision that each province should continue to operate its old franchise provisions – and that none except Europeans should sit in parliament. The effect of that provision was that there were no Coloured, Indian or African voters in the Transvaal or O.R.C., that there were only a tiny handful of non-white voters in Natal, and that four out of five voters even in the Cape were white. There was obviously no hope for a politician or a party who was popular among Coloured and African voters (or non-voters) unless he was popular among the overwhelmingly white electorate. The surviving rights of African and Coloured voters were 'entrenched' in the constitutions, by the clause which dictated that a two-thirds majority of all members of parliament was necessary in order to change the franchise system. It was much more likely that the electorate would choose members who would abolish the non-white electorate than that they would elect a government which would extend those rights. If the racial provisions of the constitution ensured that there would be a white government responsible to a predominantly white electorate, then a further provision ensured that Afrikaners would enjoy an immense advantage as against non-Afrikaner voters. That provision was the clause which laid down that rural constituencies need only have 85 per cent of the average number of electors; whereas urban constituencies might have as many as 115 per cent of the average number. Since the rural areas were overwhelmingly Afrikaner, and the urban areas overwhelmingly English-speaking, the effect of this clause was to give the Afrikaners more constituencies than their numbers alone would justify. The franchise provisions were therefore likely to produce not only a white government, but very likely an Afrikaner one.

One other fact of electoral arithmetic must be mentioned. In 1910, it is likely that numbers of white Afrikaners and non-Afrikaners were roughly equal, but the birth rate of Afrikaners was substantially greater than that of the English-speaking whites. From that, it followed that the composition of the electorate would become increasingly Afrikaner, unless the government encouraged either British immigration, or the Anglicisation of Afrikaner school children. Even if the political present were in doubt, the political future clearly belonged to the Afrikaners, and it was therefore expedient for other political leaders to come to terms with them. Another aspect of the demographic change taking place was that Afrikaners were beginning to flow from the rural areas to the towns, and especially to the mining towns. While the rural constituencies would remain Afrikaner strongholds, the urban constituencies would increasingly be dominated by Afrikaners as well – unless, of course, the urban Afrikaners lost their political identity and abandoned the Nationalist leaders. These, then, were the 'rules' governing the games of political power in the white parliamentary arena. The future lay with those politicians who could most effectively rally the Afrikaner voters, though there might be some time in which English-speaking voters and leaders would exercise some influence on affairs. It was impossible to foresee a time in which African, Coloured or Indian voters would be worth worrying about.

The first Union Government, formed out of the South African Party by its leader General Botha, attempted a rather different means of achieving and retaining political power. The S.A.P. was a very loose, incoherent coalition of all the provincial Afrikaner parties, with some slight support from English-speaking sections in the Cape, Natal and the Transvaal. Botha's intention was to increase his share of English-speaking voters, while retaining the support of the Afrikaners, so as to bring to an end the vicious hostility between the two major sections of the white community. Nowadays it is possible to see that Botha's tactics were misconceived; that it was impossible to win new English-speaking support without sacrificing some Afrikaner Nationalist enthusiasts. In 1910, however, that was not at all clear. Continued expansion of mining in the Transvaal might produce an ever-expanding community of British immigrant workers; and the passage of time might dampen the enthusiasm of the Afrikaner nationalists. For whatever reason, Botha and his party looked forward to greater harmony between the white communities: of the non-white communities they preferred not to think at all, except as 'problems'. Since many Cape members of the party were relatively 'liberal' in race relations, and since many northern members were vocally 'illiberal', it was wise to avoid the 'Native problem' altogether, lest it divide the party. Unfortunately the 'Native problem' was inescapable, since it was not a separate problem at all, but impinged upon every aspect of government.

General Louis Botha, J. X. Merriman and General J. C. Smuts

The essential tension within Botha's Goverment was between those who regarded the act of Union as the last word in Anglo-Afrikaner and racial relations, and those who regarded it as a means towards some greater end. Botha and his chief lieutenant and perhaps the brains of the Government – General Smuts – regarded Union as the last word. They, after all, had largely dictated the document, and they regarded it with parental possessiveness. On the other hand some of the Cape members of the party regarded the racial exclusiveness of the document as something which required reform; many northern members regarded the Cape franchise as something which required abolition. In another dimension, there were those who regarded South Africa's Dominion status as a step on the road towards full republican independence, while others regarded the Union's international status as sufficiently independent already. Most importantly, the leaders as a whole considered that 'equal opportunity' for Afrikaners and other whites was enough; whereas General Hertzog quite rightly argued that Afrikaner culture, the Dutch and Afrikaans languages, and individual Afrikaners themselves, required further assistance in order to take advantage of the equal opportunities offered. What equality could there possibly be for Afrikaners while South Africa's civil service, predominant language, external relations and even intellectuals, looked towards Great Britain? It was this tension which first produced division within the Government. By 1912, the speeches made by Hertzog in the country districts were alarming the English-speaking whites and were embarrassing the other members of the cabinet in their attempts to win further English-speaking support. In 1912 Botha resigned as Prime Minister, and formed a new Government which excluded Hertzog from the cabinet. The S.A.P.'s fate was sealed in that instant, when Botha showed that he valued Anglo-Afrikaner conciliation more highly than Afrikaner unity. The future now lay with Hertzog.

At first, though, it looked as if Botha's calculations were correct. Hertzog left the S.A.P. altogether and formed the National Party. In his own province, the Orange Free State, he enjoyed overwhelming support: but the O.F.S. was one of the smallest provinces, and in the Cape and Transvaal the vast majority of Afrikaners continued to follow the old leaders. Unless and until Hertzog could make some impact in the more populous provinces, his party was of no importance in affairs of state. Paradoxically, Hertzog's decision to rely upon a policy of Afrikaner exclusiveness made it necessary for him to find non-Afrikaner allies if he was to come to power at all, since so many Afrikaners remained loyal to the S.A.P. Similarly, the decision exposed him at first to the charge of dividing Afrikanerdom, a charge which could only be answered by gaining the loyalty of a majority of Afrikaners for the party. The twin objectives of the new Nationalist Party were therefore to win majority support among Afrikaners, and yet to find English allies.

In achieving these objectives, the Nationalists were materially assisted by the ineptitude of the S.A.P. Government, which first alienated an English-speaking party to the extent that it would consider an alliance with

Hertzog; and then alienated many of its own Afrikaner followers. Botha and Smuts had come to power in the old Transvaal Colony in 1907 partly through the urban support of working-class English-speakers; but since then the workers had steadily been disillusioned. In the same year as the election itself, the Government had broken a strike on the Witwatersrand. In 1913 there was renewed unrest on the Witwatersrand, when white workers struck against their mining employers. Since the Government was stranded without para-military support, the strikers won most of the points in dispute – but their victory rankled in the minds of the employers, and of the Government which had been powerless in an industrial crisis. More seriously, some of the organisers of the trade unions were dabbling in socialist and syndicalist ideas, which visualised a general strike as a means of bringing about substantial political change. Whether this was a serious threat or not, the Government certainly regarded it as menacing. During the second half of 1913, the Government created the Union Defence Force, and by the end of the year was prepared to deal with any further outbreak of industrial unrest. In January 1914, the crisis blew up once again, with a renewed strike by white workers in the mines of Natal and Transvaal. This time the Government sent in a commando – led by General de la Rey, a hero of the South African War – which aimed its cannon at the headquarters of the trades unions, and thereby brought the strike to an abrupt close. Smuts followed up that action by deporting nine of the strike leaders in secret and without legal justification, sending them off to Britain. Many of the strikers would perhaps have accepted the Government's action in breaking a political strike had it not been for the illegal deportation of these leaders. When Provincial Council elections were held in the Transvaal in March 1914, the Labour Party swept into power with an absolute majority of seats – and there was reason to suppose that the same might happen when Union elections were held in 1915. Significantly, in parliament itself, the Government was supported by the Unionist Party opposition, whose leaders were commonly big businessmen – while Hertzog made common cause with the Labour Party. It was the political shape of the future.

There is a curious and revealing parallel to be found between South African party politics immediately after Union, and Kenya immediately after independence. The role of President Kenyatta, like that of General Botha, was the charismatic and mature elder statesman of the nationalist movement. The role of Mr Mboya, like that of General Smuts, was the bright, young, overseas-educated policy maker, slightly detached from the grass-roots sympathies of the nationalist movement. And the role of Mr Oginga-Odinga, like that of General Hertzog, was that of urging economic independence in order to make political independence more substantial. In both cases, the opposition leader accused the governing party of paying too much attention to big business and non-members of the nationalist movement. The parallel seems to arise not only from the accident of political personality, but from the nature of the problems which present themselves in a new state recently removed from Imperial control. Clearly

Afrikaner nationalism and Kenya nationalism are very different phenomena, but they did inherit roughly similar problems.

Any new alignment was deferred by the outbreak of the First World War in August 1914, an event which placed the Government in a delicate and dangerous position. Technically, when King George declared war, the whole Empire was at war – but each Dominion was obviously free to determine the degree of its participation. Some urgency was attached to the decision by the fact that there was a German colony on South Africa's door-step – South-West Africa. Yet Afrikaner opinion was deeply divided on what ought to be done, so that there was great need for the Goverment to move cautiously. At one extreme were Botha and Smuts and their most loyal followers: for them, there seemed an identity of interest between Britain and the Union in fighting against Germany. South Africa might gain South-West Africa, but in any event by taking part the Afrikaner generals felt they would vindicate the 'magnanimous gesture' of the British in restoring the ex-republics to Afrikaner authority. Hertzog, though appreciating the importance which Botha and Smuts attached to their own arguments, nevertheless recommended that the Government play a minimal part in hostilities: so soon after the war against Britain, it seemed unnatural to be dragged into an Imperialist war, and in any case the necessity for preserving Afrikaner unity over-rode the necessity for repaying what some regarded as a debt of honour.

At the other extreme stood the commander of the Union Defence Force, General Beyers, another of the South African war heroes, whom Smuts had pushed into the army in order to keep him out of politics. Beyers not only declined to fight for Britain against Germany, but also – when forced to a decision – preferred to fight with the Germans against the Union. Before his defection, he attempted to induce another old general – de la Rey – to accompany him. Before de la Rey had made up his mind, he was accidentally shot dead, driving through a police barrier.

The Government was nonetheless determined to take a full share in the war. That decision polarised opinion. Beyers and yet another general – de Wet – determined to rebel and to declare a Republic. There was now no way of preventing civil war, though the Government took pains to limit the number of casualties. Government authority had been challenged: as in 1913, that authority had to be vindicated. That, too, might have been understood after some time, had it not been for the execution of Jopie Fourie, an Army officer who defected to the Germans without removing his uniform or resigning his commission. The execution of Fourie provided a martyr for the republicans. Again, Botha and Smuts might have been forgiven for conquering South-West Africa which was later added to the Union itself, had it not been for the further campaign to conquer Tanganyika from the Germans, a campaign from which the Union derived no obvious benefit. Finally, Botha and Smuts might have been forgiven for preserving the authority of the South African Government, had it not been for their obvious enjoyment of being in London and members of the Imperial War Cabinet. To take an active part in an Imperialist war was one thing: to appear to enjoy it, despite the necessity for shooting fellow-Afrikaners, was unforgivable. The rebellion of 1914, and the Government's part in the war as a whole, recruited numerous Afrikaners to Hertzog's party, even if it delayed the eventual alliance between the Nationalists and the predominantly British (and pro-Imperial) Labour Party.

The subsequent elections demonstrated the trend of white opinion against the S.A.P. Government. The Labour Party, whose hopes had been so high in 1914, won only 4 seats in 1915, in a house of 130 members. The reason was not hard to seek: as happened to so many Labour Parties in the First World War, this party was divided. One faction regarded the war as an Imperialist one, in which workers should play no part whatever: another faction regarded it as a German war of aggression, in which all good men should support the British. Creswell, the leader, belonged to the pro-British faction. The eclipse of Labour was, however, only a temporary matter, likely to be ended as soon as peace returned. More significant was Hertzog's success in winning 27 seats, not only in his own Free State but also in the rural districts of the Cape and the Transvaal. Essentially, the Unionists were holding their own against Labour, but S.A.P. support among Afrikaners was being eroded by the Nationalists. The S.A.P. was reduced to 54 members – less than an absolute majority, and necessitating the unofficial support of the Unionist opposition to ensure the life of the Government. The Government's dependence upon the Unionists – whom the Labour Party accused of being the Chamber of Mines in political disguise – suggested that the two remaining parties should form a similar alliance. However, so long as the National Party was hostile to the Imperialist war, it was unable to co-operate with the Labour Party in its jingoistic mood. It was difficult enough for the National Party to keep itself together, containing as it did a mixture of attitudes ranging from republicanism to international neutralism.

But the only extent of the shift in white opinion was revealed only in 1920. By that time Botha was dead, and had been succeeded by Smuts, whose Cambridge education and international eminence made him less plausible than Botha as an Afrikaner leader. In the election the S.A.P. was reduced to 41, while the Nationalists won 44 seats; the Unionists were reduced to 25, while Labour captured 21 seats; there were 3 Independent members who brought the total up to 134. Smuts governed for almost a year with the support of the Unionists and the Independents, who gave him the narrowest of majorities. The situation was not stable, and the S.A.P. required a permanent alliance. Talks intended to reunite the two Afrikaner parties failed – Hertzog now being too sure of eventual success to compromise – so Smuts absorbed the Unionists into his own party. Choosing his time with care, he dissolved parliament and fought another election early in 1921. This time the National Party gained only one more seat, and the financially poor Labour Party, being unable to muster an effective campaign so soon after the 1920 election, was reduced to 9. Smuts now had secured a safe majority of seats in the Assembly – but by means of a predominantly English-speaking party. The majority of Afrikaner voters had already moved over to Hertzog's Nationalist Party.

The size of the S.A.P.'s majority, however, was largely an illusion, created by the temporary inability of the Labour Party to attack in the urban constituencies. The Rand revolt and its suppression revitalised the Labour Party and made it once again an effective political force. In 1921, in the face of a declining price for gold on world markets, the gold mining industry decided to reduce the proportion of white, and increase the proportion of black, mining labourers. This decision was expected greatly to reduce working costs, since African workers were so much cheaper than the unionised whites. However, the white Trades Unions were fully aware that such a decision might lead to the permanent loss of kinds of employment traditionally reserved for them. Early in 1922 a general strike began, which affected the whole of the Witwatersrand area. Among the strikers were some who wished to establish a white workers' state. For whatever reason, in March the strike escalated into an insurrection which required considerable force to suppress. The strike as well as the insurrection was broken, and the mine-owners had their way – but in the days of the Rand Revolt the powerful slogan was born, 'Workers of the World Unite – for a White South Africa'. Furthermore, the events demonstrated that the Labour Party was the only means whereby the white workers could regain their partially lost privileges. When the election campaign of 1924 came round, the Labour Party was well organised and impassioned by its desire to ensure the safety of white workers. The Labour Party doubled its representation from 9 to 18; the Nationalists continued to gain seats in the rural districts, and moved up to 63; and the S.A.P. was reduced to 53. The two opposition leaders, Hertzog and Creswell, who had collaborated in fighting the election, now set about forming a Government.

The Labour–Nationalist combination was a peculiarly dangerous one from an African point of view. Labour had agreed to avoid socialism in order not to offend the Afrikaner farmers; the National Party avoided republicanism in order not to offend English-speaking Labour members. What, then, was left? For the first time – but by no means the last two parties found a basis of agreement in their determination to secure white privilege at the expense of existing African rights and interests. In this case the agreement was summed up in the single word segregation. For Labour, that meant the preservation of the rights of white workers as a labour aristocracy, and the permanent exclusion of African workers from positions of responsibility in industry. For the National Party, it meant the employment of poor unskilled whites in jobs which had previously been occupied by Africans and Coloureds. In either interpretation, it meant that the South African economy would have to provide a livelihood for a greater number of less productive whites. The employers particularly resented that development – but it was the cheap, productive African workers who would ultimately have to support the additional burden. In 1925, the Government passed the Mines and Works Amendment Act, which gave the Ministry of Labour the power to implement a 'civilised labour' policy. The Labour Party had at last achieved its objective, namely complete legislative sanction for a white labour aristocracy. Having achieved its objective, it swiftly sank from sight as a significant political power. Most of its members – by the 1920s most of the white working class was Afrikaans-speaking – then joined the National Party.

By 1929, Hertzog was ready to attempt a further assault simultaneously upon the S.A.P. and upon existing African interests. Early in that year he introduced into parliament two bills, one altering the Cape's franchise system so as to place African voters on a separate roll, electing separate Assemblymen; the second similarly tackling Coloured voters. In order to amend the franchise system, it was necessary for Hertzog to assemble a two-thirds majority of both houses, a task manifestly beyond his present ability. The merit of the scheme was to force the S.A.P. into the position of defending Coloured and African interests, thereby discrediting them before the predominantly white electorate. The tactic was extremely successful: the National Party was seen to be the inflexible defender of white interests, while the S.A.P. began to look ambiguous in its racial attitudes. Since the S.A.P., unlike the Nationalists, included a number of old Cape liberals among its ranks, as well as some outspoken and un-ambiguous white racialists, race relations were the weakest point in the S.A.P.'s armour. The 1929 election justified Hertzog's faith that the electorate would respond to a 'black peril' cry, and his Party at last achieved an absolute majority irrespective of the behaviour of Labour. The Labour Party was once again split between those who resented being a tool of Hertzog, and those who accepted the relationship. Pro-Hertzog Labour brought in another five seats for the Goverment, while anti-Hertzog Labour took three seats to Smuts in the Opposition. That election began the tradition whereby Afrikaner nationalism came to be identified in the voters' minds with a policy of discrimination and extreme repression against non-whites. Until then, Afrikaner Nationalism had at least found room for members whose racial attitudes were slightly more tolerant.

Nevertheless the election left Hertzog without anything like a two-thirds majority. Worse, the world economic crisis of the 1920s found the Government unprepared to cope, and by 1933 economic conditions were extremely disturbing. The initiative passed to the Opposition once again, and in the 1933 elections the Nationalist majority was reduced almost to nothing by splinter groups which recommended a variety of eccentric economic policies. The struggle for power in parliament had by that time reached a stalemate. Smuts and the S.A.P., representing a diminishing proportion of the electorate, were unlikely ever to return to power on their own: Hertzog, though he could remain in power indefinitely, could not for many years expect a two-thirds majority to achieve the changes which he still had in mind. Furthermore, after more than twenty years, the voters were becoming bored by the Smuts–Hertzog duel, and the number of new parties contesting the 1933 elections was an indication of a desire for something new in politics. Accordingly, in 1934, Smuts and Hertzog brought their respective parties together to form the United Party, formally bringing to an end the contentions of the past quarter of a century.

Ideally, the two leaders would have liked to command the support of every member of the House of Assembly. In practice, each party contained a minority of members who could not tolerate the compromise involved. In the S.A.P., the English-speaking members were often suspicious of Hertzog as a Republican, and several members broke away from the new United Party to form the Dominion Party, dedicated to preserve the links with the rest of the Commonwealth. At the other extreme in the National Party were some, led by Dr D. F. Malan, who regarded Smuts as an unreliable Imperialist, and who saw the United Party as a means whereby Smuts was trying to compromise the determination of true Nationalists. These members formed themselves into the Purified National Party – purified by shedding the weaker members whose nationalism could be corrupted. Nevertheless the United Party enjoyed massive support inbetween the two extremes: in the 1938 election they returned the record number of 111 members while the Dominionites returned only 8, and the Purified Nationalists only 27, and Labour only 3. That strong central combination might have remained in power almost indefinitely, but once again a World War disrupted the ordinary course of South African politics.

Once again, when war broke out in 1939, the issue was whether the Union should support the Commonwealth. By this time the Commonwealth links were much looser, and technically South Africa could have remained neutral without illegality. That was what Hertzog advised. However, when the question was debated in the Assembly, it transpired that all the English-speaking members, and a considerable minority of Afrikaner members of the United Party, led once again by Smuts, wanted to participate fully in the war against the Germans. It may seen extraordinary that so fascist a state as South Africa had become, had grounds for conflict with the European fascist powers – and in many ways it is indeed extraordinary. However white South Africans did not regard themselves as fascists, and in fact insisted that they were democrats – among themselves, of course. At any rate, South Africa went to war once again, and Hertzog departed to the political wilderness. There was no further role for him to play. Smuts's United Party men occupied the war platform; Malan's Purified Nationalists occupied the peace platform – and what other policy was there to recommend? Eventually Hertzog founded a new party, the Afrikaner Party, but he was too old to start a new campaign. After his death, the Party was unable to win a single seat in the 1943 elections, and politics reverted to the old pattern: all the English-speakers and a minority of Afrikaners on one side following Smuts; the majority of Afrikaners on the other side – this time following Malan. This time as well – as had happened in the First World War – there was disagreement in the ranks of the opponents of the war. Some, like Malan, simply wanted neutrality; others, including Verwoerd, would not have objected to a Nazi victory; yet others (including Vorster, who was interned during the war at Koffiefontein) would positively have welcomed such a victory; and a few were even prepared to attempt acts of sabotage in order to help bring about that victory. During the 1943 elections therefore it was very easy for the United

Party Government to expose the internal feuds of the Nationalists, and thereby to preserve itself in power, retaining 89 seats, while its Dominion allies won 7, Labour 9 and Independents won two other seats. The Nationalists had to be content with 43 seats for the duration of the war.

But this lasted no longer than the war. The war, among other things, held the governing coalition together, just as it kept the Nationalists apart from each other. After the war the old tensions between British and Boer, between liberalism and repression, both came to the surface. Once again the Nationalists could taunt the United party with the timid liberalism of some of its members – Jan Hofmeyr especially, who had broken taboos to the extent of tolerating an inter-racial rugby match during a Christian Youth conference. Furthermore, Smuts was now 78 years old, and the United Party itself looked somewhat senile. The timid liberals, like Hof-

Dr D. F. Malan, founder of the Purified National Party and Prime Minister of the Union, 1948–54

meyr, recommended a move to the left; most of the members preferred a move to the right, to take the sting out of Nationalist criticisms; as a compromise, the party stood still. Smuts, who expected to win the election, wanted to postpone any liberal moves until he was securely in power. It is axiomatic in South African elections that a party with nothing to recommend in the way of racial repression, except maintaining the existing state of affairs, is at a great disadvantage. In this case, the Nationalists and their slogan of 'apartheid' were as successful as Hertzog and 'segregation' had once been. To everyone's surprise, in 1948 – despite a Royal Visit in 1947 to encourage Commonwealth solidarity – Malan came to power. He had only a minority of the voters (36 per cent for the Nationalists and 3·6 per cent for the Afrikaner Party allies) but he gained a clear majority of seats (70 Nationalists and 9 Afrikaners), whereas Smuts won 65 seats and his Labour clients won 6. For the first time a cabinet was formed exclusively of Afrikaans-speakers, responsible to an exclusively Afrikaans-speaking majority party in the Assembly, and dedicated single-mindedly to the achievement of 'apartheid' – whatever that might prove to be.

It is commonly argued that 1948 marks an important turning point in South African history. In practice, the break was less sharp than is often supposed, and much of what the Nationalist Government had done since then simply continues along lines laid down by a variety of earlier governments. But it was a turning point at least in this sense that it marked the end of serious competition for power in parliament. Every election from 1948 to 1970 gave the Nationalists a greater majority of seats than it previously possessed: in 1958 it even achieved a majority of voters, and during the 1960s increasing numbers of English speakers abandoned the United Party for membership in the Government itself. Since 1948, the important struggles have taken place outside the House of Assembly; some within the ranks of the National Party, others outside parliament altogether.

The parliamentary power of the Nationalists has not since then been in danger; nor have we any reason to believe that an alternative government will ever be returned to power by parliamentary and constitutional means. For that reason it seems appropriate to terminate this chapter in 1948, when the outcome of the parliamentary struggle became known.

SOUTH AFRICAN ASSEMBLY
ELECTION RESULTS 1910–1950

Year						Seats
1910	S.A.P. 68,		Unionist 37,	Labour 5,	Independent 11	121
1915	S.A.P. 54,	Nat. 27	Unionist 39,	Labour 4,	Independent 6	130
1920	S.A.P. 41,	Nat. 44	Unionist 25,	Labour 21,	Independent 1	132
1921	S.A.P. 79,	Nat. 45		Labour 9,	Independent 1	134
1924	S.A.P. 53,	Nat. 63		Labour 18,	Independent 1	135
1929	S.A.P. 61,	Nat. 78		Labour 5+3,	Independent 1	148
1933	S.A.P. 61,	Nat. 75		Labour 4,	Others 10	150
1938	United Party 111		Purified Nat. 27,	Dominion 8,	Labour 3, Ind. 1	150
1943	U.P. 89,	Nat. 43	Dominion 7,	Labour 9,	Independent 2	150
1948	U.P. 65,	Nat. 70	Afrikaner 9,	Labour 6,		150
1950	(South-West Africa only) Nat. 6					(6)

Chapter 13

The struggle for land

A theme which has been central in Southern African race relations is the struggle for possession and use of the land. Until the discovery of minerals in the 1860s to be landless was to be without the ability to produce wealth or independently to sustain life. Despite the growth of industries during the late nineteenth and early twentieth centuries, the overwhelming majority of all South Africans were dependent upon agricultural production for at least part of their incomes. Africans particularly have been debarred from flowing freely into the urban areas, and remained much more a rural community than did whites. In 1911, when slightly more than 50 per cent of whites were urbanised, only 1 in 8 Africans lived outside the country districts. By 1946, when almost three-quarters of the white population was urbanised, less than a quarter of the Africans had moved into the towns. For Africans therefore, even more than for whites, the land remains a central pre-occupation. The manner in which that land has passed out of their hands deserves some attention. In 1652, when the first Dutch settlement was founded in Cape Town, white people owned and used none of the land; by 1952 they owned over 80 per cent of it. Here, then, is one of the central themes of historical change in the sub-continent.

A point which it is necessary to emphasise, in order to explain the process, is that the frontiersmen and later the Afrikaners were not efficient users of land. Until scientific agricultural technology was made widely available early in the twentieth century, the African societies were rather more efficient in land use than the white. For one thing, until well into the twentieth century, the white frontiersmen were not really agricultural at all, but would plant and harvest crops only on a large enough scale to satisfy purely domestic needs. The African communities, on the other hand, devoted a far greater proportion of time and land to agricultural purposes. The explanation for the massive acreages of the white farms in the interior was the need for grazing rather than arable country. Only in the vicinity of Cape Town, with its Mediterranean type of climate, were vineyards and substantial wheat fields to be found. Cape Town, of course, was the market for such agricultural produce and farmers beyond the neighbourhood of Cape Town were unable to overcome the high costs of transport. (For the same reason, incidentally, white settlement in Australia could not at first introduce cultivation beyond the immediate vicinity of the harbours.) Compelled by hard economic facts to rely upon pastoralism, the frontier farmers were unable to apply their European agricultural traditions, and were ill-equipped with knowledge of how to run animals efficiently. The fact that thousands of acres were required in order to sustain a frontier white family at a relatively low standard of living is indicative of economic inefficiency. African agriculture, by contrast, could sustain dense rural populations, even though it did not permit the accumulation of large agricultural surpluses for export. Both white and black agriculture adapted to the tough environment: but the African adaptation and the African agricultural traditions enabled them to sustain a massively greater rural population than their white competitors.

As a result, the tradition was quickly established that the white population was a community of land-owners rather than land users. Every white farmer was an employer of African or Coloured labour, and the physical inactivity of the landowner meant that he rapidly became dependent upon the labour of others. Alternatively, the land which the white frontiersmen acquired (sometimes by purchase, sometimes by conquest, sometimes by interpreting a lease as a sale) could be leased to African tenants, either in whole or in part. Many African families became labour-tenants working part of the time for the landlord, in exchange for rights to live on and use a part of the farm. Conversely, many white landlords moved on altogether, leaving the land to be used by tenants who would pay in kind whenever the landowner passed by. All of these methods of using the land re-inforced the same trend: that white landlords very seldom acquired intimate knowledge of the processes of production while the Africans (either as tenants or as squatters) remained the community which actually understood what could be done with land. In this manner, white ownership of land, in many cases, developed into a veneer of white ownership, superimposed upon actual African land use. With the passage of time, two further possibilities arose: the African tenant might acquire sufficient cash or sufficient goods with which to buy out the white owner; or he might prove himself so efficient and so capable of producing a good annual rental, that he acquired in effect a long-term lease. These possibilities were dangerous for the Afrikaner landowners: without any other skills, if they were not farmers then they were nothing. In the long run a non-productive planter-type community cannot resist political and economic pressure from an efficient peasantry.

Though it was widely admitted that African acquisition of white-owned land was a menace to the white community as a whole, there was no denying that it was a financial advantage to each individual white landowner. The landowners' interest as a class was to preserve control over the land; but his interest as an individual farmer was to lease or sell the land to productive African peasants. The conflict of interests was an acute problem for the early Afrikaner legislators. One way of dealing with the threat was to enact laws which either prohibited or made difficult the process of 'kaffer-farming' – in other words the process of alienating land to Africans. One such law, which was enacted by all the republican governments, was a

'Squatters Law', which declared that no white landowner should have more than a certain number of African families living on his land. The intention of a Squatters Law was twofold: to distribute African labour evenly among all landowners, and to prevent the growth of African communities which would actually run the farm instead of the landowner himself. Another common idea was to outlaw the practice of selling land to Africans and to reinforce this law by laying down that no African should own land as an individual. These pieces of legislation, if effective, would certainly have put a stop to the alienation of the land-owners from the process of production. Unfortunately for the framers of these laws, there was no means of enforcing them. Until the republics could afford to employ detectives and policemen to enforce governmental decisions, the laws were little more than statements of intention, which each citizen could observe or ignore as he pleased.

While the individual Afrikaner or British farmer might have some racialist scruples about alienating his land to Africans, the land companies had none. Land companies moved into Natal soon after the trekkers moved out in the late 1840s, and began to acquire large tracts of land for future speculative sales. The intention was to hold on to the land until such time as increasing white settlements drove land prices high, when the companies would make substantial capital gains. The acquisition of such blocks of land tended of course to discourage the creation of a large settler community and partially defeated its own object. While the white settler population was expanding, however, it was found that the most rewarding way of gaining a return on the land was to lease it to African tenants. While in theory the bulk of Natal's land was owned by white colonists, or by white companies, in practice it was occupied and utilised by the Africans who began to return to the Natal midlands and coastal belt as soon as the Afrikaner trekkers intervened between them and the Zulu. From a white racialist point of view the practice was clearly objectionable: the economic future of the Colony would be towards a class of absentee landlords living in the towns, while the land reverted to African occupation. Nevertheless it was difficult to devise a system of controlling the process without infringing on the property rights of the companies involved – and it was unthinkable in a British Colony of the nineteenth century to interfere with property rights, if the proprietors were white.

Land companies began to appear in the Transvaal on a large scale only after the beginnings of gold-mining in the 1880s. The gold mining companies then began to acquire large blocks of land in case precious minerals or stones were ever located there. Once again the companies discovered that the most profitable short-term use for the land in their possession was to lease it to African tenants, who were more efficient and better able to pay rent, than white tenants. The Republican officials were extremely disturbed by this development, since it coincided with the first appearance of landless Afrikaners. The restriction of the frontier of Afrikaner expansion, by Rhodes's take-over of the Mashona and Ndebele, had put an end to the traditional practice of landless Afrikaners trekking further into the interior. Looking around them, they observed with disgust that there was still land available, but that the land companies had settled African peasants on it. To make the situation even more infuriating for the officials, they lacked the legal expertise to prevent the practice: the company lawyers tended to be smarter than the government lawyers, so that the practice continued despite governmental disapproval.

Towards the end of the nineteenth century, two new kinds of people began to be seen in the country districts: poor whites and individual African land-holders. So long as the Afrikaners remained a predominantly clannish society, it was possible to cope with the landless members of the community. These people steadily became 'bijwoners' – tenants-at-will – living on the property of wealthy kinsmen. The bijwoners, being white, refused to perform the manual labour which Africans performed; and not being the owners, could not perform the organising role of the landlord. Their economic role was non-existent, and their social status humiliating. On the other hand, the new African individual landowner was an equally new and non-traditional person. He was found especially in the eastern Districts of the Cape Colony. Rhodes, in power as Prime Minister, had passed 'Glen Grey' legislation in the early 1890s intending to permit Africans to purchase 'tribal' land, thereby forcing the majority of the peasants off the land and into the diamond mining compounds. The result was to initiate a tendency for the eastern Cape Africans to divide into individual land-owners and large numbers of landless. However, the new African landowners seem to have emerged elsewhere in Southern Africa as well: in the Cape the law recognised their position; elsewhere they seem to have acquired land despite the laws which prohibited such acquisition. In the north, land was purchased not only from 'tribal' but also from white landowners. The two phenomena add up to only one conclusion: that the Africans were beginning to challenge for land, even on terms dictated by white legislators. The situation had the ingredients of crisis.

Around the turn of the century the tide began to turn against the new African land-owners. White farmers, with the encouragement of the various governments in differing degrees, formed themselves into Agricultural Associations, through which modern ideas could be spread – amongst the white farming community, but not beyond it. At the same time the Transvaal after the South African War established a Department of Agriculture, whose function was also to disseminate new technical knowledge to the white farming community. In effect, the profits of industry were devoted to assist the white farmers in their struggle with Africans over ownership and utilisation of land. Furthermore the machinery of government could be used to impede African attempts to purchase land, and to facilitate white efforts to retain control over it. The reason why the turn of the century brought matters to a crisis was that during the South African War of 1899–1902 many bijwoners took up arms against their kinsmen, and in favour of the Imperial army, in the hope of being rewarded with land thereafter. After the war many bijwoners were therefore unwelcome on their old properties, and drifted into the towns. The war shook them loose from an economic relationship which was already humiliating and unproductive.

Similarly, the destruction of farm-houses and live-stock reduced many land-owners to poverty such that they could no longer afford to sustain bijwoners. The war therefore turned loose hundreds of families who wanted land and who could not obtain it – and all the adult men were potential voters. Again, the destruction caused by the war forced many white farmers into bankruptcy, so that there was a glut of land on the open market during the first years of this century. This was the greatest opportunity yet presented for Africans to acquire the land being sold.

And yet they failed. The British officials in the ex-republics purchased land and attempted to resettle the bijwoners upon it. They also tried their hardest to prevent the acquisition of land by individual Africans, by insisting that such purchases be registered in the name of a white man or of the government itself. Such was African suspicion against the white community that the condition was unacceptable. African independent church congregations attempted to purchase land for themselves, by forming themselves into land companies. The advantage of that technique was that companies – unlike individuals – did not have to mention their 'colour'. However, by various legal and administrative measures, the governments contrived to prevent large scale acquisition of land by Africans, for the duration of the glut of land for sale. Soon the spread of technical knowledge among a minority of prosperous white farmers enabled them to recover from the effects of war, and to purchase whatever land came onto the market. By 1907 and 1908, when Afrikaner (and therefore farmer) governments came back to power in the Transvaal and Orange River Colony, the immediate crisis was passed. Nevertheless the threat of African land acquisition remained.

One of the first major legislative actions initiated by the Union Government was to tackle the land problem. Having in Union much greater governmental resources at their disposal than ever before, the white farmers tried to accomplish all that had previously eluded them. The purpose of the 1913 Natives Land Act was to prohibit any further acquisition of 'white' land by Africans, and to curtail the practice of allowing Africans to manage and operate white estates. This Act, however, proved more interesting as an indication of white anxiety, than effective as a means of securing white control. The Cape was excluded from the Act, since the Cape's franchise system was based partly upon land ownership, and since any interference with the franchise required a two thirds majority of both houses of parliament. Elsewhere, it was still possible for individual Africans to acquire land by such stratagems as forming themselves into 'colourless' companies and congregations. The most important effect of the Act was to reduce the practice of allowing Africans to occupy and to cultivate white farms as labour-tenants. The relationship between white and black on the land became much more strictly that of employer and employee, rather than that of landlord and tenant. The effects of the Act were so limited, and so much less than the intentions of the legislators, that Hertzog determined to initiate farther-reaching legislation as soon as he had the two-thirds majority required for that purpose. What happened was that little damage was done to existing African land rights, but that the extension of African land-ownership was severely inhibited. The 7 per cent of total land area reserved for African occupation and ownership was even then inadequate as a means of subsistence: with the passage of time it became even less adequate.

Why was it that white opinion was so determined to limit African land-ownership? Individual white farmers had no objection to it, since it enabled them to sell land at reasonable prices. Urban whites were not directly affected by the colour of land-owners. While it is easy to understand how African voters could seem dangerous, it is less obvious why African land-owners were seen as public enemies. White farmers corporately regarded African land-ownership as dangerous for two main reasons. First, it closed land which might otherwise be open for acquisition by landless Afrikaners, who were presently obliged to drift into the towns and sometimes to lose their politcal identity. Second, African land-owners and tenants were not willing to become labourers on white farms. If the African labour force could support itself without working for white employers, no one was going to enter agricultural employment at the very low wage-levels which prevailed. Nevertheless farmers by themselves could never have contrived to assemble the two-thirds majority in parliament which was required to deal with the situation in the Cape. They were materially assisted by urban members of parliament representing white middle class and working constituents. Now all urban voters, to varying degrees, depended upon a system of migrant labour. Migrant African workers came and worked in the mines, eventually in factories, and often as domestic servants in white homes. White employers desired a series of rural ghettoes, in which the families and dependents of the migrant could live, but which would not be capable of sustaining all the African population. Too much African land would make it unnecessary for potential workers to come to urban employment at all; too little land would make it necessary for the workers to bring their families with them. While many urban voters would have opposed any *reduction* of the area of African land; most would agree to restrict any *increase* of that area.

Opportunity for further measures did not present itself until the 1930s. As we have seen, from Union in 1910 until the fusion of parties into the massive United Party in 1934, no party could hope to achieve a two-thirds majority. Once the United party was created, however, the necessary majority existed, and inevitably one of the measures introduced by this Government dealt with land. Hertzog's plan was rather more ambitious however, and was nothing short of a legislative package-deal which would tackle every aspect of race relations and would once-and-for-all 'solve' the 'Native Problem'. As early as 1929, following his elections victory, Hertzog had set up an inter-Party Committee of members of parliament to consider African representation in parliament. The report of that Committee matured only in 1936, and then it proved necessary to pacify the Cape liberal members of parliament. Instead of simply abolishing the Africans' existing voting rights therefore, the Government compromised. Part of the compromise was to permit Cape African voters to remain on a separate voters' roll, and to elect three white members of the Assembly: four white Senators were to be elected indirectly by Africans throughout the Union. The other part of the compromise was the passing of the Native Trust and Land Act. The intention expressed by the Act was to compensate Africans for the reduction of their political power, by providing for the release of land for African occupation. If the promise of the Act had been kept, Africans would have acquired a further 7,250,000 morgen of land, bringing their share of the total land surface up from 7 to about 12 per cent. In practice, the enthusiasm for African land purchase did not survive the session of parliament itself, and during the next eight years only some 1,500,000 morgen were actually acquired by the Trust. Altogether it took the trust over twenty years to approach the target figure – by which time the African population had increased by almost 50 per cent. In other words, African land acquisition under the 1936 legislation did not even keep pace with the population explosion.

With the passage of time, pressure on land increased as a result of mounting population. When that happened in the white community, the poor landless whites flowed into urban slums, from which in due course they were rescued by the government. Employment could always be found or created, to cope with white indigency. On the other hand, the strongest objection was taken to Africans following suit. The mechanism for preventing Africans from flowing into the urban areas has traditionally been the Pass laws, which lay down that Africans must be in possession of a pass if they are in urban areas. Passes would be issued only to Africans actually employed, and those without employment (and therefore without valid passes) could – and can – be sent back to the countryside. Depending upon the determination of municipal pass control authorities, this mechanism could be a potent means of preventing the influx of rural Africans. Since the Pass laws were generally effective in controlling movement of people, there was no way out of the impositions imposed by other legislation. That exposed Africans in rural areas to such legislation as the Native Service Contract Act of 1932, which laid down that it was a criminal offence for an African labour tenant (or any of his dependents) to absent himself from the property of the land-owner. One effect of this legislation, among others, was that an African child might not go away to school without the permission of the landlord on whose land the family lived. Labour tenants therefore became enmeshed in unequal contracts with the landlords, were unable to accumulate capital or acquire skills in order to make a living elsewhere, and had the whole weight of Governmental authority against them if they attempted to evade the conditions imposed on them. Those conditions commonly included the obligation of most of the family to work for 90 or 180 days per annum for the landlord. Steadily the labour tenants were bound hand and foot and exposed to the mercy of the landlords. No wonder that white agriculture recovered so well from its disabilities in the nineteenth century. Given free market conditions, African peasants had managed to begin to win back the land and their independent means of livelihood. As the State increasingly reflected and executed the wishes of the white farmers, so African peasants and tenants were increasingly hampered and harassed in their efforts to gain their economic independence. First prevented from increasing their land-holdings, then isolated from the new agricultural technology flowing in from Europe and America, ultimately even their relative independence as labour tenants has been undermined. In African reserves live the men and their families who are in perhaps the most depressed economic and social conditions of the whole sub-continent.

Chapter 14

Labour struggles

The style and the content of South African history is well illustrated by the success of white workers, and the failure of African workers, to secure for themselves a comfortable standard of living and reasonable working conditions. The explanations for this difference in the success and failure of working men to better themselves, is almost entirely a matter of political power. Both white and black workers have tried and failed in their industrial strike actions; but the white workers have been able to fall back on political action, whereas the voteless Africans have not. Since white workers were the first to initiate trade unions, and the first to initiate political action on behalf of working men, we should look first at the methods they employed before considering the attempts of African workers to achieve the same objectives by similar techniques.

Until the mineral revolution in the second half of the nineteenth century, such industry as existed in Southern Africa was on an extremely small scale – wagon-making, newspaper-publishing, wine-making, were all undertaken by organisations which were too small to encourage the emergence of trade union organisation. The history of industrial tension and negotiation properly begins in Kimberley, when diamond-mining for the first time brought hundreds of workers together in the same place for the same purpose. Certain peculiarities of the diamond industry should be observed at once: diamond mining was not only the first major industry in Southern Africa; it was also the industry where the pattern for future industrial relations was laid down. Gold mining in the Transvaal and coal mining in Natal both proceeded upon the basis that was established in Kimberley diamond mining. First, the diamond mines attracted white and black and coloured labourers, but these labourers were treated differently right from the start of serious mining. The African labourers came from the Transkei, the Ciskei and Basutoland, and they came unskilled, illiterate, unfamiliar with such large scale economic operations. The European labourers were normally new immigrants from Europe rather than migrants from the neighbouring districts, and they came skilled, literate, and fully familiar with large scale industry. Many were Cornish immigrants from the tin-mining industry, whose families had been miners for many generations. By contrast, the young African men came from families which had been farmers since time immemorial. The Coloured men who came to the diamond fields were in an anomalous status. they were often literate, sometimes skilled in industrial techniques, though completely unfamiliar with the industrial system which was employing them.

Second, as we have seen, diamonds are intrinsically worthless, and therefore they are only expensive if the supply is closely regulated. For that reason the diamond producing companies eventually merged into one massive and monopolistic company – De Beers. Unity of ownership of the industry encouraged workers to combine in order to negotiate, and to agree to uniform terms right across the industry. Since the white miners were already familiar with the processes and techniques of industrial negotiation, they were well placed to bargain with the employers: the same was not true of the African workers. Third, diamond mining is concerned with a high-priced, small scale product, which tempts people to steal. Coal mining, for example, faces no such problem – a worker would have to carry away tons of coal in order to make theft worth-while. Diamonds, however, are ideally designed for theft, and Kimberley was soon notorious for Illicit Diamond

A section of a modern mine compound where African workers live while on contract

Buying – I.D.B. – or the purchase of diamonds from whomever had been lucky enough to steal from the owner. The diamond mining managers devised a useful technique for preventing I.D.B., namely to herd all the workers into compounds, and not to allow them out, except at the end of the contract, and only after a thorough search of the worker and his belongings. That technique saved a great deal of trouble, since the only alternative would be to search each worker thoroughly every time he came off duty. Now the African workers, unfamiliar with any kind of industry, were not aware that this was a unique restriction on their liberty; white workers, familiar with other mining systems, were fully aware of the outrage. Furthermore, white workers were prepared to take drastic action against such isolation, whereas African workers were unfamiliar with strike techniques, and being unskilled were in any case less essential to the mining process. Very rapidly therefore, migrant African workers came to be treated differently from white workers, and in a manner which emphasised the difference of treatment. Finally, the African workers at first were so unskilled that they could exercise no control over the industry: if they abandoned the mines or went on strike it was easy to find unskilled replacements. The skilled and semi-skilled white workers, however, could not easily be replaced if they struck work. The difference between the two categories of employees was in the first place that between skilled and unskilled. Unfortunately, that distinction also coincided with race, with the result that in practice African employees were exploited because they were African, not just because they were doing unskilled work.

Another phenomenon, which was later to become well-known, also originated in the Kimberley diamond mines: white working-class racialism. An essential tenet of European trades unionism in the nineteenth century was that all workers in any industry must unite in order to negotiate with (or to overthrow) the management – otherwise the management could divide the employees amongst themselves. In Southern Africa, however, it became normal for white workers to ignore the interests of non-white employees. How did the variation occur? An important point to grasp is that share-holders and managers of such industries as De Beers tended to take a cool and unemotional view of the industry. While they might agree in principle that white racial privileges should be defended against African or Coloured intrusion, they were not personally prepared to pay for that defence. When white workers appealed to the racial instincts of the employers, the reply was often extremely uninterested. African workers were paid very little, and they made very little trouble since they had no trade unions to organise them. White workers were relatively well paid, and tended to make a great deal of trouble if their interests were ignored. Employers therefore tended to prefer African employees to whites, and often attempted to increase the proportion of African labour employed. Their motive was to increase profit, rather than to extend industrial opportunities to an underprivileged group of workers – but the effect was the same. Conversely it followed that white workers regarded Africans as potential and dangerous competitors for employment. Against the argument that Africans were cheaper and more productive, the white workers could only reply that Africans were in some way inferior. That argument became increasingly difficult to demonstrate as numbers of Africans began to acquire knowledge of the skills and techniques involved in mining, and as poor and unskilled whites began to come to the mines as well. The result however, was that the white workers began to express hostility against African workers, instead of attacking the management itself. From the point of view of the managers, that was an excellent result. Furthermore, the racialism of the skilled white workers fitted in very well with the racialism of the white frontiersmen, and the racialist language of the frontier began to be spoken in the mines as well. In an important sense that was appropriate. There was indeed a racial frontier in industry, just as there had been on the land; and in each case the white frontiersmen were determined that no African should cross the frontier into the area of white privilege. The similarity can even be taken a step further. The governors of the Cape Colony, sitting in Cape Town several hundred miles from the frontier, were seldom impressed by the racialist arguments of the frontiersmen; and the managers and owners of the mining industry, whose own posts were a long way from the African competitors, were equally unimpressed by arguments based upon racial interests. Of course, if Africans had wanted to be governors of colonies, or managers of industries, the governors and managers might have felt differently. As matters stood, however, it was common to discover mine owners expressing paternal opinions about African workers, while the white skilled labourers were the outspoken racialists. That pattern was often to be repeated.

It was repeated almost at once, when gold mining began in the Transvaal. The Transvaal Republic already practised an ideology of race, based upon the fundamental dictate that there should be no equality between the races, in any sphere of life. Mine owners and skilled white artisans, often travelling to the Witwatersrand from Kimberley, were prepared to accept that ideology when it was applied to the mining industry. Managers knew from their Kimberley experience that a segregated work-force was a docile work-force; artisans knew from their Kimberley experience that the only reliable way of preventing cheap African labour from undermining their positions was to insist upon an industrial colour bar. One further argument was brought forward in the Witwatersrand situation, namely that of economic necessity. The price of gold was relatively stable, and it was not possible for producers to monopolise production. In order to work at a profit therefore, it was argued that only a small proportion of the working population could be paid at 'European' levels. In practice, white artisans came to accept that their high wages depended upon the existence of a badly-paid mass of unskilled African migrants. The only arguments which broke out between managements and white artisans related to the relative proportions of black and white in the labour force. Decisions made in, and for, the mining industry, later applied in the manufacturing industry when that began to grow during the second quarter of the twentieth century.

Despite the tacit agreement between management and white labour that there should be a white labour aristocracy and an African migrant labour force to sustain it, it was a long time before the precise position of the industrial colour bar was agreed upon. Until the end of the nineteenth century the dispute was muffled. For one thing, both the mining magnates and the white artisans in the Transvaal Republic felt themselves to be oppressed by the Republican government, and the tension between the two white communities throughout Southern Africa tended to overshadow industrial disputes. Secondly, in the early days it was still possible for white miners to hope that they would become millionaires, either by clever investment in the volatile share market, or by successful prospecting. Since the artisans did not entirely believe that they would always remain artisans, there was little incentive to take drastic action on behalf of other artisans. Furthermore, many of the artisans were target workers, working for a few years in order to go home to Britain with their savings. The fluid nature of the working population made trade union organisation very difficult. Not until 1902 was the Transvaal Miners Association formed, and before that the unions had boasted very small membership indeed. Finally, until the end of the nineteenth century there were almost no African workers in possession of paper qualifications required for responsible positions. There was no school of mines in the sub-continent: those who were qualified had usually obtained their training in Europe. While there were no qualified Africans, there was no urgency about restricting their rights. All that was required was to insist that employees be in possession of paper qualifications. Many of these circumstances changed after the South African War of 1899–1902.

For one thing, the British victory in the war meant the removal of the Republican Government, and thereby the removal of the external pressure which had held magnates and workers together in a common bond. Each group expected the Crown Colony Government to favour its particular interests. In practice the Government favoured employers as against employees – but whichever direction the Government had taken, it would have annoyed one or other section of the British industrial community. Then again, as time passed and as the mining industry became more stable and predictable, it became foolish for white artisans to expect to become millionaires. Prospecting was now undertaken by the companies and the stock-market was stable enough to cut out the possibility of great wealth being made by poor investors. Finally, the mine-owners began to think in terms of altering the existing employment ratios, so as to employ a larger proportion of African, and a smaller proportion of white employees. As soon as gold mining resumed after the war, the mine managements – working through the Chamber of Mines – began to try to extract greater productivity from the white artisans. Small scale strikes of white employees took place in 1902 and in 1903, reflecting the new hostility in relations between managements and white workers.

The new militancy of managements was not, of course, conceived as a pro-African policy (though it was sometimes defended in those terms). One of the immediate consequences of the British victory was that mine-owners, who expected to be allowed to recruit African labour throughout British

Colonial Africa, agreed to offer African workers Shs.30/– per month instead of the pre-war rate of Shs.55/–. Sir Harry Johnston, for example, had encouraged the mine managements to believe that thousands of Baganda would be willing to travel down the Uganda railway to ships in Mombasa which would take them to Lourenço Marques whence they would travel by train to the Johannesburg compounds. In the event, no new recruiting areas were opened up. The Belgians in the Congo and the Portuguese in Angola wanted their own African labour for forced labour purposes. Rhodesia was already anxious to monopolise Southern and Northern Rhodesian African labour for local purposes. A thousand Nyasa labourers were recruited experimentally, but so many of them died in the cold climate of the mining areas that the experiment was terminated and not repeated for many years. In Southern Africa itself, the post-war years saw so much harbour-improvement and railway construction that Africans could find employment in safe work on the surface, rather than work cheaply underground. The mining industry was therefore placed in the embarrassing position of having cut wages sharply, without ensuring that there were labourers who would accept such conditions of employment.

The response of the African labour force is instructive in demonstrating the possibilities at their disposal. They could not go out on strike: Africans were not permitted to form trade unions, and in any case an unskilled, migrant labour force was unable to bring much pressure to bear upon employers, without endangering their own material interests. A migrant labour force, drawn from every African community south of the Limpopo, was extremely difficult to organise at all, even if trade union organisation had been permitted. Two options remained. One was to withdraw labour from the mining industry and to discourage other labourers from accepting employment there; the other was to rebel against the colonial authorities who encouraged recruiting. The withdrawal of African unskilled labour quickly precepitated a crisis in the industry as a whole; at the end of 1902 – six months after the end of the war – there were less than half as many African workers in the mining compounds as there had been in 1899 before the war. Furthermore, only those Africans who were absolutely destitute (and often half-starved by the time they arrived on the Rand) came forward at all. The unskilled labour could, of course, be done by white workers, especially the ex-soldiers who were demobilised after the war, but that meant a far greater cost to the employers.

The second alternative – revolt – was put into practice in Portuguese East Africa. The Portuguese administration operated a very profitable system, whereby they encouraged as much recruiting as possible, since they received a cash payment of 15 shillings per head for every African recruited for work in the Transvaal. Foreign journalists in Lourenço Marques described the system as a modified form of slavery, so little choice did the recruits have in their recruitment. Two thirds of the total mining labour force was recruited from Portuguese East Africa. During the war there was no such recruiting, since the mines were closed. Immediately after the war when the authorities attempted to resume recruiting, and indeed began to recruit further north than ever before, they encountered severe and effective resistance under arms. Not until about 1906 were some areas sufficiently 'pacified' to permit labour recruiting on the desired scale.

For a few months the policy of withdrawal seemed to be working. Under pressure, the mines gradually increased the rate of wages offered, until early in 1904 wages had returned to roughly their pre-war level. However, a further measure had been adopted to meet the crisis: the importation of contract labourers from China, some 50,000 of whom arrived during 1904 and 1905. What this amounts to is that the mine-owners were able to recruit labour anywhere in the world, to deal with a purely local labour crisis: unskilled African migrants had no such contacts and as soon as the Chinese began to arrive, African wages once more began to fall. That was the end of resistance: in 1907 and 1908 the labour force once again flowed into the Rand, as the Chinese left. The main beneficiaries from the Chinese labourers were their employers – but it is very significant that the white artisans contrived to benefit also. Being sophisticated in the nature of industrial relations, they realised that an abundant supply of cheap Chinese labour could be used by managements to fill semi-skilled and skilled positions, and to oust white artisans from their privileged position. They also feared that Chinese might prove more efficient than African workers, since there was a widespread belief that the Chinese were fiendishly clever in such matters. Furthermore, white artisans had trade unions to make representations, they expected eventually to be voters when elections were held, and they had important political contacts with trade unions in Britain. Using these pressures, they came to an agreement with the managements that the Chinese would only be employed in positions which required absolutely no skill, and which had never ordinarily been filled by white workers. That was the first legal colour bar in Southern African industry, and it was later applied to exclude Africans as well as Chinese from responsible positions. Chinese labourers remained on the Rand for only five years, but the experiment, which was made necessary by African efforts to improve their industrial prospects, in practice enabled white artisans to obtain legal sanction for the previously non-legal colour bar.

White artisans, despite this success, were nevertheless so suspicious of their employers that they voted against them at the first opportunity. That opportunity came in 1907 in the Transvaal, when the first post-war elections were held, to create a Responsible Government answerable to the white community. The main line of battle was between Botha and Smuts and the Afrikaner Nationalists on one hand, and the English-speaking Progressive Party on the other. White artisans ignored that inter-ethnic dispute by voting either for the Labour Party or in many cases for the Afrikaner Nationalists, who therefore won a majority of seats in the new parliament. The Labour Party itself fared very badly, since it had rather too many leaders, too many ideologies, and not enough grass-roots organisation. However, immediately after the elections, during 1907, the mine managers renewed their pressure upon white artisan wages and conditions. Worse still, the new Afrikaner Government called in British Imperial troops to

CHINESE LABOUR.

TRUTH—AT LAST.

JOHN BULL—" No, the Chinaman is only to do un-
   skilled work in the Mines, and he knows it.
   He can't and won't sneak your business, Mr.
   Trader, and he can't buy the land that you
   want, Mr. Farmer, and he can't get your job,
   Mr. Skilled Workman.

   " Tell all your friends to come out now

THE UNSKILLED LABOUR PROBLEM IS SETTLED."

A page from a leaflet issued by the Tory party of Great Britain reflecting the fears of the white
artisans about Chinese workers

help control the strike. Only then did the artisans realise that in order to be sure of their interests they would have to support their own white Labour Party, rather than rely upon either the magnates in the Progressive Party or the Afrikaner government. It took a long time to achieve that political power, but by 1914, as we have seen, as a result of further industrial trouble, the Labour Party was able to control the Transvaal Provincial Council. Had it not been for the war, they might have taken a share of the Union Government as early as 1915. The failure of the strikes of 1914, 1913 and 1907 all pointed to the necessity of white artisans entering the political arena in order to ensure their industrial privileges.

The Rand Revolt of 1921 further underlined that lesson, with the result that the white workers rallied to the polls and returned 18 members of parliament in 1924, which was enough to enable them to form a coalition government with the Nationalists under Hertzog. The subsequent decline and extinction of the Labour Party from that position of strength is a most intriguing phenomenon. Primarily, the Labour Party so entrenched the interests of the white workers behind the industrial colour bar, that they ran out of reasons for existence. White workers were then so secure that they could turn their attention to other political questions unrelated to their economic interest – such as the desirability of a Republic. Almost as important is the fact that the white industrial working force was becoming increasingly an Afrikaans-speaking community, which preferred to keep close links with other Afrikaner parties – especially the Nationalists – rather than combine with other English-speaking urban political groups. They were encouraged in that direction by the activities of an Afrikaner secret society, the Broederbond, which constantly emphasised the point that the workers' first loyalty must be to their race and language, rather than to the working class as a whole. Afrikaner workers, coming from country districts where the separation of races was axiomatic, were even less likely than the English-speaking workers, to form alliances with African migrant labourers. Nevertheless the essential lesson to be learned from the extinction of the Labour Party is that it measures the absolute success of the white workers in entrenching their economic interests by means of the vote.

African industrial workers were in a very different position. They were not permitted to form unions in the mines, so that the only way they could organise themselves was to ally with a union whose base was outside the industry. They were so close to subsistence level that strikes were almost out of the question: there was simply not enough money available to sustain the workers during a prolonged stoppage of work and wages. On the other hand industrial action was absolutely essential, since the workers had no voting power whatever, and could not exercise influence except as workers. In 1919 Clements Kadalie, a migrant worker from Nyasaland employed in Cape Town, observed the modest success of Coloured trade unions and the growing power of the white unions, and came to the conclusion that Africans could and should be organised in the same manner. Starting in the Cape and later expanding into the Transvaal, he inaugurated the Industrial and Commercial Workers Union, better known as the ICU. At its peak, this

144

union had over 100,000 members and many thousands of sympathisers, and was by far the largest concerted organisation of Africans in Southern Africa so far. During the 1924 elections such eminent politicians as Hertzog and Malan, both destined to become Prime Ministers, took care to be courteous to Kadalie, lest he turn the Cape African and Coloured voters against them. Naturally, that courtesy did not last long after the election, but it still represents an index of the potential power of the ICU in 1924.

Such an organisation had no precedent in Southern African history. The white Governments, never having expected any such threat, lacked legislation with which to suppress or domesticate it. During the early 1920s therefore it was comparatively simple to bring the ICU to life and to prominence. However, once it was created, all manner of problems beset its leaders in deciding how to use this instrument. The white Labour Party was not a useful guide: apart from being hostile towards the ICU, it had won its success by means of the ballot, and that avenue was closed to the African workers. Political action must therefore mean extra-parliamentary and probably illegal action, and Kadalie hesitated to commit his followers to the extreme course of insurrection, especially as the outcome of such a policy might very well be disastrous. On the other hand, much might be done by concerted pressure upon the employers of labour, to improve the working conditions and wages of African workers. Unfortunately, Kadalie never quite made up his mind which way to go, and indeed at the height of the ICU's strength he decided to go to Europe to seek advice from European trade unionists. He was certainly well received in western Europe, but the advice he received was not very helpful for the unique circumstances in which the ICU operated. A Scottish trade unionist, Ballinger, was sent to advise him on trade union methods, and was immediately horrified at the financial chaos of the ICU's accounts. Soberly and sensibly he set himself to bring order to the ICU's finances – but it is questionable whether sober accountancy was relevant to the ICU at such a time. Members were rapidly becoming disillusioned at the inactivity of the Union, and were beginning to drift away. If the ICU failed to act swiftly, it would soon lack the membership to act at all. In the event, the Union broke up altogether. Harry Champion of Zululand split off to form the ICU yase Natal, a predominantly Zulu organisation. Ballinger and Kadalie broke from each other, each forming a separate section of the remaining ICU. None of these sections resolved the dilemma of being at the same time a political party and a trade union. Once the ICU was split, it was comparatively easy for the Government to suppress the component sections separately.

Yet the failure of the ICU in South Africa was not entirely due to the policies adopted by the leadership. An episode which occurred after the disintegration of the ICU illustrates the general difficulties involved. By 1930 Kadalie had moved to East London, where he led the dockworkers in a strike to support their demand for a minimum wage of $6\frac{1}{2}$ shillings instead of 3 shillings per day. Agents of the ICU toured the Eastern Cape discouraging potential workers from filling the places of the strikers; and Kadalie appealed to the white Trade Union Congress in

Johannesburg to prevent their members from 'scabbing'. Appeals were also sent to the International Transport Workers' Federation in Amsterdam, and to the Anti-Imperial League in Berlin. Locally, every effort was made to keep up the determination of the strikers: wives vowed that they would not prepare food for men who broke the strike, and prayer-meetings were held in order to impress upon the strikers the importance of avoiding violence, lest the authorities have an excuse to use counter-violence. Everything which the ICU and its members could do, was done. On 17th January, some 1,500 men were away from work, and meetings of up to 4,000 people were held during the following week.

The employers were nevertheless able to resist the strikers. The Railways and Harbours, being a Government agency, could afford a prolonged stoppage of work since they were not obliged to make profits, while the ICU had not the funds to feed the strikers who were soon close to starvation. In the impoverished reserves and townships, the authorities were able to recruit African casual labourers who needed money too badly to resist the temptation. They were also able to recruit white casual labour, and African labour from Zululand, which was not affected by Kadalie's organisation. Also the employers were the Government, and could use the instruments of government in the struggle. Soon after the strike began, special (white) constables were enrolled, and provocative patrols of the locations instituted. Eventually, on 26th January 1930, Kadalie and eight other leaders were arrested and charged with incitement to public violence, or alternatively promoting hostility between the races (a crime recently invented by the Hertzog-Creswell government). Bail was first refused, and later set so high that Kadalie could not pay it. From jail, on 28th January, less than two weeks after the strike began, Kadalie called the strikers to return to work. Many of them had already done so, since they could not afford to stay out of work any longer. What the episode indicates is that the government had the legal and physical resources required to beat a strike, and that the ICU was unable to organise workers over a large enough area, or beyond the African communities, or to sustain a strike for more than a very few days. Like the white trade unionists, they discovered that a strike by one race only was an ineffective means of bringing about change.

The tragedy of the ICU was that it could have enjoyed some success as a trade union, or it could have taken a chance in the political sphere, and that this was to be the last occasion on which it would be possible to create the organisation for attempting either of these courses of action. African workers were so disillusioned by this episode that no comparable action was taken for almost twenty years.

During the Second World War, the divisions within Afrikaner Nationalism were so severe that the Smuts Government from 1939–1948 contained an unusually large proportion of moderately liberal white politicians. Foremost among these was Jan Hofmeyr, who became the Minister of Finance and, while Smuts attended to the conduct of the war, Hofmeyr more or less ran the home Government. It was also a Government dear to the hearts of the mining magnates, whose economic interests coincided with Hofmeyr's cautious interest in removing some of the disabilities from African, Coloured and Indian workers. Furthermore, since the war against the fascists was perceived to be a war against evil (and particularly racialism against Jews) both Smuts and Hofmeyr made speeches reflecting a rather incautious approval of a generalised liberty of people to determine their own affairs. These comments were not intended to apply to the South African situation, but it was hard to draw a distinction between liberalism in Europe and liberalism in Southern Africa.

The measures taken by the Government were hardly likely to cause a revolution: some provision was made for pensions for African and Coloured and Indian, as well as for white citizens – though not on equal terms. A larger grant was made available for the financing of African education – though not in proportion to the real African contribution to general revenue and prosperity. Nevertheless these measures taken in conjunction with the speeches of the Government leaders, all created great expectations in the minds of the Africans as a whole, and of industrial workers in particular. In August 1946, 50,000 African mine-workers came out on strike along the Witwatersrand. Police fired upon the strikers in an attempt to force them back to work, and there were several fatalities. It really did not matter which government was in power, since even the most liberal government within the possibilities of the electoral system was not prepared to tolerate industrial strike action. During the Second World War the normal wage for African mine-workers was still Shs. 2/- per shift – before the South African War it had been Shs. 2/- per shift. Few categories of industrial labour in the whole world can have derived so little benefit from their employment – white workers in the same industry during the same period had more than doubled their rate of pay, despite Chamber of Mines warnings that any increase in wages would bring ruin to the whole industry. Only in the 1960s, when industrial expansion was faster than the availability of white skilled labour, were restrictions on African employment relaxed. Even now, it is a matter of relaxing regulations rather than abolishing them, and as soon as the number of skilled white workers is once again sufficient – through the assisted immigration of European artisans – the regulations can and will be re-imposed.

Chapter 15

Internal white power, 1910–1948

So far, we have considered the years 1910 to 1948 as a period in which different interest groups of the white community jostled each other for positions within the privileged enclosure. Perhaps more significant than that theme is the one which will be traced in this chapter, namely the increasing power of the white community as a whole, over all other communities, using the government as the agency for establishing that control. The account begins in 1910, since the Union of South Africa for the first time provided the white community with the machinery to achieve absolute command of the situation. As late as 1905–1906, for example, the Natal Government had been obliged to call in Imperial troops in order to suppress the Bambatha revolt: such reliance upon external military power was clearly a limitation on the ability of the local white communities to look after their own interests.

The creation of the Union in 1910 did not, by itself, make the white community secure from all possible challenges internally, but it did provide that community with the means of enhancing its power. Let us first consider the purely military aspects of the question. In 1913, as we have seen, the Union Government was once again obliged to call in British Imperial troops in order to deal with a white miners' strike on the Witwatersrand: but immediately after that shock, Smuts took the lead in creating the Union Defence Force, which was staffed predominantly by Afrikaner generals who were too numerous to go into political life, but too prominent to be ignored altogether. The immediate crisis provoking the creation of the UDF was a white disturbance, but the Force immensely strengthened the hand of the Government in dealing with opponents of any colour. During the years 1907 to 1913, for example, Mahatma Gandhi had developed the weapon of Passive Resistance – Satyagraha – as a means of advancing the interest of the Transvaal and Natal Indian communities. The absence of a readily available and numerous force of troops had meant that the Passive Resisters had been extremely difficult to deal with. Many years later it proved difficult to deal with them even when force was available, but undoubtedly the modest success of Gandhi's campaign leading up to the Indian Relief Act of 1914 is partly attributable to the Government's military weakness.

Armed force was not required for purposes of coercing Africans until after the First World War. A small congregation of an African separatist church calling themselves Israelites and led by Enoch Mgijima as 'Bishop, Prophet and Watchman', settled on common land in Bulhoek location in the eastern Cape. The congregation was unpopular with the other African inhabitants of the location, whose common ground they were occupying. They also refused to obey Government instructions to disperse. By May 1921 they had become an embarrassment to the local officials, who called in a detachment of police to disperse them by force. Eight hundred armed police had no difficulty in routing 500 Israelites armed with spears and sticks, but excessive force was used, and 163 Israelites were killed in the battle. Even among white parliamentarians that degree of bloodshed was considered rather unnecessary to disperse a community which was a nuisance rather than a threat to peace.

Slightly over a year later, in May and June 1922, the UDF was involved in a more substantial encounter in South-West Africa, which had become a League of Nations Mandate Territory after the War, administered by the Union Government. The Bondelzwarts were a Coloured community, one of several who had trekked out of the Cape during the nineteenth century and set up their own systems of government beyond the borders. During the Nama-Herero wars against the Germans early in the twentieth century, a leader of the Bondelzwarts community – Abraham Morris – had gone into exile in Bechuanaland Protectorate. In 1922 he returned, without the Government's permission. That incident brought to a head a series of grievances felt by the Bondelzwarts against the new administration, grievances which included high taxes and unanswered claims to land expropriated for German settlement. Tactless officialdom escalated the issue out of all proportion, the Bondelzwarts became more militant, and in May 1922 the Government attacked the settlement. The Bondelzwarts were prepared for guerilla war in the nineteenth century tradition, but were defenceless against the aeroplanes which the Government sent against them. Once again there were over a hundred casualties, and the Government's military advantage was such that the campaign lasted only a week. These two incidents were widely reported – the Bondelzwarts even as far as the Permanent Mandate Commission of the League of Nations. Quite apart from the various moral and tactical issues involved, the incidents proved beyond doubt that the Government would not hesitate to commit its forces to the suppression of African protests – indeed, that the Government was if anything over-anxious to commit its forces to such purposes. That knowledge is an important part of the background to all subsequent political life in the Union.

It need hardly be said that, in the armed forces of the Government, only white members carried arms. During the Second World War, General Smuts caused something of a scandal by asserting that he would arm Africans in the event of a Japanese invasion. The eventuality did not occur, however, and the rule continued in force that African and Coloured servicemen would act as labourers, porters and other non-combatant employees.

Because of this military colour-bar, the defence forces were absolutely reliable instruments in dealing with internal non-white protests.

That in itself might have been considered sufficient defence for white privilege. However, the laager mentality – a local variation of seige psychology – made many white citizens fear that none of them were really safe so long as any Africans, Coloureds or Indians belonged to the privileged community of voters. The fact that non-white citizens were unable ever to use the franchise in order to gain other advantages was overlooked: what was much more obvious was the fact that the link between franchise and land preserved Cape Africans from the full rigour of the 1913 Land Act. Individual politicians like John Merriman and others especially in the Cape might argue that the best means of white defence was to absorb the potential African and Coloured leaders; but that kind of argument did not commend itself to Governments whose political traditions stretched back to the days of the land frontier and the fighting laager. In the circumstances of nineteenth century South Africa, it was obviously true that the white trekkers had to be exclusive in order to survive: in the twentieth century it was less true, but by that time the attitude had become deeply entrenched in white (and especially in Afrikaner) political phiolosophy.

As we have already seen, the political parties were so evenly balanced for the first twenty years of Union, that none could muster the two-thirds parliamentary majority required to tamper with African and Coloured votes directly. The Natal franchise, which had theoretically provided for the enfranchisement of some Africans, Coloureds and particularly Indians, was permitted to change its character over time: no new voters were enfranchised unless they were impeccably white, and the old non-white voters died. That still left a substantial number of Cape Coloured and African voters: as late as 1929 12·3 per cent of the Cape's electorate was Coloured, and 7·6 per cent African. However, even then it was possible to restrict the numbers of non-white voters, by instructing the officials in charge of registration to apply the regulations strictly against Coloured and African applicants. In 1930, also, the value of the African and Coloured votes was cut in half by the passage of the Women's Enfranchisement Act, which extended the franchise to all adult females – so long as they were white. The number of white voters was automatically doubled, while other voting groups continued steadily to decline in numbers as a result of strict rules governing registration. By the 1930s the 'qualified franchise' in the Cape was no more than a token of political integration: all white adults were enfranchised, and the qualifications had only to be met by non-white candidates. Their less than 10 per cent of the Cape electorate was in fact a trivial proportion of the whole Union electorate.

Nevertheless the existence of a qualified franchise in any form became a matter of principle for the Government to extinguish. While the lead was taken by the Afrikaner nationalists, it should be mentioned that without English-speaking electoral support they could not have had their way, and that they were positively assisted by some rabid racialist English-speaking parliamentarians whose anti-Indian sentiments reinforced the general fear and scorn directed towards the Africans and Coloureds. In the 1930s, with the formation of the massive United Party and its almost automatic two-thirds majority, the opportunity had risen for stern action. A legislative package was passed through Parliament including the Native Trust and Land Act (whose limitations we have already mentioned) and the Native Representation Act which removed Cape Africans from the common roll and provided three separate seats instead, in the House of Assembly. The number of seats in the Assembly increased in proportion to the number of electors, and by the 1930s the Assembly had grown to over 150 members. At the same time, the Government set up a curious body described as the Native Representative Council, none of whose members were directly elected, and which had purely advisory powers. The NRC proved absolutely powerless, since the Government itself did not regard it as representative, unless its advice happened to coincide with what the Government wanted to hear. The three seats in a house of 155 were unlikely to be of any value unless the two major parties in the Assembly had almost equal numbers of members, and even then the major parties might hesitate to ally themselves with representatives of Africans. Previously, at least in theory, African voters could influence the election result in a score of constituencies; now the white candidates could altogether ignore African electoral opinions. The political segregation was not yet complete of course: the Coloured voters remained as they were, and there was still at least a notional African presence in the House of Assembly, even if the three representatives did have to be white. It was sufficient, however, to pacify white opinion until after the Nationalist victory of 1948.

A more delicate problem was to deal with the handful of white citizens who so far forgot their racial interests as to speak in favour of African, Indian and Coloured interests. Among the fruits of the Nationalist–Labour Pact was the Immorality Act, which asserted that a sexual union which cut across colour lines was not only immoral but also illegal. The puritanism implicit in such legislation is in character with much legislation which has been passed by Nationalist Governments, but in practice the puritanism is somewhat imbalanced in execution. Cases involving the Immorality Act have generally been heard by magistrates rather than by judges, and have therefore reflected public white opinion to an unusual extent. It is not uncommon, therefore, for unequal sentences to be passed upon the convicted parties, with the white accused receiving a milder sentence than the other party. However, the basic intention of the Act is to limit inter-racial contacts, and by imposing a constraint upon such contacts the Act has largely achieved its object. Ordinary social contact within a racial group is not usually inspected by crime squads of the Police Force: social contacts between racial groups are, and the risk of Police investigation is a severe discouragement. Finally, such legislation tends to encourage public opinion to regard all inter-racial contacts as being more or less improper; and without personal contacts across racial categories, it is difficult for any group to form a realistic assessment of the opinions of another.

In the same year as the Immorality Act – 1927 – the same Government also passed the Riotous Assemblies Act. Having witnessed the decline of Clements Kadalie's ICU, the Government resolved to equip itself with powers to prevent a repetition of Kadalie's career by any other trade union leader. The Riotous Assemblies Act provided the Government with the power, by request from the judiciary, to prohibit public gatherings which the Government thought likely to lead to a breach of the peace, and thereby to control the risk of a gathering of Africans (or indeed anyone else) for the purpose of staging a strike or organising a protest. More important than the actual provisions of the law (which has been amended to make it stronger and more arbitrary since then) is the effect which it produced on public opinion. White citizens were encouraged to believe that any gathering of Africans was a potential threat to white safety; and Africans and others were encouraged to believe that any sort of gathering might involve them in illegality. Like the Immorality Act, therefore, it expanded the existing definition of a crime, and thereby enhanced the power of the state over each of its citizens. One of the consequences of the Government's increasingly absolute powers was to alter the climate of public opinion so that members of inter-racial groups felt that they were somehow guilty if they met at all. In any case, the increasing restrictions upon Africans and Indians and Coloureds working alongside white men, and the similar restrictions against their living near each other, made it immensely difficult for inter-racial groups to form at all, except in circumstances which underlined the artificiality of the meeting itself. Once casual contacts were minimised, they had to be replaced by organised meetings, which simply reinforced everyone's feeling that such a meeting was unnatural.

It is tempting to ask why, in view of the mass of discriminatory legislation which was passed in the first twenty or more years of Union, governments felt driven to new excesses of discrimination. If twenty years or more of legislation had failed to secure the white community in its power and privilege, what purpose could be served by continuing along the same road in future? Security by means of controlling all the actions of all the citizens was in fact an illusion – there would always remain some citizens free to perform some actions which might conceivably endanger an over-sensitive government. Governments have therefore constantly attempted to allay the fears of the white electorate by fresh assaults on the interests of the non-white communities.

One such episode relates to the attempt of the Indian community to gain some sort of status and recognition within the government of the country. In their negotiations they enjoyed the support of the Indian Government. which in 1927 appointed an Indian Agent-General to the Union Government. Since India was well along the road to Dominion status, and since India was so important a part of the Empire held by very fragile bonds, the Indian Agent-General could be sure of a hearing. That was especially true when Smuts was in power, since Smuts venerated the Commonwealth and valued its peaceful continuation – but it was also true no matter who was in charge of the Union Government. Agreements were signed, for instance, in 1927 at Cape Town, and in 1944 at Pretoria, which had something of the status of international treaties. However, respect for the Empire-Commonwealth was not sufficient to overcome white suspicion at Indian immigration, Indian economic activity, and Indian political aspirations. Even in Natal, where the Dominion Party stood ostensibly for Imperial links as against republican independence, it proved that the Dominion Party stood for white power first, and Commonwealth solidarity only if that was compatible with white power. In 1944, therefore, the Dominion Party in Natal successfully sabotaged the Pretoria Agreement by refusing to carry out Government policy at the provincial level. At one point in the tangled negotiations, the Indians were actually offered parliamentary representation on the same basis as the separate African representation; but they turned the offer down on principle, and no similar offer was ever repeated.

The career of the Native Representative Council is quite instructive in this respect. Created as a result of Hertzog's United Party legislation in 1936, it was an advisory body, with neither judicial, nor legislative, nor executive powers. Those disabilities might have been overcome had it not been for the fact that the Council was also unrepresentative. Had its members been directly elected, they might have co-ordinated African opinion, and their comments might have commanded more attention. As it was, the members tended to be men of great integrity and tact, but obliged to plead since they had neither the power nor the mandate to command. Since organised African opinion was critical of the institution on principle, and discouraged its members from serving in the NRC, it also followed that the African members were unusually 'moderate' in their approach to political change. Composed in this manner, the NRC was precisely the sort of institution with which a white government could have co-operated in complete safety – had the government been at all willing to co-operate with African leaders.

Since politely phrased appeals proved unavailing, the NRC members steadily reinforced their demands beyond the range of political reality. In 1944, for example, they demanded the abolition of the Pass Laws and the abandonment of segregation as a Government policy, two recommendations which the Government could not have accepted without precipitating the suicide of the governing Party. Matters came to a head at the session in 1946. On that occasion the Pretoria City Council, which had usually allowed the NRC to meet in the Town Hall, refused to allow its facilities to be used by Africans even if they were members of the NRC, a piece of bureaucratic vindictiveness which was becoming increasingly common. In the offices of the Department of Labour, where the meeting did take place, there were no lavatories for Africans. Furthermore, the Minister for Native Affairs was absent, as was the senior civil servant of the Department, so that the meeting was actually chaired by a junior bureaucrat. These circumstances underlined the long-standing complaints of the members on two counts: that Government policy at home was at variance with the resounding liberal statements of the Atlantic Charter, and that no one was interested in listening to the NRC's opinions. The members compared themselves to a toy telephone, to which one could say anything, but the words could not be heard. So saying, they adjourned the meeting indefinitely, until such time as the Government adopted a different approach to race relations. The change of Government in 1948 brought no such different approach, and the NRC never again assembled. Eventually the Nationalist Government abolished it entirely.

The entrenchment of white power within the Union was not only a matter of governments passing a series of discriminatory Acts. Since union, the white electorate has become increasingly intolerant of a diversity of racial opinions, even within the white political parties. At the time of union there were eminent white politicians who were described as 'liberal': their policies, on closer inspection, were seldom radical, but at least they were different from the straightforward racialism of the majority of white electors. Merriman had been Prime Minister of the Cape; F. S. Malan became deputy leader of the South Africa Party under Smuts; Sauer held ministerial office. Admittedly party discipline obliged them to suppress their liberal opinions when it came to voting for governmental proposals, but nevertheless they were in parliament, and it was respectable to express racial opinions which were more tolerant and permissive than the parliamentary norm. By 1948, that tradition was represented in office by only one man, J. H. Hofmeyr. What had happened during the intervening years?

Superficially, the answer is that the old Cape liberals died, and were not replaced by similar parliamentary recruits. That, of course, begs the question of why there were no comparable recruits. Perhaps the significance of the old men is that their political education was acquired during the nineteenth century and in the Cape, when few articulate Africans challenged the political structure, and where it was possible to regard Africans as *external* to the centre of life. The western Cape, as we have seen, was settled by very few Africans at any time in its history. Africans indigenous to the western Cape – the Khoikhoi people – had been conspicuous for moving away, rather than challenging the new white community. In the western Cape, therefore, racial relations were fairly easy. Once Union had been formed, however, there was no comparable political climate. Africans were clearly *internal*, and race relations an urgent concern rather than a philosophical problem for thoughtful but remote white politicians. The real capital of the country was Pretoria (though parliament met in Cape Town), and the real economic centre of the country was Johannesburg (even though the country districts elected most of the parliamentarians).

Nevertheless the old Cape tradition did not die altogether. In the English-speaking cities white radicals could still be found, people who were determined to remain available and accessible to African, Indian and Coloured individuals who shared their interests. The real change was that these individuals no longer found their way into parliament. The political parties would no longer countenance such deviation amongst parliamentary candidates. In that change of mood, the 1924 election was of paramount importance. As we have seen, the alliance between Labour and the Nationalists was a difficult one to establish: Nationalists had to stop advocating republicanism, and Labourites had to stop advocating socialism, so that the only common ground left for them to exploit was racial privilege. The success of the slogan 'segregation' in 1924 demonstrated that whichever party was most vehement in its racialism had a great advantage in elections. Party managers therefore realised that they could no longer afford to create the impression of racial tolerance in any of the members of the party. Increasingly, it became difficult to see precisely how one party differed from another, since no party would offer a liberal alternative to the electors. The common argument was that any liberal in the party must suppress his opinions lest he give ammunition to the opponents and thereby extinguish liberalism altogether. Among the consequences of this tactical decision was the fact that liberalism, even within the white community, came to be regarded as discreditable and disreputable ideology. The white public was cut off from easy contact with other racial communities, was led to believe that racial mixing of any description was a prelude to crime and immorality, and was then deprived of any parliamentary voice reminding them of the freedom which they, as well as other citizens, had lost. The intellectual climate was changing towards greater exclusiveness than ever before, and that is what enabled the white electorate to tolerate increasingly intolerant governments.

The prime example, and perhaps the leading victim, of this development, was Jan Hofmeyr. A child prodigy, he took his B.A. at 15, with Honours, a second degree at 16, and an M.A. at 17, before proceeding to Oxford for yet another degree. At 22 he was a Professor, and at 24 the Principal of the University of the Witwatersrand. At the age of 29 he was appointed Administrator of Transvaal Province, and at the age of 35, in 1929, he entered parliament as a SAP member. Until that time he had been known as a brilliant mind and an able administrator, but it began to be clear also that his mind moved in rather different directions from those of the other members of parliament. A successful political career was interrupted in 1938. Hertzog appointed a close political colleague to be a Senator to represent Native Interests. The man in question had neither knowledge of, nor sympathy for, his supposed constituents, and Hertzog had merely appointed him in order to get a valued friend into parliament after he had lost his seat in the recent election. Hofmeyr's growing tendency towards liberal principles made him resign from the cabinet in protest – though he did not resign from the United Party. In 1939, with the break-up of the United Party, Smuts called upon Hofmeyr to look after South African affairs while Smuts himself went off to the war. During the war years Hofmeyr smuggled through parliament a few social reforms which tended to ameliorate the condition of non-white citizens, and by the end of the war he had become very conspicuous as the leader of liberal white opinion in the country at large. For that reason the Nationalists seized upon Hofmeyr in the 1948 election, declaring that he was so liberal as to be a great danger to the white community. The white electorate, by throwing out the United Party Government, again served notice that a reputation for liberalism was political death. More seriously, the United Party hierarchy itself took a poor view of Hofmeyr, and it was only Smuts's intervention which saved Hofmeyr from a public humiliation at the hands of his own party. In the same year he died, the last influential liberal to sit in the South African parliament as a representative of white voters. He was also one of the last influential Afrikaners to assert the old tradition of the individual's right to eccentric opinions. During the hundred years following the trek, the Afrikaner community steadily established legal and social control over dissenting individuals, and became one of the most coherent, disciplined and single-minded communities in the world.

During the 38 years from Union until the Nationalist election victory in 1948, the foundations were laid for totalitarian government. The white community armed itself and became militarily safe from African rebellions, and even from African protests. Existing African electoral rights were eroded until they were negligible, though the Coloured voters lingered on the common roll until after 1948. The once powerful African trade unions were rendered harmless while white workers entrenched their position of economic privilege. Inter-racial contacts became difficult and disreputable, and at the same time the white community became infected by a siege mentality, and therefore tolerant of increasingly harsh and arbitrary methods. Most of the actions of the Nationalist Government since 1948 have therefore been to take existing institutions and existing ideas to their logical (or illogical) extreme.

Chapter 16

South Africa's neighbours

The re-alignment of states in 1910, whereby Union was formed, left the other dependencies in the region divided, vulnerable to the increasing strength of the Union, and unable to devise any form of association which would provide an alternative source of power and influence. During the first half of the twentieth century, the position of the neighbouring states, *vis-a-vis* the Union, steadily deteriorated, partly because of the growing strength of the Union itself, but largely because of the inability of the Imperial powers – Britain, Portugal and Germany – to develop or strengthen their dependencies. Portgual, without capital, could do little more than hold on to her existing possessions in Africa; Germany, losing the First World War, lost her African possessions as well; Britain, continuing to regard the Union as the corner-stone of British influence in the sub-continent, neglected to build up a rival association until it was too late to do so successfully.

During the negotiations leading up to Union, it was commonly believed that other British possessions in the region would eventually join the first four colonies, in a substantially enlarged Union. Rhodesia actually sent observers to the drafting convention, so likely did it seem that the Union would expand to include territory to the north. Provision was made in the Union constitution for the admission of the three High Commission Territories of Bechuanaland, Basutoland and Swaziland, so that machinery should exist when that admission should be considered. In 1910 it was entirely reasonable to look forward to a time when Rhodesia and the protectorates would be absorbed: they were all British dependencies, all part of the same economic, commercial and currency system, and their white and black populations were very similar to those in the Union. In practice however, all have retained separate constitutional identities, even though they have increasingly moved into the orbit of South African influence. The only territory to become absorbed into the Union was German South-West Africa, a development which no one in 1910 anticipated. The constitutional relations between the southern African states do not provide a complete picture of the real relationships, but they do provide a starting point in understanding the changes brought about during the first half of this century.

When the First World War broke out in 1914, as we have seen, the Union Government resolved to play a major role in the African campaigns despite the reluctance of many Afrikaners to take part in an Imperial war on the side of their recent enemies. The immediate target inevitably was German South-West Africa, because of its proximity and the assistance which it might continue to provide to rebels within the Union. Once the 1914 rebellion had been suppressed, therefore, Generals Botha and Smuts took personal control of the South-West African campaign early in 1915. Smuts took charge of a three-pronged invasion by land from the south, where there was sufficient pasture for the horses, and water for the troops and animals. Botha captured the harbour of Walvis Bay, and led the direct attack inland to Windhoek, the capital of the territory. Despite the natural protection offered by the Skeleton Coast and the escarpment of hills, Windhoek fell in May, and the German forces surrendered in July 1915. The conquest was surprisingly easy, and it encouraged Smuts to undertake a second campaign in German East Africa, where the British and their Belgian allies had been unable to achieve a conclusive result. Once a rudimentary administration had been established for South-West Africa therefore, Smuts set off for East Africa. There the German forces were commanded by a brilliant officer, von Lettow Vorbeck, who conceived it his task not to win the campaign, but to tie down as many enemy troops as possible and prevent them being deployed in Europe. His rear-guard actions were so successful that he was still at liberty and potentially dangerous when the war ended in 1918. Despite the military interest of that campaign however, it was essentially a side-show from South Africa's point to view. If Smuts had anticipated the later development of Tanzania, the South African Government might have demonstrated more interest in East Africa: as it was, the main interest centred in South-West Africa, whose constitutional fate was decided in the post-war settlement.

The end of the First World War ushered in a new experiment in international relations, namely the ill-fated League of Nations, established in order to minimise the risk of a further outbreak of world war. Among many other functions, the League assumed responsibility for ex-German colonies. A mandate system was devised, whereby the Permanent Mandates Commission of the League authorised particular countries to administer the ex-German colonies, and to report to the Commission on their activities. Although in practice the victorious allies parcelled the German colonies amongst themselves, some semblance of respectability was created by insisting that the new administrations administered only on behalf of the international community as represented in the League of Nations. In East Africa and West Africa, German colonies were taken over by Britain, Belgium and France: in the case of South-West Africa, administration was entrusted to the Union Government. Union officials had been administering the territory since the occupation in 1915. They continued to do so, under various minor restrictions imposed by the League of Nations, such as submitting annual administrative reports to the Permanent Mandates Commission. The League of Nations was the sovereign power, but the location of actual responsibility was somewhat mysterious. The League possessed no mechanism whereby it could actually control events in the Mandate Territories in the event of the trustees proving unsatisfactory. Such a confrontation was extremely unlikely though, since the Permanent Mandates Commission was manned by representatives of other imperial and colonial powers, who were unlikely to insist upon radical change. The administration was able to do very much what it liked. For instance, there was a small outcry against the South African authorities after the Bondelzwarts campaign in 1922, but no action was taken (or even planned) against the Union Government. Essentially, the Commission acted as if it were an advisory body, recommending policies to the officials in charge of administration, but not enforcing its recommendations.

This curious and ill-defined relationship might have continued indefinitely, without creating ill-feeling between the Union Government and the League's officials, so long as the Commission restricted itself to an advisory role. However, the outbreak of the Second World War terminated the feeble life of the League, and thereafter it was replaced by the United Nations Organisation, potentially more powerful, and comprising a larger and more diverse membership. The Trusteeship Commission took over from the Permanent Mandates Commission, and proved rather less conservative in its approach to colonialism. More and more ex-colonial states took seats in the organisation, and brought to the General Assembly an explicitly anti-colonial point of view. Even by 1948, Smuts as Prime Minister of South Africa was coming under attack from the ex-colonial states, and the electoral victory of Dr Malan's Nationalists in 1948 accelerated the increasing disreputability of the Union in the world forum. Malan took refuge in the ingenious theory that the United Nations was not, legally, heir to the League of Nations. From that premise it followed that the Union Government had no obligation towards the United Nations Trusteeship Commission, unless it voluntarily acknowledged the authority of the Commission. There was also the electoral consideration that the white population of South-West Africa would probably support the Nationalist Government in the Union, if they were given machinery with which to do so, and Malan in 1948 was operating in parliament with a tiny and rather unreliable majority of members. The Nationalist Government thereupon incorporated South-West Africa into the Union, as the fifth province, a coup which simultaneously shed United Nations complications and gave the Nationalists a reliable majority of members of parliament from 1951 onwards. The United Nations naturally objected, but has been unable to establish its authority in the territory.

Constitutional manipulations are of rather less importance than the real economic and social and political links which have enmeshed South-West Africa in the Union's web since 1915. When the First World War broke out, there was a German population of some 15,000, many of whom left or were deported after the war. By 1970 the white population had grown to exceed 100,000, mainly through immigration from the Union. For landless whites, South-West Africa offered land, for unemployed whites it offered employment in the mining industry, and thousands have responded to these inducements. Mining was undertaken by mining companies already based and operating in the Union, and especially by the Anglo-American series of companies. Africans in the territory, and especially the relatively dense population along the northern boundary, were drawn into the white-dominated economy as migrant labourers. Because the South-West African administrators were responsible to the Union Government, it was simple to transfer laws and institutions and attitudes from the Union itself to its South-West African Mandate. In short, the incorporation of the territory as a fifth province was little more than a formality, expressing the real economic and political incorporation which had already taken place during the previous thirty years. Only a few anomalies, like the survival of German as one of the three official languages, distinguished South-West Africa from the first four provinces. Before the outbreak of the Second World War, there was some residual sentiment among surviving German settlers, in favour of re-establishing links with Germany, but once that idea was discarded South-West Africa became so closely bound up in South Africa that change in one cannot be achieved without change in the other. The German Imperial Factor has been unreal since 1915 and inconceivable since 1945.

The survival of the Portuguese Empire in Africa is one of the most astonishing phenomena of the twentieth century, especially in view of the widespread belief in the imminent collapse of that Empire, ever since the scramble in the late nineteenth century. The establishment of a rudimentary Portuguese authority over the whole of Angola and Mozambique was probably as late as the First World War, by which time the long control over the coastlands had reached the interior as a result of a series of substantial military campaigns. As late as 1940, there were only some 70,000 Portuguese settlers in the two territories, of whom less than half were resident in Mozambique. The Portuguese lacked the capital, the technology and the managerial skills of other colonising powers, and were therefore unable to bring about even the very modest economic development which characterised some of the British, French and even Belgian colonies of the same period. The Portuguese Republic fell in 1926 to the fascists, and from 1932 until 1969 when he resigned, Salazar constructed and consolidated the 'new state' in its place. In 1930 the new regime enacted a Colonial Act which embodied Portuguese policy towards the colonies; but it mattered little what Portuguese policy was, since Portugal lacked the techniques and the power to do more than hold on. Under the new state, even more than under the Republic, popular participation in government of the colonies was unthinkable. In consequence, lack of capital could not be made good by mobilising the energies and abilities of the colonial peoples. Until mid-century, Portuguese possessions continued to stagnate much as they had done since the decline of the slave trade, for lack of any invigorating economic activity.

Portuguese Africa was therefore ideally suited to the interests of the Union, and Mozambique quickly became an economic dependency of the

Union. Much revenue was derived from the two railways which ran to Lourenço Marques from the Witwatersrand and to Beira from Rhodesia. The other major source of revenue derived from the recruiting fees and earnings of African workers recruited for the Witwatersrand gold mines. Briefly, between about 1905 and about 1908, substantial numbers of Portugal's African subjects rebelled against the migrant labour system, but have consistently been regarded simply as a labour reservoir for Union labour requirements. The expansion of the labour recruiting system during the first years of the twentieth century also marked the end of an experiment which the Portuguese had hoped would transform the stagnant Mozambique economy. Chartered companies, similar in powers and scope to Rhodes's company, were commissioned to exploit three vast areas of Mozambique. That experiment, in turn, was a development out of an earlier failure, the *prazo* system, whereby large chunks of territory had been made over to individuals, who ruled them in essentially a feudal fashion. Unfortunately neither small-scale prazos nor vast-scale chartered companies could overcome the chronic difficulties posed by the absence of capital, technology, or economic rationale. When the chartered companies agreed to serve simply as labour-recruiting and labour-organising bodies, ancillary to the demands of the Witwatersrand mining complex, any prospect of an independent and viable Mozambiquan economy was driven out. Angola, similarly, developed into a supplier of labour for the Portuguese island possessions in the Bight of Benin, until the diamond and cocoa boom which followed the Second World War. As in the hey-day of the slave trade, so in the early twentieth century, Portuguese economic activity in southern Africa amounted to little more than providing labour for the use of employers, on terms and for wages determined by the employer, and with the Portuguese as the middle-men rather than the producers. Such a function was neither productive nor particularly lucrative, and for these reasons it seems fair to say of the Portuguese as late as the Second World War, that their hold over their African possessions was an extremely tenuous one. The fascists in Portugal were shunned by western European opinion, and starved of the capital required to make any impact on the colonies; in Africa, the Government was unable to settle any substantial number of white settlers on the land, and equally unable to employ a significant number of settlers in industry; its economy in Mozambique depended upon a subordinate relationship with the Union; and the African communities acquiesced without enthusiasm in the authority of Portuguese officials. Much was said about Portugal's civilising mission, which in practice boiled down to an assimilation policy reminiscent of that in French West Africa, but which after 400 years had still produced less than 1 per cent of an assimilado population. After the Second World War Portugal was admitted to the North Atlantic Treaty Organisation, and able to acquire sophisticated arms, but until that time its control over the Portuguese African territories was limited in extent and mainly negative in quality. Portuguese Africa offered no alternative to a sub-continent likely to be dominated by the rapidly developing South Africa, but continued to depend very largely upon the services it could provide the Union Government and South African economy.

For some years it looked as if Rhodesia might break loose from the umbilical cord which bound the settlers first to the Cape and then to the Union. In practice, it proved easier to oppose the British Imperial factor than to avoid increasing entanglement in the affairs of the large and apparently amiable neighbour to the south. The formal protagonists in Rhodesian politics were the Imperial Government, the Chartered Company, the settlers and the fluctuating African political associations which sprang up in the early twentieth century. In this contest, the settlers enjoyed immense advantages against all other parties. The Imperial Government, having determined in the 1880s to function through the Chartered Company, was inhibited from assuming direct responsibility for so troublesome and unpromising a colony. The Chartered Company, as early as the Shona-Ndebele rising, had been obliged to make massive concessions to the settlers, to ensure their loyalty in the crises which afflicted early settlement. That alliance was required not only to put down any African resistance, but also to present a united front to the Imperial Government on the few occasions when it felt disposed to interfere. Formally, therefore, Rhodesia was ruled by the Company, which in practice used the settlers as its economic and political collaborating and innovating class. With the death of Rhodes in 1902, the Company also lost any remaining political ambitions, and turned its attention to making the profits which had eluded it ever since its foundation. Increasingly, the Company was willing to hand over political power to the colonists on condition that the Company be allowed to continue in its privileged economic role. In 1911, for instance, the Company permitted the settlers to elect a majority of members to the Colony's legislature, where the major political and economic decisions affecting the Colony were made. By that time the settlers had already taken for themselves a lion's share of the land, and had established a social system very similar to that of the Cape whence most of them had come.

The balance of power, whereby the Imperial Government allowed government to devolve upon the Company, and the Company allowed it to devolve upon the settlers, broke down in the early 1920s, when the Company's Charter expired and was not renewed. The alternatives presented to the Imperial Government were to assume authority directly and rule Rhodesia like a tropical African dependency, or to let it be merged in the Union of South Africa, or to permit a kind of constitutional development similar to that of the Union but outside it. The problem presented itself at precisely the same time as the problem of the long-term destiny of Kenya, and the differences between the two Imperial decisions are striking. In the same year – 1923 – the same government announced that in Kenya African interests should be paramount, but that in Rhodesia the existing electorate should be allowed to choose between incorporation with South Africa or Responsible Government on their own. Admittedly the paramountcy of African interests in Kenya was something of a myth, but at least some restraint was imposed upon settler ambitions. It is impossible to avoid the conclusion that Rhodesia's proximity to South Africa was one of the decisive considerations, and that the settlers' relative freedom from Imperial control was a consequence of having an already powerful white neighbour.

In view of the similarity between the white populations of Rhodesia and South Africa, the settlers might well have chosen to join the Union, and indeed Smuts as Union Prime Minister was very anxious that they should do so. However, the predominantly English-speaking white population of Rhodesia was alarmed at the possibility of being submerged in a predominantly Afrikaner political system. Accordingly, some 9,000 voted against incorporation, while some 6,000 voted in favour, and so in 1923 Responsible Government was inaugurated. A separate constitutional identity was maintained, but this was largely through the existence of the Union, which could act as a counter-weight to Imperial interests in the region. For the next thirty years the Imperial Government was content to leave Rhodesia very much to its own devices, and intervened very little in its affairs.

Perhaps the most striking feature of white Rhodesian politics in the period from Responsible Government until the Federation scheme after the Second World War was its dullness. By the end of the 1930s there were still only some 20,000 voters, which was too small a number to produce very remarkable politicians or statesmen. The small number of Afrikaner voters produced the consequence that Anglo–Afrikaner rivalries were nothing like as important as they were further south. Although Rhodesia's franchise system was based upon that of the old Cape, and therefore permitted the enfranchisement of some Africans and Coloured people, African voters amounted to only about 1 per cent of the whole electorate, and therefore posed no serious threat to white electoral supremacy. Nor could such a small electorate support a strong party system, and formal white politics tended to be a matter of personality rather than interesting principle. The white community was strong enough militarily to be able to suppress any African rising, and well enough entrenched constitutionally to be able to withstand any African political movement. Just as elsewhere in colonial Africa between the two great wars, nothing seemed to be happening in Rhodesia.

The appearance of inaction was an illusion in Rhodesia, as much as elsewhere in the continent at that time. Relations between the Colony and the Imperial Government were admittedly frozen, since the settlers already enjoyed sufficient control over their political system and their security forces, and were not anxious to sever the remaining ties between them and the Imperial Government, lest they fall a prey to the Afrikaners further south. On the other hand, important changes were taking place in race relations, and in the approaches of the Africans towards gaining a share of influence upon government. The Ndebele, after the failure of the Ndebele-Shona Rising in the 1890s, devised the Matabele Home Society, as a pressure group dedicated to re-establishing the Ndebele monarchy with Nyamanda (the eldest son of Lobengula) as king. The Society was also anxious to regain Ndebele ownership of the land which had once been theirs, and in general to preserve as much as possible of the fabric of earlier

Ndebele life. Because of the emphasis upon Ndebele issues, the Society was necessarily divisive, and had little appeal to the Shona majority. More interesting was the development of the Rhodesian Bantu Voters Association, comprising the more westernised and affluent Africans who were able to meet the property and educational qualifications required for the franchise. Mfengu migrants from the Cape, who had come to Rhodesia with the white pioneers, and who were irritated at the rejection of their claim to full equality with those settlers, were prominent in the establishment of the RBVA, but they soon broadened the membership so as to include as many as possible of the new indigenous African élite. Like the African National Congress in South Africa, however, it was reluctant to broaden its membership beyond the élite group, or to depart from a gradualist approach to African advancement within the existing structure of white government and white society.

On the key issues of land and labour, events in Rhodesia differed slightly from those in South Africa. The vital aspect of the land issue, for example, was not so much land ownership as land usage. During the 1890s and thereafter, as we have seen, settlers acquired vast tracts of land for themselves, but there were too few settlers to alter the real land position appreciably. In many areas, African land-occupation and usage continued as before, except that the settler-owners took a large share of the profits. After the First World War, the Matabele Home Society was able to enlist the support of returning ex-servicemen, in requesting a greater area of land for African ownership. Nevertheless the issue was not sufficiently urgent to provide the focus for a militant mass movement, and the Society was in any case unable to exert any significant pressure on the Government. In 1930 the legislature passed the Land Apportionment Act, defining the whole land area in terms of its intended ownership. African reserve land was left as it was, and a 'Native Purchase' area declared, in which individual Africans could acquire land. Admittedly the settlers seized the most attractive areas for themselves, leaving the least useful land for the African reserves and individual owners. Nevertheless, as late as the 1950s, white owned land amounted to no more than 50 per cent of the land area, and as a result the land ownership issue was never as explosive in Rhodesia as it was in South Africa. A much more serious issue was raised in 1951, in the form of the Land Husbandry Act, a major encouragement to African militancy. Massive assisted white immigration after the Second World War imposed a considerable strain on the land resources of the colony, and the legislature had the clever idea of reforming African agriculture in such a manner that Africans would require less land on which to live, thereby releasing more land for white settlement. That decision coincided with similar demands made upon African peasants by colonial administrators throughout colonial Africa after the Second World War, and as in the rest of colonial Africa so in Rhodesia, the peasants were infuriated by this interference with their means of livelihood. The Land Husbandry Act strove to encourage individual land owership by Africans, in place of communal land holding, and also tended to deprive absentee-owners (including the men working in the cities) of their title to land in the rural areas. However, the legislature perceived the danger of continuing in its course, and the Land Husbandry Act has never fully been implemented. In 1961, for example, the Land Apportionment Act was slightly revised, so as to release a little more land for African ownership and usage, in the hope of taking some of the steam out of the nationalist movement. Africans have therefore continued to exercise more control over the land than is the case in South Africa.

Labour movements have also, apparently, enjoyed greater success in Rhodesia than in South Africa. In 1927 Clements Kadalie encouraged the establishment of Rhodesian branches of the ICU, and organisations appeared in Bulawayo and Salisbury, the two main industrial centres. The first organiser of the Rhodesian ICU, Robert Sambo, was deported to his native Nyasaland, but the Rhodesian ICU survived, and its major difficulty arose in deciding upon tactics rather than in government harassment. Without a mass following, it was foolish to attempt a large strike; and yet without the publicity of a large (and preferably successful) strike it was extremely difficult to build up a mass movement. Again, it was obviously necessary to play down ethnic differences and to establish an inter-ethnic trade union movement; but that approach made it difficult to appeal emotionally to many of the African working population. In that respect the Rhodesian ICU faced a similar dilemma to that of its South African counterpart. Even more striking a similarity is its early attempt to establish an alliance with white trade unionists. As in South Africa, however, white trade unionists could win their cases by political action, and therefore saw no advantage in co-operation with disfranchised workers. By the end of the 1930s, the Rhodesian ICU had faded into insignificance. Trade Union activity revived only after the Second World War. Charles Mzingeli revived a reformed ICU; the Rhodesian African National Congress began to exhibit some interest in trade union activity; and most important, the African railway workers in Bulawayo held a successful strike in 1945. That strike not only won the wage demands of the strikers, but demonstrated that they were a considerable pressure group when adequately organised. In 1948, a general strike broke out in Bulawayo and Salisbury, but that was over-ambitious, and marked the end of a short phase of trade union militancy and effectiveness. With the emergence of a nationalist movement in the 1950s, the separate role of African trade unions was effectively eclipsed. Joshua Nkomo, for example, who had become prominent as a railway workers' leader, became in the 1950s the leader of political nationalists rather than a continuing trade union movement geared to industrial disputes. At the same time, substantial white immigration after the Second World War enabled the government to adopt a much tougher approach to African protests of any kind. In short, by mid-century, political and economic developments in Rhodesia could be regarded as following in much the same path as those further south. Trade union activity had been tried and that approach had failed through the refusal of white workers to co-operate; élite politics had developed, and had so far failed to advance the interests even of the small élite group; and over time the white population had increased and entrenched itself on the land, in the security forces, in parliament and in employment.

Faced with crises similar to those of the Union, the Rhodesian settlers devised remedies which were also very similar. The Land Apportionment Act, like the Natives Land Act in the Union, attempted to restrict the expansion of African land-ownership and to protect the often inefficient settler farming population from African competition. Land was divided into four categories: white land (which could not be alienated to Africans) amounted to 49,000,000 acres; native reserves (which could not be alienated either) amounted to 21,000,000 acres; the native purchase area (in which Africans could buy land individually) amounted to 7,500,000 acres; and 17,750,000 acres were unassigned. The much smaller white agricultural population did not demand nearly as great a proportion of the land as did the white farmers in the Union, but in other respects the legislation is very similar. Again, in face of labour troubles, the settler Government enacted the Industrial Conciliation Act of 1934, which made it difficult for Africans to form trade unions, and which established machinery for the representation of white trade unions in industrial disputes. The South African Pass Law system was also copied in legislation enacted during 1936 and 1937, with the effect of limiting the mobility and therefore the bargaining power of African workers. By the end of the 1930s the Rhodesian settlers had voluntarily established a system very similar to that in operation in South Africa, except for the colour-blind franchise system which survived as a relic of the Rhodes influence upon the foundation of the state.

At first sight it is remarkable that no constitutional links were established between the Union and other settler-dominated British colonies in Central and East Africa. Settlers from elsewhere in Africa certainly had sentimental links with the Union: they would often spend their holidays there, invest their money in South African concerns, send their children to school and to university there, and generally hold up the Union's tough racial policies as an example to be emulated by other settler communities. Yet for some reason these sentimental ties were never consolidated in constitutional forms. Perhaps the explanation is two-fold. First, the settlers were anxious to preserve their identity as British settlers, and were therefore nervous of too close an association with an Afrikaner-dominated political structure. The electoral victory of Hertzog in 1924, and then the success of Malan in 1948, both seemed to point to the triumph of an exclusive Afrikanerdom in which English-speakers could have no important place. Settlers, no less than anyone else, could allow their interests to be blurred by ethnic considerations. Secondly, until perhaps the 1950s, there seemed to be no imminent risk of the Imperial Government failing to defend the settlers against African aspirations. By the time the 'winds of change' began to be noticed, it was too late to establish links with the Union, and impossible to reverse the trends of the previous half century.

If changes in Rhodesia and in South-West Africa favoured the interests of the Union, and if Portuguese Africa dove-tailed so neatly with those interests anyway, it must also be said that the absence of any important development in the High Commission territories placed them increasingly at the mercy of their massive neighbour. From 1910 onwards, the Imperial Government seems to have expected that the High Commission territories would ultimately be incorporated in the Union, and was therefore reluctant to take any action at all, beyond the preservation of some kind of order and the balancing of budgets as often as possible. Basutoland continued to export labour to South Africa, Bechuanaland continued to export labour and cattle-products to the Witwatersrand, and Swaziland exported asbestos in addition to labour. Though the Union Government occasionally pressed the Imperial Government to permit incorporation, by and large the Union tolerated the existence of these enclaves, on the grounds that they already served South Africa's interests well enough. The mere passage of time and the growth of population increased their dependence upon the Union's economy.

The development of the Union's economic strength enabled it increasingly to control the destinies of its neighbours, in which economic development either did not occur at all, or else occurred too slowly to rival the power of the Union. For convenience, two types of economic influence may here be considered; one is the process whereby some territories became wholesale suppliers of labour; and the other is the process whereby some became recipients of South African investment capital.

We have already traced the origins of the migrant labour system to the opening up of intensive diamond mining in the Kimberley region during the 1870s. During the 1880s gold-mining operations began in the Transvaal on a large scale, and by the end of the century there were massive mining enterprises throughout the four colonies, extracting gold, coal and diamonds. Rhodes's dreams of substantial gold-mining in the Rhodesias were never realised, and after the pillaging of existing supplies of gold in and around Zimbabwe, the supply of Rhodesian gold dried up to a small trickle. Copper mining began on a large scale in what is now Zambia during the 1930s, but until then the Union mining enterprises were by far the largest employers of labour in the entire sub-continent. We have also traced the origins of the industrial colour bar to the Kimberley diamond mines in the 1870s. Diamonds being a very highly-priced commodity, it was possible for the diamond mines to offer relatively good wages to its unskilled labourers; but the profit margin in the coal and gold mining industries was not large enough for them to do the same. What they demanded, therefore, was a low-paid labour force. The only other alternative was a highly-paid but very efficient force – but that could not be harmonised with a policy of migrant labour, since the migrant workers seldom remained long enough to acquire useful skills.

At first, the area south of the Limpopo River was sufficient to provide the required numbers of unskilled workers in the diamond mines, but as soon as gold-mining began on a large scale that source was too small. Furthermore, if recruiting were restricted to that area, the demand for unskilled labour would exceed the supply, and it was likely that wages would be raised in order to attract the labourers. On the gold mining properties, for example, each mine competed with the others, throughout the 1890s, by raising the wages offered to the workers. Then the mine managers would come together to deal with the problem of rising wage bills, and would agree to reduce the level of wages throughout the industry. That agreement would last for a few months until a particularly hard-pressed mine manager would abandon the agreement, raise the level of wages in his mine, and initiate a fresh cycle of wage increases. Eventually the mines came to a more binding arrangement during their idleness in the South African War, but it was nevertheless clear that, unless other sources of labour were discovered, there would always be a danger of wage increases. The mines could probably have afforded to pay more, but were understandably reluctant to do so. The white trade unions could be expected to compel the mines to increase white wages, so it would be foolish voluntarily to give wage increases to African labourers who were not permitted to form unions, and therefore unable to exert pressure on the managements.

During the 1890s, a fresh source of labour was discovered in Portuguese East Africa, and by the end of the century some two-thirds of the gold-mine labour supply came from the east coast. After the South African War, recruiting was regulated, and the Portuguese administration was paid a recruiting fee for each of the recruits it provided for work in the Transvaal. As we have seen, that system provided an incentive for chartered companies to take political control of most of Portuguese East Africa, and to transform most of the territory into a colossal labour reservoir for export to Johannesburg. The result was a labour recruiting system which was very similar to slavery, except that the labourers could return home after the contract period (usually between 6 and 12 months). For the Portuguese authorities that was very fortunate: since the recent suppression of the slave trade on the east coast, the Portuguese had found no economically useful way of exploiting their east coast possessions. For the labourers, it was a less fortunate development.

By the turn of the century, the Basutoland protectorate had followed the same path, and had become a dormitory territory from which thousands of labourers were drawn every year for contract work in the Union. Bechuanaland and Swaziland, whose own economic resources were better than those of Basutoland, offered only a much smaller number of migrant workers. During the twentieth century Nyasaland protectorate also became a major source of labour for the mines, and smaller numbers came also from Southern and Northern Rhodesia. In 1943, for example, there was a total African work-force of 360,000 men in the mines operated by the Chamber of Mines. Of these, half – 180,000 – were recruited within the Union (and two-thirds of those came from the Cape, whose eastern districts were grossly over-populated); 45,000 from Basutoland, 10,000 from Bechuanaland, 8,000 from Swaziland; 87,000 from Portuguese East Africa; and 30,000 from the Rhodesias and Nyasaland. Without external recruiting, the mines would have been hard-pressed to recruit the same number of labourers without raising wages or introducing a labour system involving direct compulsion.

If the mines depended so heavily upon external supplies of labour, however, how is it that the labour-exporting territories were dependent upon South Africa? First, the system itself inhibited the colonial governments of the territories from encouraging other kinds of economic development. The governments wanted revenue and wanted to relieve unemployment wherever that existed: the easy 'solution' to both 'problems' was to encourage recruitment for the South African mines. The government derived revenue directly from recruiting fees, and indirectly from the taxes paid by recruits out of their savings; while there was no limit to the number of unemployed or under-employed men who could be recruited. Other kinds of economic development required capital investment – which few colonial administrators could normally obtain – and hard thinking: the labour-reservoir policy required neither. Before long the expedient became indispensable: the African population came to depend upon the earnings of its adult men, and there was seldom any local alternative for employment. The advent of independence did not necessarily alter the basic situation: Lesotho, for example, is just as dependent upon labour recruiting now, as it was while a British protectorate – any suspension of labour recruiting would render the population almost entirely unable to feed itself. It is still true that the mines (and therefore much of the South African economic structure) depend upon external labour resources, but it is practically impossible for the various reservoirs of labour to combine in order to extract concessions from their economic masters – whereas it would require a very simple administrative decision for the mines (or the state) to close the borders to recruits from any one of the labour-exporting territories.

To use a geographical analogy, the mining industries in South Africa have become a pool for labour; and into that pool flows labour from all areas within the watershed. The precise location of the watershed has of course varied enormously: until the 1880s it included no more than the Cape, Basutoland, Bechuanaland and the two Afrikaner republics; by the end of the century the watershed had moved outwards to include southern Mozambique; and by the 1920s it included Nyasaland as well. However, the copperbelt region of Zambia and Congo also constitutes a pool for labour, which similarly draws labourers from an area bounded by a watershed. As the copper mining industry of Katanga and Zambia has expanded, so its watershed has also expanded, and the area dependent upon South African employment has correspondingly decreased. If and when there is further expansion of industry in Central Africa, South Africa's influence in the region may be expected to decline, as independent countries will be able to adopt a tougher policy towards the recruiting agents.

However, another aspect of economic inter-dependence must be taken into account, namely the influence brought about by capital investment. The economic empire constructed by Rhodes included the British South Africa Company (which governed Northern and Southern Rhodesia until 1924), De Beers centred upon Kimberley, and various gold mining companies in the Transvaal. The B.S.A. Company (often named the Chartered Company), through its political control, acquired valuable economic interests in the Rhodesias, including all the mineral rights. Rhodes's economic empire has survived its political extinction in 1924 (when Southern Rhodesia became a

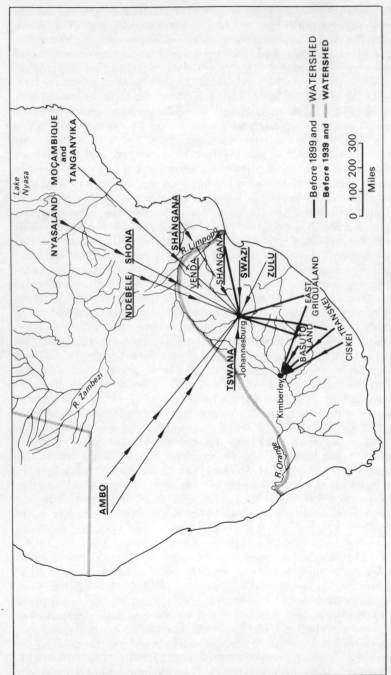

Labour 'catchment' area, illustrating the direction and distance of labour migration to mining centres

settler self-governing colony, and Northern Rhodesia a Crown colony) and has been the channel for substantial South African and other capital investment in both the Rhodesias. In Zambia, for instance, the largest economic enterprise is Anglo-American, a firm which is mostly capitalised in South Africa, despite its title. It was largely South African capital which financed the expansion of copper mining in Northern Rhodesia during the 1920s and 1930s – and white South African managers and artisans who were brought in to occupy the highly paid and responsible positions. The Chartered Company itself was usually content to take a share of the royalties, rather than to operate the industries itself: nevertheless its South African connections facilitated the growth of South African investment and management over the economies of the two territories to the north. And so long as the two states are anxious to attract more capital investment for other economic development, they are obliged to treat South African investors with some respect: that constraint naturally inhibits such countries from dopting too outspoken a policy towards the country from which the capital flows, and makes the Zambian Government extremely cautious in planning to take control of the mining industry.

A further, though probably less important, aspect of South Africa's developing economic influence to the north, is the growth of the manufacturing industry. Manufacturing on a large scale is a very recent occurence in South Africa. Until the mineral revolution of the late nineteenth century, there was a negligible volume of manufactured production, since there was a negligible market for manufacturing products, and because Britain at that time was able to produce most manufacturing requirements more cheaply than anyone else. Even as late as the First World War, only 100,000 workers of all colours were employed in manufacturing, and that total includes many thousands employed by government in railway and harbour services. Considerable expansion in manufacturing occurred only during and after the Second World War, when the population (and particularly the white population) had become prosperous enough to construct factories and to purchase their products. Since the 1940s, however, the South African manufacturing industry has expanded enormously, both in quantity and in the diverse range of products sold. Because of proximity, most South African manufactured produce is cheaper in Southern Africa than the products of any other industrialised country, and the cheapness of the products is obviously a very tempting consideration even in independent countries. Such economic attractions, however, are double-edged: factories depend much more upon consumers than mines depend upon unskilled labour, which could if necessary be replaced by mechanisation.

The power of a developed, sophisticated economy, is illustrated by the Cabora Bassa project in Mozambique. Here the Portuguese propose to build a massive dam, and to use the electric power and irrigation to build up a vast settler population. The capital and the technology for this vital scheme are both to be recruited mainly from South Africa. Economic power is thereby to be transformed into another bulwark for the survival of the white south.

Finally, South Africa has gained control over much of the income of the three 'hostage' states of Lesotho, Swaziland and Botswana. That control dates back to a customs and railways agreement of 1903. In that year, shortly after the British assumed control of the Transvaal and Orange River Colony, and while Imperial prestige and power were at their height, the British colonies of Southern Africa were called together to consider ways and means of collecting and distributing railway rates and customs duties. One of the side-effects of this round of negotiations was that the white colonies agreed to collect customs duties for the three High Commission territories, since almost all of the goods which paid customs duties came through the colonial ports. That agreement remained intact not only despite Union, but also despite the political independence of the three territories concerned. Furthermore, the proportion of total revenue to be handed over was fixed at the estimated proportion of 1903. At that time the customs duties to be paid to the three territories was a very small sum indeed, since they imported very little. Nevertheless, the fact is that the three territories developed economically at a much slower rate than did South Africa, from 1903 onwards, since they became economic appendages of the Union's economy, and sources of unskilled labour for South African economic development. In 1969 the proportion of total receipts to be paid to the newly independent states was almost doubled. At present, therefore, the states are paid a much larger proportion of total Southern African customs receipts than their imports would justify – and the payment has gradually become an annual South African subsidy to the poor relations. Naturally, the Governments are unwilling to terminate that arrangement.

A glance at the economic circumstances of Lesotho, Botswana and Swaziland at independence will demonstrate the importance of the economic links with South Africa. In Swaziland during the financial year 1967–1968, total revenue amounted to R 15 million. Of that revenue, British Government and other forms of aid amounted to R 5 million; and customs payments (from the Republic of South Africa) totalled R 2·6 million. During that year, over 6,000 Swazi were employed in the Republic. The economic dependence of Lesotho was even greater. For the same year, revenue totalled R 11 million. Of that revenue, over R 6 million came from Britain in the form of aid. Customs receipts therefore formed a massive proportion of Lesotho's guaranteed income. At any given time during the year, some 80,000 Basotho were in employment in the Republic. Botswana's total revenue in 1965–1966 was R 15 million, of which almost R 10 million was aid, mainly from Britain; and Customs receipts amounted to R 1·3 million. Over 30,000 Tswana were employed in South Africa; and cattle and meat, exported mainly to South Africa, formed almost all of Botswana's export revenue. All three states, in other words, are bound economically to South Africa: customs revenue forming a major link, labour (especially from Lesotho) forming another, and markets (especially from Botswana) yet another.

The steady growth of these economic links between South Africa and the other states of Southern Africa very largely explains the continuing importance of the South African Government in the affairs of neighbouring communities. So long as most of the neighbours were British dependencies, and so long as the British High Commissioner in charge of them resided in Pretoria, South Africa obviously had direct influence. Seretse Khama, for example, was dismissed from his post as chief in Bechuanaland, when he committed the (South African) crime of marrying an English girl: his deposition was urged by the South African Nationalist Government, and executed by the British Protectorate authorities. The independence of the territories, however, brought that kind of influence to an end, and replaced it by the present economic influence, exercised with much greater sophistication but with equally impressive success.

At the basis of all this economic influence lies the economic power of the Republic, as compared with the relative poverty of most of its neighbours. That, in turn, takes us back to the mineral revolution of the late nineteenth century. A hundred years ago, the white communities of the South African interior were economically indistinguishable from the African states of the same region: without the discovery and exploitation of precious metals and minerals, it is difficult to see how those communities could have developed beyond a mean and poverty-stricken existence, and it is even conceivable that they would not have survived at all. In the last hundred years, however, the white communities have established their control over an immensely powerful economic system, built upon the mineral wealth of Kimberley and the Witwatersrand. And with the resources made available to governments by those industries, the white population first established its control over the African societies of those states, then united amongst themselves and dispensed with British protection and control, then applied the resources to establishing themselves as an economic aristocracy, and have finally established themselves in a dominant position as against their neighbours further north. The question which now looms large, is whether that dominant position can be maintained.

Chapter 17

Government moves out of parliament

Since the 1920s in Portugal, since 1948 in South Africa, and since perhaps 1953 in Rhodesia, the power of parliaments has declined, and they have steadily lost their earlier position as the arena and the focus of decision-making in the Southern African subcontinent. The process is two-fold: while Governmental decisions have increasingly been taken outside parliament, so have Opposition decisions and Opposition activities. For convenience, we may consider each part of the process in a separate chapter, but it is important to bear in mind that each side is complementary to the other. With that reservation we may turn to the shift of political power within the governing groups.

Although it is true to say that the Nationalist Government in South Africa from 1948 onwards has carried previous lines of policy to their logical conclusion, the year 1948 does represent a break in the continuity of white South African politics. For the first time an exclusively Afrikaner cabinet representing exclusively Afrikaner interests had a monopoly of political power within the constitution. From that time onwards, important decisions have increasingly been made within the parliamentary party, and debated by different factions within the Afrikaner community. In parliament, the United Party opposition survived, with a smaller number of seats after every general election from 1948 to 1970, and with rapidly diminishing hopes of ever forming an alternative government. In every important respect except the formalities, South Africa became a one-party state, with the ruling party using its parliamentary majority to rubber-stamp its decisions.

Dr Malan's Party in 1948 was a twice-distilled essence of Afrikaner exclusiveness. Hertzog had broken with the main body of Afrikanerdom in 1912, in order to pursue the interests of Afrikaners more narrowly – but he had normally defined Afrikaners in such a way as to include English-speaking whites as well. Malan had broken away from the main body of Afrikanerdom in 1934 with the same purpose – and incurred Hertzog's annoyance for claiming an exclusive legitimacy for Afrikaners. The two breaks in the ranks of Afrikanerdom not only separated conciliatory Afrikaners from the rigid exclusiveness of the party, they also demonstrated the peril of Afrikanerdom if they ever again allowed themselves to be put out of office or divided amongst themselves. However, the main stream of the Nationalist Party had flowed through some rather murky countryside in the years immediately preceding the surprise election victory of 1948. The emergence of Hitler in Europe during the 1930s had encouraged some Afrikaners to emulate his policies and adopt his methods. The Brown Shirts, the Black Shirts, and the Grey Shirts, all extra-constitutional forces, had formed themselves in South Africa and South-West Africa during the late 1930s, consciously imitating fascist methods of affecting public opinion. Afrikaner sentiments, which had previously been free of anti-Semitism, were infected by Hitler's belief that the Jews and the Communists were allied in threatening democratic institutions. More generally, it became respectable to argue that parliament was an outdated relic of a past era, and that the people – in this case the Afrikaner *volk* – should seize power by force rather than by electoral procedures.

When war broke out in 1939, therefore, there was a considerable pro-German sentiment at work among Afrikaners. The Ossewa-Brandwag (Oxwagon-Guards), which had been formed for ornamental purposes during the celebrations of the Voortrekker centenary in 1936, steadily became a well-armed and well-trained irregular army; its off-shoot the Stormjaers (shock-troops) was involved in several acts of sabotage during the war, with the purpose of disrupting the Government in its participation in the war against the fascists. So strong was the OB that Malan feared that it might replace the Nationalist Party itself, as representative of Afrikaners in politics. Oswald Pirow, once cabinet minister under Hertzog, also formed an organisation called the New Order, whose policy was to bring about a fascist system of government. Eventually in 1942 Malan turned against these organisations, and asserted the leadership of the Nationalist Party; and in the course of the war most of the organisations either folded up, or vanished when the fascists began to look like losing, or were declared illegal. Nevertheless the flirtation with fascism infected the quality of Afrikaner thinking thereafter, and provided an ideological rationale for policies which were adopted in the first place out of racial self-interest. In any case, the Nationalists re-asserted their prime importance among Afrikaners by absorbing some of their opponents into the party itself: H. F. Verwoerd, who later became Prime Minister, was found by the courts during the war to have disseminated Nazi propaganda; J. B. Vorster, who succeeded Verwoerd as Prime Minister, was interned by the Smuts Government for his fascist activity. Ironically, while the present Rhodesian Prime Minister was fighting against the Germans in the air force, the present South African Prime Minister was confined to detention at Koffiefontein.

Even by 1948 these internal squabbles had not entirely been resolved. For the first two or three years of the Nationalist Government's reign, for example, they had to rely upon the Afrikaner Party (which was the remnant of Hertzog's followers) for a secure majority: not until the six Nationalist M.P.s for South-West Africa joined parliament in 1951 was Malan assured of his majority, and there were constant rumours that the Afrikaner Party might join the opposition United Party to bring down the Government. The tiny Afrikaner Party, in its weakness, had joined forces with the OB, and thereby brought an ideologically fascist strain into parliament and into the Government. That was one of the tensions within the party. Another strain was whether – and if so how – to bring about a Republic. Some members of the party considered that an absolute majority of voters was necessary to justify the change; others considered the Nationalist parliamentary majority sufficient. But more seriously there was disagreement as to the precise nature of 'apartheid', the slogan which had helped bring the party to power. On one hand were the party ideologists, including Verwoerd, and supported by the South African Bureau for Racial Affairs, who were anxious to press ahead to full territorial separation for all races; on the other were those more interested in preserving the existing situation, and who regarded 'apartheid' as no more than a useful election slogan, which it was not necessary to implement at all. These were the real divisions of opinion, and they were discussed not in parliament but in the caucas of the parliamentary Nationalist Party.

At first the ideologists were in the minority, and Malan's legislative programme set about completing the existing trends in Government policy, rather than setting up a different style of Government altogether. During the 1948 session, Indian voting rights in Natal (which had not been used since they were granted in 1946) were abolished; and stricter conditions were imposed upon Cape Coloureds in the exercise of their franchise – so that under 20,000 actually voted in 1958, whereas almost 50,000 had voted in 1948. Dependent upon the unreliable Afrikaner Party, Malan could not proceed any further. In 1949, mixed marriages between the races were prohibited, the majority of Africans were excluded from unemployment insurance payments, and the Labour Department was strengthened in order to restrict the influx of Africans from the countryside seeking urban employment. In 1950, a Population Register was established, to determine the race of every citizen – and which re-captured many Coloured people who had slipped across the racial border into the white community. During the same session the Suppression of Communism Act was passed giving the Government power to suppress not only communism but virtually any other extra-parliamentary political group as well; and the Group Areas Act set about separating the races in the urban areas, so as to prevent different races living in the same area. Also in the old Smuts-Hertzog tradition, the Immorality Act was amended so as to make any combination or permutation of races illegal if they attempted to have sexual intercourse.

In 1951, however, the Afrikaner Party lost its leverage: since its leader – Havenga – was a Hertzog man, he had resisted any proposal to tamper with the 1936 legislative package; so there was a mass of legislation waiting until 1951 when Havenga lost his effective veto over Nationalist legislation. Furthermore, by 1951 both Smuts and Hofmeyr – the two leaders of the United Party opposition – were dead, and much of the Opposition's vitality died with them. The Bantu Authorities Act in the same session abolished the Native Representative Council (which was in any case permanently suspended by its members) and established local committees of members nominated by the Government.

More widely significant, however, was the beginning of a long war of attrition against Coloured voters. In 1951 the Government passed the Separate Representation of Voters Act, in order to remove Coloured voters from the common roll onto a separate roll, as the Africans already were. The following year the Appeal Court ruled the legislation invalid, as it should have been passed by a two-thirds majority in parliament. The Government retaliated by passing the High Court of Parliament Act in 1952, which gave parliament the right to over-rule the Appeal Court. The Supreme Court, in turn, ruled that the Government's policy was still invalid, since the Act of Union still existed and had full force. During 1953 and 1954, the Nationalists tried to assemble the required two-thirds majority, by encouraging opposition members of parliament to cross the floor, but that still failed to produce enough voting fodder.

Johannes Gerhardus Strijdom, Prime Minister 1954–8

The retirement of both Malan and Havenga in 1954 brought J. G. Strijdom to the Premiership, with a reputation for inflexibility even greater than Malan's. In 1955, he increased the membership of the Appellate Division of the courts and appointed some fresh judges; and at the same time went round the back of the constitution by increasing the membership of the Senate so as to give it a larger majority of Nationalist members. Finally, in 1956, the two houses of parliament were brought together once more to pass the South Africa Act Amendment Bill, and to validate the original Separate Representation of Voters Bill. Since all the constitutional rules had been observed (even if the spirit of the constitution had been ignored) the courts had to admit that the legislation was valid. Nevertheless, the Courts had played a more prominent and courageous role than the parliamentary opposition: and the whole episode demonstrated the determination of the Government to have its way no matter what the cost might be. Such a performance may seem strange for the limited purpose of removing 20,000 voters to a different voting roll, but in the process the Nationalists were anxious also to demonstrate that the Party was unchallengable, and that on matters of 'principle' such as a separate voting, it would stop at nothing.

The battle for separate Coloured voting took up so much parliamentary time, that the sessions leading up to and including 1956 had little opportunity to do anything else except legislate yet more severely against urban racial mixing. In 1956, for instance, it passed legislation prohibiting non-whites from attending church services in white areas: Africans could, of course, be employed to clean the white churches, but were prohibited from praying in them. For once the Christian Churches protested so strongly that the legislation has not in fact been applied. Its significance is that as late as 1957, the Nationalists were still involved in the very unimaginative and tough-minded process of applying existing political decisions in greater and greater detail. 1958 was taken up with another general election, and with the Party's decision to elect Dr Verwoerd in succession to Strijdom. However, with the new Prime Minister, an increased parliamentary majority and – for the first time – a majority of the electorate, the tone of legislation altered sharply. Verwoerd's selection meant, among other things, the victory within the Party of the extreme right, and of the ideologues of 'apartheid' – those who regarded separate development as a policy worth pursuing further than the immediate racial interests of the white community would require.

The new style legislation began to appear in 1959. A Bantu Investment Corporation was set up, to facilitate the investment of money by Africans in African rural areas. Though the capital at the disposal of the Corporation has never approached the capital requirements of the African areas, the Act devised a new extension of separate development, namely that each race was to be encouraged to invest only in its own areas and its own economic concerns. This legislation foreshadowed the Bantu Homelands legislation which came later in the same session. More significant was the notoriously mis-termed Extension of University Education Act, which restricted the entry of non-whites into the open universities, and proposed to set up a university for each major ethnic group. Fort Hare was immediately requisitioned for Xhosa students, and new colleges were set up in Zululand for Zulu, in the Transvaal for Venda, Pedi, Tswana and Sotho, in Durban for Indians, and in the Western Cape for Coloureds. The Government's imposition of racial qualifications upon university entrants, and its tight control over the staff and syllabuses in the new tribal colleges, stirred up considerable opposition throughout South Africa and beyond; but the Government regarded separate facilities and the restriction of racial mixing as objectives worth pursuing at the cost of unpopularity. Finally at the very end of the session, legislation was introduced establishing procedures for the creation of 'Bantu Homelands' – in other words limited self-government in the African reserves. Conservative and racialist white opinion regarded this policy as grossly irresponsible and it may properly be regarded as a departure from the old style of straight-forward repression, into different avenues of political relationships. It was a demonstration that Verwoerd controlled the Party, that the Party controlled parliament, and that the Government was firmly in control of internal affairs.

In 1960, the Government at last felt confident enought to hold a referendum on the desirability of creating a republic: the white electorate provided a majority of votes in favour; the Commonwealth Prime Ministers objected to South Africa's continued membership of the Commonwealth; and in 1961 South Africa became a republic outside the Commonwealth. When various opposition groups objected to such a decision being taken only by the electorate, and when various protests were bloodily dispersed, a state of emergency was declared and the two major opposition groups – the African National Congress and the Pan-Africanist Congress, were outlawed. That left very little time during the two sessions for the passage of any legislation except defence bills and emergency regulations designed to strengthen the Government's hand against any kind of internal opposition whatever. In 1961 began the process whereby, even in times of peace, individuals suspected by the Government or by the police of being dangerous enemies of the Government (or of the State, though the difference between State and Government is difficult to draw any longer) could be interned. In 1961 the limit was 12 days. In 1962 that limit was extended to 90 days: it now stands at 180. On the other hand, time was found in 1963 to push through the Transkei Constitution Act – Verwoerd's answer to the ills of the whole community, ushering in a policy which will be dealt with in a later chapter.

The question arises: if the Party has such complete power, why does it bother with parliament at all? For one thing, parliament is now a harmless diversion, where the United Party goes through the motions of a western European parliamentary opposition but without making the slightest impact on Government policy. On the other hand the harmless fiction of democratic government makes it easier for the South African Government and its international apologists to defend South African policies. There is no risk of losing power, there is a place for loyal party workers to retire to, and there is a marginal propaganda gain to be derived. In reality, the contest for power and for policies takes place elsewhere: within the Party, the ideologues dispute with the straightforward repressors; and outside parliament the

179

security forces have been doing battle with the Opposition which has also moved its activities out of parliament. The only significant act to take place in parliament in the past ten years or more was the assassination in 1967 of Dr Verwoerd by a mentally deranged white parliamentary messenger – and that had not been on the agenda. Even that act had little consequence, since the succession of Vorster simply perpetuated the steady drift towards right-wing extremism within the parliamentary party and within the white community as a whole. Vorster, since his days in the detention camp, had entered parliament, become Minister of Justice and author of the repressive legislation enacted to deal with extra-parliamentary opposition, and now exercised supreme authority.

In Southern Rhodesia, one of the consequences of the election of the anti-British Nationalist Government in South Africa was to encourage the settlers (and to induce the British authorities) to consider Southern Rhodesia as part of a Central African complex. The outcome of this new perspective on Rhodesian affairs was the proposal to federate the dependencies of Southern and Northern Rhodesia and Nyasaland into a Central African political system. In principle, such a federation had much to commend it: an amalgamation of the three territories might save all of them from dependence upon South Africa; the economies of the territories were inter-twined by labour migration and flows of capital from one area to another. It was not the general concept of a federation which annoyed African nationalist opinion so much, as the clear indications that such a federation would be an instrument for the influence and control of white settlers generally, and of Southern Rhodesian settlers in particular. Furthermore, the northern territories were anxious to remain as much as possible outside the sphere of influence of Southern Rhodesia, whereas the Southern Rhodesian Africans occasionally wondered whether white control might conceivably be diluted and weakened by being spread over three territories instead of one. That suspicion was encouraged by the publicity given to the federation, which was widely described as inaugurating a policy of racial partnership, and a departure from the practice in Southern Rhodesia of racial exclusiveness. White Rhodesian politicians, at any rate, were obliged to preach the coming era of partnership in order to pacify African suspicions, and simultaneously to reassure Rhodesian voters (who remained overwhelmingly white) that these assurances meant very little. Whether those politicians were genuinely in favour of a real partnership, or were genuinely determined to entrench white Southern Rhodesian interests, is neither here nor there – in either event, they were obliged to dissimulate their real intentions. An era of political unreality and double-talk was ushered in.

Conceived in duplicity, the Federation was obliged to carry on in the same vein, since the British Government retained ultimate control, and was in a position to review events taking place in Central Africa. In the 1950s, the British Government's reputation was one of liberal gradualism, and it was widely believed that that Government would insist on liberal integrationist policies. The Federal Government must therefore quieten British fears and local African objections, while nevertheless retaining the confidence of an

180

electorate which was overwhelmingly white and conspicuously intolerant of liberalism and integration. The ordinary solution to the politicians' dilemma was to act as if they were right-wing white settlers, but to speak as if they were white liberals. Two very early decisions by the Federal Government illustrate this habit of mind. First of all the Federal capital was placed in Salisbury: good administrative reasons could be produced for putting the capital in the largest city, but the fact that Salisbury was also the Southern Rhodesian capital was probably more important. Again, the Federal Government resolved upon a massive hydro-electric dam, and had to choose between Kafue (in Northern Rhodesia) and Kariba (on the Zambezi between Northern and Southern Rhodesia). The smaller project at Kafue was recommended by economists: but the larger project at Kariba was undertaken since the publicity would be great and the control left in Southern Rhodesian hands since the power station would be on the southern bank of the river. In each of these cases Southern Rhodesian white opinion was gratified, but the decisions were explained in non-political terms. Also in 1953, the foundation-stone of a multi-racial university was laid, to serve the three federated territories. However it was sited once again in Salisbury, where the local laws had to be amended in order to permit the university to function. While a multi-racial university was an appropriate development in terms of racial partnership, it is curious that Salisbury – where the political climate was least favourable – was awarded the honour of being its site.

More importantly, the franchise qualifications were changed in the three component territories and in the Federation itself. Since the Federal Government was anxious to be given full independence by the British Government, and as the British Government was expected to insist upon evidence of advance towards an integrated society, the constitutional changes had to look like liberal legislation. At the same time they must not actually be liberal, since that would alienate the white electors to whom the politicians were responsible. In Northern Rhodesia and Nyasaland, the Colonial Office had allowed more power to be shared by the local electors, though nothing had been done to increase the African share of the electorate. In Southern Rhodesia and for the Federal parliament, an immensely complex system was devised. The system purported to reconcile two incompatible principles: one-man-one-vote and white minority control. In essence, a substantial number of Africans were declared eligible to enroll on the B roll of voters; while the A roll was reserved for citizens possessing capital, a large income, or educational qualifications. In each case, however, the number of seats which B roll electors could control was a much smaller number than was controlled by the A roll electors. While these schemes were publicised (for the benefit of liberal British opinion) as advances towards multi-racial partnership, the African Affairs Board quite correctly reported that such constitutions actually diminished the degree of control exercised by Africans over their governments.

The final and conclusive evidence against a real change of heart among the white electors, and against a real change in the balance of power between the various races, came in the elections which were held during the years of Federation. In Southern Rhodesia, the ruling United Rhodesia Party became increasingly suspicious that the Prime Minister – Garfield Todd – really intended to achieve racial partnership, so in 1958 he was ousted from his post and replaced by Edgar Whitehead. Later that year the re-constituted governing party won 17 seats in the Southern Rhodesian parliament; Todd's new and overtly liberal party won no seats whatever; and the overtly racialist Dominion Party won 13. The election demonstrated quite clearly that the only parties which stood any chance of success at the polls were the overt racialists and the covert racialists: a non-racial party stood no chance. Later in 1958 Federal elections were held, in order to strengthen the hand of the Federal Premier, Welensky, in attempting to gain full independence for the Federation. Since the Federal Government was not seriously accused of liberalism, and insisted that the real issue was independence, it won a massive majority of 46 seats, while the racialist Dominion Party won 8, and Todd's liberals won 3. At the same time, an attempt was made to introduce similar constitutions for Northern Rhodesia and Nyasaland, which would be likely to produce the same sort of governments. That was too much for the African nationalists in the north to tolerate, and they set about the task of demolishing Federation and achieving separate independences on the same style as the ex-colonies in West Africa. Federation and 'partnership' had failed to reconcile the conflicting interests of majority rule and white racial supremacy.

Government within the Federation had never enjoyed much African participation: early in 1959, following confrontations with African nationalist parties in the two northern territories, the basis of government was revealed as being coercion. In Southern Rhodesia, Whitehead declared a State of Emergency in February, arrested five hundred African activists, and passed laws which outlawed the most effective African organisations and which enabled the Government to detain indefinitely its political opponents. A week later the Government of Nyasaland also declared a State of Emergency and initiated a system which the British Devlin Commission later described as a police state. In March, Kaunda's Zambian Congress was proscribed in Northern Rhodesia, and in April the elections returned the United Federal Party as the strongest single party in the Northern Rhodesian parliament. In the short run, this repression ensured the survival of the Federation despite African resistance to it; but in the long run it was clear that federation had not won significant African support and would not be a means of achieving independence for the territories involved. Since federation failed to release the Southern Rhodesian white settlers from British control, the white settlers also turned against it. In the north, the Africans wanted to abolish Federation in order to achieve independence for themselves – now the same was true of the settlers in the south. The British Government sent the Monckton Commission to report on the Federation in 1960, but its report – that Federation still stood a chance of success if racial discrimination were brought to an end – was not very realistic since the white settlers were firmly in control of the Southern

Rhodesian parliament and would only tolerate Federation so long as they controlled the Federal Government. Though Federation survived until the end of 1963, it was clearly dying from 1959 onwards, when the initiative in political affairs passed out of the hands of the parliamentarians into the hands of the settlers in the south and of the nationalists in the north.

Compared with the changes and constitutions of the rest of Southern Africa in the 1950s and 1960s, the Portuguese territories at first sight appear unchanging. During the early years of the twentieth century, when relatively liberal governments sometimes ruled in Lisbon, there was some reality in the Portuguese policy of alleviating the worst brutalities of forced labour, and of extending full and equal rights to Africans who assimilated Portuguese culture. The policy of Europeanising Africans was obviously open to some objection, but in the early twentieth century it was a more interesting, more promising and more radical policy than was being practised elsewhere in Southern Africa. However, the establishment of a fascist state in Portugal during the 1920s and 1930s brought that promising era to an end. Since there was no liberty for Portuguese citizens in Portugal, it is hardly surprising that there was none in the colonies either. The incorporation of Portuguese colonies as overseas provinces of metropolitan Portugal may appear similar to the incorporation of France's overseas colonies as provinces of France: but whereas it was possible for Francophone Africans to exercise some slight influence in Paris, it was quite impossible for Portuguese African citizens to do the same. During the forty years of Salazar's dictatorship, the proportion of 'assimilated' Africans actually declined, and the attitude of the assimilated grew increasingly hostile to the Portuguese and to the system of administration. Being one of the poorest countries in Europe, Portugal had neither the economic strength to do without colonial profits, nor the political sophistication to disarm its enemies by granting early and useful concessions to them. In 1959 the politics of the Portuguese African colonies moved directly from resentful acquiescence to armed rebellion, without an intervening stage of constitutional argument. In 1969 Cactano succeeded the ageing Salazar without any change in Portuguese policies and attitudes towards its 'overseas provinces'. For forty years the Portuguese have ruled consistently without any pretence of parliamentary legitimacy: the only thing that has changed is the increasing militancy of the African opponents of that rule.

By the late 1950s therefore, the three most powerful communities in Southern Africa – the Union, the Federation, and the Portuguese colonies of Angola and Mozambique – had all abandoned any attempt to conciliate African opinion by sharing power with African leaders. Though the political style of Salazar differed from that of Verwoerd and that of Welensky and Whitehead, all these Governments shared in common their determination to resist African advancement by all means possible. Since parliamentary methods were no longer applicable, African nationalist movements were obliged – whether or not they so wished – to change their tactics. How they adapted themselves to the new situation will be considered in the next chapter.

Chapter 18

Opposition moves out of parliament

The tendency for increasing numbers of decisions to be taken outside parliament, and then ratified by parliament, has had the clear effect of making parliamentary and constitutional opposition futile. A brief survey of the constitutional oppositions in Southern Africa since mid-century will sufficiently demonstrate that trend. To take the Union first, parliamentary opposition comprised the United Party and splinter groups which broke away from it, and the representatives of African voters (abolished in 1960) and of Coloured voters (abolished in 1970). The United Party leadership decided upon the tactic of attacking details of Nationalist legislation, rather than the principles of racial segregation, in the hope of winning the support of dissident Nationalist voters. The continuous decline of the United Party's fortunes after 1948 demonstrated the futility of such an attitude, and encouraged some members to break away and form more determined parties. During the crisis over the removal of Coloured voters to a separate roll, for example, the United Party objected to the techniques used in achieving separation, rather than the principle of separation itself. The main opposition came from the Torch Commando, an *ad hoc* association of ex-servicemen which vanished after the crisis had passed. In 1953, some ex-members of the United Party, supported by some representatives of African voters, formed the Liberal Party, which eventually resolved upon a policy of one-man-one-vote but failed ever to win a seat in parliament. Other former UP members created the Federal Party, whose intention was to safeguard and increase the rights of the provinces against the central government – a policy which also failed to win significant support. And in 1959, following yet another electoral failure by the UP, 11 members of parliament broke away to create the Progressive Party, reviving the policy ascribed to Rhodes, of equal rights for all 'civilised' people. Despite the conservatism of that policy, however, only one of the Progressives survived the next general election. Even conservatism made little impact on white electoral opinion. Significantly, the party which caused most annoyance to the Government is the *Herstigte* (Re-formed) Nationalist Party, created in 1969 by Albert Hertzog, son of a Prime Minister and a former cabinet minister. Though the splinter party did not win any seats in the 1970 election, it represented a continuing threat to the Government by denouncing the sophistication of separate development in favour of the older and simpler policies of straight-forward racial superiority. Nevertheless Hertzog failed to bring back to parliament an effective voice in governmental decisions, even though he publicised the degree of power exercised by the Bureau of State Security (BOSS) without any reference to parliament whatever, and showed to what extent South Africa has become a police state. The party did seize the initiative in the 1970 election and – by distracting the governing party – enabled the UP to record a slight gain in parliamentary seats.

White opposition in Rhodesia and in the Federation proved equally incapable of seizing power or influencing government. When Garfield Todd was ousted from the Prime Minister's office and from his party, under suspicion of liberalism, he joined Sir John Moffatt in forming the Central African Party. In the late 1950s this party contested Federal, Northern and Southern Rhodesian seats. Against Welensky in the Federal elections they won three seats; against Whitehead in Southern Rhodesia they won no seats at all; and in Northern Rhodesia they won four. African voters preferred African nationalist candidates when these were available; white voters on the whole preferred racialist candidates, who were always available; and there was no middle group to support the compromise policies of the Central African Party. In Southern Rhodesia after Federation, even Whitehead's disguised racialism was insufficient, and the Rhodesia Front party won power, moving steadily to the political right, up to and after the illegal seizure of independence in 1965. The only parliamentary opponents who could win seats were those contesting the minority of B Roll seats which had predominantly African electorates, and the Nationalists declined to contest those seats. Finally, in Portugal the possibilities of parliamentary opposition were absent from the 1920s onwards. Even Galvao, whose opposition was liberal rather than radical, resorted to violence in 1960 to publicise his opposition by capturing the ship *Santa Maria* in the Atlantic.

Effective opposition, therefore, had to be mounted elsewhere than in parliamentary lobbies. In South Africa the obvious vehicle for African political expression was the old African National Congress. Elsewhere in Africa, such old-fashioned and conservative élite organisations were adapted to nationalist purposes during the 1950s, because they enjoyed the priceless asset of a territory-wide organisation. In Tanganyika, for example, the old Tanganyika African Association was transformed by Julius Nyerere into the Tanganyika African National Union. By the 1940s, however, the ANC was not an obviously useful organisation for the purpose. Throughout its career it had been ignored or attacked by Africans who wanted to achieve real results at high speed. In the 1920s it had been eclipsed by Kadalie's ICU; in the crisis of Hertzog's bills in 1935–1936 it had been circumvented by the All-African Convention; and it was somewhat discredited by association of some of its members with the Native Representative Council. Its great weakness had been that it represented only the interests of the élite group which enjoyed the franchise and often owned land individually. It galvanised itself into militancy only when those interests were attacked (in the 1913 Land Act, and the 1936 Voters legislation) but lapsed into silence when those interests were secure. Until its revival in 1935, for example, some observers thought it was dead. Nevertheless it possessed an organisation which covered the whole country, and was therefore the chosen instrument of African political leaders after the Second World War.

ANC was undergoing change even during the early 1940s. The Second World War, ostensibly a war against fascism and racialism, encouraged hope that the resounding liberal principles of the Atlantic Charter might be implemented, that Afrikaner nationalism might be discredited by association with the Fascists, and that Smuts and Hofmeyr might move in a more permissive direction than their predecessors. At the same time Dr A. B. Xuma, acting as President of the ANC, was trying to recruit young men into the middle-aged organisation. The new generation of recruits later rose to national eminence, producing Oliver Tambo, Walter Sisulu, Anton Lembede, Nelson Mandela and others. Many of the new generation were graduates of Fort Hare University College, most of them were urban professional men, and yet many of them had ties with the rural areas as well. They were well placed to understand the difficulties not only of townsmen but also of labour tenants and peasants, and they were sufficiently familiar with the operation of international and national affairs. However, the infusion of new blood into the conservative organisation created fresh problems, since many of the old guard considered the new generation irresponsible and unrealistic. In order to provide themselves with a platform from which to be heard, and a forum for discussion, the new recruits formed the ANC Youth Wing. The Youth Wing served also as a power-base and as a machine for recruiting more like-minded young men. Using the Youth Wing, they drafted a Programme of Action which was eventually adopted by ANC as a whole in 1949, thereby committing the ANC in principle to a more determined and consistent struggle for equal rights within the institutions of South African government and society. The acceptance by Congress of the Programme of Action also marked the beginning of a transfer of power from the old to the young members, and new leaders were elected who were more likely to listen to the voice of the Youth Wing – namely Dr Moroka and Walter Sisulu himself.

However, the emergence of the Youth Wingers brought Congress face to face with a serious dilemma. The old guard continued to occupy many important posts within the Congress, and continued to comprise much of the backbone of membership. Some means had to be discovered whereby Youth Wing programmes could be implemented without alienating too many of the older generation from Congress altogether. Division within ANC was seen as being the most dangerous risk to Congress effectiveness, since a militant programme without substantial membership would be just as ineffective as the old lack of purpose which had characterised ANC. What was required was a charismatic leader, who would not necessarily resolve differences of opinion, but who would ensure co-operation between the contending factions. He would have to lead the older men into more militant attitudes, without too great restraint upon the enthusiasm of the young. Such a figure slowly emerged in Natal – the least likely place to produce a militant nationalist, since the Zulu retained a great imperial hangover from the days of Zulu greatness, and were sometimes contemptuous of the abilities of other African communities. Pixley Seme, the founder of the Congress in 1912, had begun his political thinking as a Zulu nationalist before concluding that a wider base of organisation was required.

The President of the ANC Natal branch at that time was none other than A. W. G. Champion, who had broken away from Kadalie in the 1920s and formed ICU yase Natal. Since that time his respectability had increased, and he was extremely unlikely to tolerate (let alone encourage) a more militant approach to politics. His experience led him to believe that nothing could be achieved by mass action in any case, and his pessimism made him an obvious object of Youth Wing attack. Casting around for an alternative President, the Natal Youth Wing came upon Chief Albert Luthuli, and persuaded him to stand for election in 1951. At first sight Luthuli was also unpromising as a militant: he was already over 50 years old, had joined Congress only in the 1940s, was a Government-appointed chief and a member of the Native Representative Council. He had previously organised nothing larger or more significant than an African Cane-Growers Association around his home at Groutville. Nevertheless he had the character required, and enjoyed a reputation as an arbitrator between contending factions. In 1952 he was duly elected Natal President, though without much enthusiasm either from himself or from his supporters. It was the Defiance Campaign of 1952 which enabled him to emerge as a national figure.

For forty years ANC had been busy with petitions and appeals to the government. The Defiance Campaign against Unjust Laws was the first departure from the old tactical tradition, and was opposed by the more conservative of the members. Champion, for example, believed that no good could come of the project, and declined to inform his own members of the national executive's decisions. The Campaign nevertheless came to life. Its intention was to encourage people to defy racialist laws by means of token assaults upon segregated institutions. The Indian Congress at that time was also involved in a struggle between conservative and radical leaders, and also decided to enter the Campaign. So did some white liberals and radicals, so that the Campaign was characterised by an unusual degree of inter-racial co-operation. Together the activists entered doors marked for other racial groups, sat in offices and on benches reserved for 'Europeans Only', and made similar non-violent token demonstrations.

A few optimists may have expected the Campaign to bring the whole structure of discrimination tumbling down, by filling the gaols to bursting point, and by imposing a massive strain on the police force. The real achievements of the Campaign, however, were much more modest. In Durban, for example, there was a legacy of ill-will between Africans and Indians, as a result of African riots in 1949 when Indians had been attacked and their shops looted. The Campaign helped to heal that wound, and

Albert Luthuli, President-General of the African National Congress and winner of the Nobel Peace Prize

demonstrated that the hostility had been an aberration. As the ANC leaders understood the situation, they regarded non-racialism as the most effective response to white racial arrogance, and the inter-racial co-operation of the Campaign helped to publicise the non-racial aspirations of the Congress and its allies. Secondly, in the early days of the ANC revival, the Campaign served to attract attention to the existence and activity of the ANC, and to encourage recruiting. If mass support was required, the masses had to be informed. Third, it was considered desirable to demonstrate that racial discrimination really did affect every South African at every point of his or her life and to demonstrate this before a world audience. In that respect the Campaign was extremely successful.

Tragically, the Campaign was infiltrated by agents provocateurs anxious to discredit Congress, and race riots broke out in Port Elizabeth, which spread to East London and Kimberley. These disastrous riots provided the Government with an excuse for taking severe measures against an otherwise peaceful movement. The Criminal Laws Amendment Act was rushed through parliament, giving the Government powers to impose heavy sentences upon persons involved in breaking trivial regulations for a political purpose. That legislation was closely followed by the Public Safety Act, which allowed the Government to declare an emergency and rule by decree if necessary. In addition, the Government acted against individual leaders, by dismissing them from government employment (and so Luthuli was deprived of his Chieftaincy) or by banning them in terms of the Suppression of Communism Act (which defined Communism so widely that almost anyone could be described as Communist or in favour of Communist policies). However, Luthuli's dismissal simply served to attract more attention than before to his new stature as a national leader, even though it complicated the task of building a mass organisation.

The following years, in the middle 1950s, marked the building of an inter-racial alliance against the Government's racialism – an alliance which the Congress leaders considered necessary not only for tactical reasons but also because such a policy came naturally to many of them. It was the kind of policy which accentuated Luthuli's qualities, since he possessed the ability to address and persuade diametrically differing audiences. The predominantly white Liberal Party was induced to adopt an explicitly liberal (rather than gradualist) stance, after which it began to attract African and Indian and Coloured members. More important, a formal alliance began to emerge. The associates were the ANC, the Congress of Democrats, the South African Indian Congress and the South African Coloured People's Organisation. The Congress of Democrats in many ways acted as successor to the Communist Party which had been banned in 1950, and which had abandoned its support of the white trade unions. Once the Communists had concluded that the white trade unionists preferred racial to class solidarity, they had been quite successful in creating for themselves a new role as organisers of small inter-racial unions, and as advocates of a 'black republic' as a necessary step towards a workers' state. Nevertheless ANC suspicions survived long after the change of heart of the 1920s, and only in the 1950s did a significant number of ANC members accept many of the tenets of the Congress of Democrats' faith. The South African Indian Congress inherited from the days of Gandhi an ambiguity regarding the proper role of its members in South African racial affairs. By the 1950s, radical and non-racial leaders had achieved leadership positions from which to alter the older policy of seeking accommodation only with the white authorities. The South African Coloured People's Organisation, similarly, inherited the ambiguity of Dr Abdurahman's African People's Organisation. Because of the nature of the Coloured community, it could sometimes be persuaded to support white against African aspirations, though often the leaders realised that hostility between Coloured and African was only to the advantage of the white supremacists. By the mid 1950s, at any rate, the three other Congress movements were ready for co-operation with ANC.

Representatives of the four Congresses met in 1954, and arranged to hold a Congress of the People in 1955. That meeting, at Kliptown near Johannesburg, adopted a Freedom Charter which defined the aims which the allies would pursue. It proposed equal rights for all citizens, and vaguely referred to a moderately socialist economic policy. Although this meeting marked the inauguration of a formal Congress alliance, it did not actually do anything, and it attracted the unfriendly attention of the Government. That attention was all the more unfriendly because the ANC was involved in an anti-pass campaign in Johannesburg at the time. Since the Congress leaders had not actually done anything striking, it was difficult for the Government to do more than simply harrass the individuals concerned. But in 1955, soon after the adoption of the Freedom Charter, the Government decided to act more strongly. 156 leading opponents of the regime, of all races and of many different political opinions, were arrested and taken to trial in Johannesburg on a charge of high treason. There was little reason to expect conviction, and indeed every one of the accused was eventually acquitted. The real effect of the Treason Trial was to disrupt leadership, since the trial lasted for four years, during which period the political leaders were unable to devote much time to political organisation. The dynamism and momentum of the Congress alliance was largely lost during those four years.

Pressure of persecution put additional strains on the cracks within the alliance itself, and in the ANC especially. In order to bring about an inter-racial alliance, ANC leaders had been willing to allow their Congress allies equal representation in decision-making, despite the grave inequality in the size of the respective allies. As against that policy, there was a strong body of opinion, describing itself as Africanist, and looking askance at such restraint by the ANC. It was certainly true that the smaller Congress allies brought no considerable power to the alliance, though the Africanists were probably exaggerating when they viewed the alliance as a means of subordinating ANC to Communist influence, and in any case the ANC was not in a position to be excessively fussy about the political complexion of its allies. The Africanists further alleged that the ANC was insufficiently militant, and that more action was required in the situation. Precisely what kind of action was contemplated never became completely clear. Nevertheless the Treason Trial and the paralysis it produced in the Congress alliance provided ammunition for the Africanist view that nothing tangible had been gained in exchange for the privileged position given to the allies within the alliance.

During the late 1950s events moved out of the control of the ANC leadership. On one hand, ambitious projects for mass co-ordinated action failed to muster sufficiently widespread support; and on the other, locally initiated actions occurred which had no potential for nation-wide mobilisation of large numbers of people. When the Government implemented its Bantu Education policy, taking over mission schools and imposing the kind of education which the government thought suitable for Africans, the ANC attempted to organise a boycott of the schools. In principle, that was a suitable issue to emphasise, but in practice few parents were prepared to risk have their children shut out of school altogether, and the boycott quickly broke down. ANC also objected to the separation of the universities into racial institutions, but that was an issue which affected only a small minority of Africans. In both cases, the issues appealed more strongly to white liberals than to African peasants and industrial workers. Without an effective nation-wide organisation, ANC leaders were obliged to let the initiative pass to local groups, and then decide whether or not to lend ANC support to the particular movement. In 1956, for example, when African women were included in the operation of pass legislation for the first time, women spontaneously demonstrated against the legislation, and even organised a demonstration at the seat of government – the Union Buildings in Pretoria. At that time, however, the leaders on trial had not yet arranged for decisions to be taken by anyone else. In 1957, in protest against increased bus fares, the residents of Alexandra Township outside Johannesburg boycotted the bus service and walked to work. The protest was successful, but ANC could not claim to have organised it, nor did the issue have any nation-wide appeal. In 1958, in the Northern Transvaal, there were violent protests against government policies, but the ANC was prohibited from the area, and was unable to influence events. The Africanists were able to argue that the ANC leadership was incapable of uniting urban and rural grievances into a united movement. Whether that was entirely the fault of the leaders was, of course, another matter.

The break came towards the end of 1958, when Robert Sobukwe split away to create the Pan-Africanist Congress. P-AC proved equally unable to co-ordinate urban and rural unrest, which continued in a piece-meal and sporadic manner throughout 1958 and 1959. Riots in the Northern Transvaal countryside, violent protests in Natal country districts, an attempted boycott of schools in the Eastern Cape, violent protest in Pondoland – all separately were incapable of bringing pressure to bear upon government policy. At the same time as rural mass movements were being united by élite organisations elsewhere in colonial Africa, the reverse was happening in South Africa: rural radicalism was becoming cut off from the unifying efforts of the national political parties. In retrospect it appears that government tactics were very successful: by isolating the leadership (in the Treason Trial, and by action against other individuals) they prevented mass movements from becoming concerted and effective. By the end of the 1950s both ANC and P-AC required a boost to their morale. The successful potato boycott of 1959, though a significant achievement, was not the sort of action which would make a dent in the armour of the Government.

After considerable thought, ANC resolved to stage an anti-Pass campaign at the end of March 1960, a date influenced slightly by the fact that the United Nations had declared 1960 to be Africa Year. Passes were selected for two compelling reasons: the spontaneous protests by women confirmed the view that passes were political dynamite; and passes were simultaneously a badge of inferior status and a tangible and powerful restriction on the rights and powers of Africans generally. An attack on passes would therefore be symbolic, popular, and just possibly successful, in which case South Africa would never be quite the same place again. P-AC came to the same conclusion, and resolved to stage a campaign on 21st March. On that day, Africans moved peacefully to police stations to surrender their passes, or to burn them publicly. Rallies began very successfully, and tension mounted throughout the country in a manner which had no precedent. The police, however, took a different view of the matter. Africans were behaving with dignity, with a sense of purpose – and in defiance of the law. Some response was obviously required. At Sharpeville in the Transvaal, and at Langa in the Cape, the police decided to disperse the gatherings by force. They fired upon the assembled people, and continued firing at the backs of fleeing demonstrators. Some 80 Africans were killed, and probably four times that number were injured. There were no police casualties.

These incidents provoked international outrage. In South Africa the

Sharpeville: some of the dead and wounded lying on the ground

ANC called for a one day stay-at-home in protest and in mourning. In most countries such a scandal would have led either to resignations in the government, or at least to a reprimand against the police. The South African Government decided to blame the African parties, which were immediately proscribed, while hundreds of political activists were detained without trial. In the Western Cape, Africans were coerced back to work, so that the Government could claim that normal conditions had been restored. That claim was all the more necessary since foreign capital investment had become alarmed and much of it had been withdrawn from the country's economy.

Prohibition of the parties resolved the question of tactics: the only remaining possibility was armed struggle. However, the parties were proscribed precisely at the time when they were most hostile to each other, and the division was carried over into the 1960s and even 1970s. ANC sponsored an underground organisation called Spear of the Nation; P-AC sponsored Poqo. Both organisations were involved in acts of sabotage as a means of bringing about political change. The Government responded by intensifying its policy of training the white community in the use of arms and in anti-guerilla warfare. The Government also armed itself with even greater arbitrary powers to detain and interrogate political opponents. African violent protest began to concentrate on rural rather than urban areas. In urban areas, where every African was under threat of expulsion to the impoverished countryside, organisation of resistance became extremely difficult. In the rural areas, however, protest was easier. It was easier to discover who was favourable towards the Government, and to take action against the collaborators. However, to the extent that protests became rural, they also became sectional and non-national. In 1960, for instance, much of Pondoland was in revolt; people declined to pay taxes or to patronise white shops, and some took to the hills. However, a local movement of that nature was easily isolated, and the Government had only to seal-off the area in order to starve the protestors into submission, while it was impossible for the Mpondo to spread their revolt elsewhere. A further development was the removal of the leadership, either into South African prisons or beyond South African borders.

Constant risk of betrayal within the country, and the existence of newly independent and hospitable African states, both encouraged leaders to organise outside the country altogether. For many months Nelson Mandela continued to organise branches of the ANC within the country, but the capture of Mandela and a handful of other leaders at Rivonia in 1962 was probably the end of serious political organisation based within the borders of the country. Arrest and trial of small numbers of people has continued ever since, on charges arising out of membership of ANC or P-AC, but the later trials have not brought to light any leaders of the stature of Mandela or Sobukwe. Though both ANC and P-AC continue to have members within the country, the organisational bases are now outside, in Ethiopia, Dar es Salaam and Lusaka. From these bases guerilla movements are organised and launched against the white supremacist states.

Nelson Mandela in captivity

African politics in South-West Africa were long complicated by the ethnic diversity of the inhabitants. The largest ethnic group, the Ovambo in the far north, were not involved in the Herero-Nama war against the Germans, and were not involved in territorial politics until comparatively recent times. Toivo ja Toivo on behalf of the Ovambo contributed petitions to the United Nations, but it was only in 1957 that he founded the Ovamboland People's Organisation. Jarirentundu Kozonguizi, representing younger Ovambo, consistently pressed for the creation of a territorial African organisation into which the OPO would be merged; and eventually in 1959 the South-West African National Union was created, predominantly by associating the Ovambo with the leaders of the Herero. Meanwhile further east in the Caprivi strip, where the inhabitants were related linguistically to the Lozi, a separate Caprivi African National Union was formed in 1964. Neither of these organisations succeeded in capturing the political initiative from the Herero and Nama people of the southern and central part of the country.

Among the Herero, Chief Hosea Kutako, a survivor of the Herero-Nama war against the Germans, had become involved very early in efforts with the Reverend Michael Scott to bring South-West Africa to the attention of the United Nations. SWANU was believed by many to be an unsatisfactory compromise between the Herero and the OPO, and in 1962 another organisation was created – the South-West Africa People's Organisation – to bring about a more national alignment of forces. During the 1960s and early 1970s, SWAPO proved the more militant of the two national organisations, being involved in a series of attempts at armed sabotage, and Toivo ja Toivo himself being tried in 1967 as a member of SWAPO, and therefore involved in guerilla actions launched from a military base in Tanzania, where many exiled organisations had by then set up their headquarters. Nevertheless the continuing split between the two national parties is a dangerous one, which survives despite the military alliance agreed upon in 1964.

In some respects African politics in Southern Rhodesia were closely bound up with those further south, from which they sometimes took their cue. Kadalie's ICU, for example, spread from Johannesburg to Salisbury and Bulawayo in the late 1920s. The Matabele Home protagonists had also derived assistance from the members of the early ANC movement, who saw the restoration of Ndebele kingship and land as a suitable issue, combining ancient dignity and economic realities. More significantly, many of the leaders of the first élite organisation – the Rhodesian Bantu Voters Association – were Mfengu who had settled in Rhodesia in the wake of the Pioneer Column. At first they attempted to distinguish themselves from Rhodesian Africans, but quickly fell foul of settler racialism and began to see themselves as part of a distinct Rhodesian African élite group.

There were, however, important differences between the two situations. The ethnic division of Africans into two large blocs of Shona and Ndebele, each with traditions which involved hostility to the other, made any territorial organisation vulnerable to ethnic feelings. Whereas in South Africa 'tribalism' did not prevent the formation of territory-wide organisations before Union, or Union-wide organisations after 1910, in Rhodesia ethnic feeling was concentrated into two substantial groupings which impeded close association. Secondly, the small size of the settler population made it necessary for the settlers to tread rather more delicately on the land and the rights of the African inhabitants. African voters (admittedly a tiny proportion of the whole electorate) were not harassed as brutally as in South Africa; nor was African-occupied land expropriated to such a great extent, at least until the Second World War. Nevertheless African politics in Rhodesia followed a similar course of development to those elsewhere in Africa during the first half of the twentieth century, namely the division of Africans into two distinct groups – the minority who had access to western education, clerical or professional employment, and some political rights or influence, and the majority who were not able to enter into these new relationships. It seems to be common in such a situation that mass action is not very well directed. In both Rhodesia and South Africa (and indeed East and Central Africa as well) a common expression of mass radical hostility to the colonial situation was the formation of separatist or messianic religious movements. These movements enabled people to organise themselves, but at the same time prevented them from understanding the problems they were facing, except in religious terms. Conversely, élite Africans, anxious to dissociate themselves from such 'ignorant' activity, failed to provide leadership and increasingly concentrated on their own immediate interests. Not until the 1940s were the élite and the masses able to come together.

One important spur to unity was the Second Occupation of Mashonaland, a massive assisted immigration of white settlers sponsored by the Rhodesian Government to entrench the power of existing settlers. Despite myths and legends about the Rhodes tradition and the Pioneer Column, probably two-thirds of Rhodesia's white population arrived only after the Second World War. Their arrival inevitably created more pressure on the land. Some settlers, for instance, were placed on land which had already been designated 'white' but had in fact been occupied by Africans. More seriously, the Government concluded that the solution to the land problem was to reform African agriculture so that Africans required less land to live on. That was the purpose of the 1951 Land Husbandry Act, which sought to encourage individual tenure and to insist upon more intensive cultivation. A second spur to unity was the rapid development of an industrial sector of the economy, pulling thousands of African peasants into urban employment and presenting them with all the problems of adjustment that such a change involves. The successful 1945 railway workers' strike and the 1948 general urban strike in Bulawayo and Salisbury are indications of the new militancy. Nevertheless most trade union and other political leaders considered their bargaining position to be relatively weak, in view of the lack of massive support and territorial organisation, and therefore determined to extract concessions by co-operation with the Government, rather than launch an ambitious but possibly ruinous political campaign.

Leaders who favoured co-operation were immensely encouraged by the froth of liberal sentiment which was released by the introduction of the Central African Federation. They were in any case anxious to believe that real changes could be brought about without organising and fighting for them. That optimism lasted no longer than the first two years. The Land Husbandry Act continued to be enforced, and the urban concessions to social integration had no perceptible influence on the balance of political power in the country. In 1955 young men in Salisbury broke away from the politics of apparent participation, and formed the City Youth League, whose intention was African national rather than multi-racial. When the League took up the issue of the Land Husbandry Act, it acquired an appeal to the rural areas as well as the towns. Nevertheless another two years elapsed until – in 1957 – some of the old leaders of the decayed Southern Rhodesia ANC joined with the League to re-create the SRANC, under the leadership of Joshua Nkomo, a trade union leader from Bulawayo. The new organisation was strongly represented both in the towns and in the country districts. The following year, the dismissal of Southern Rhodesian Prime Minister Garfield Todd confirmed the view that Federation did not really involve any liberal change. Congress therefore gathered in many Africans whose faith in partnership and Federation was finally demolished. Shortly after that, the Government paid Congress the high compliment of banning it, thereby acknowledging its potential power.

Undismayed, the Congressmen re-formed themselves in 1960 into the National Democratic Party; and when that in turn was banned, they created the Zimbabwe African People's Union. During these months, the movement acquired the characteristics necessary for a successful national movement: mass support in rural and urban areas, a resourceful élite leadership to maintain country-wide communication, and an historical charter in the appeal to the glories of ancient Zimbabwe. The appeal to Zimbabwe may be seen as part of a conscious attempt to build up the sentiment required to sustain an inter-ethnic political movement among both major ethnic groups and all classes of membership. In most parts of Africa such a powerful movement would have been sufficient to bring about political independence and majority rule. In Rhodesia, however, the movement came up against a determined settler minority, which held the instruments of government and military power in its grasp. By 1963, when the movement had still failed to dislodge settler power, it followed the same path as P-AC and ANC in South Africa. Those who blamed the ZAPU leadership for failure broke away and formed the Zimbabwe African National Union, under the Reverend Ndabaningi Sithole. A few months later, both movements were banned from the colony, and followed ANC and P-AC underground. By the time the settlers declared UDI in 1965, ZANU and ZAPU were both established predominantly outside the country, in Lusaka, Dar es Salaam and Addis Ababa. Nkomo had been in detention before UDI; Sithole was sent to gaol in 1969 on charges of plotting to assassinate the leaders of government and seize power.

Political developments in the three protectorates followed a very different course altogether. Political independence was attained despite the relative weakness of the nationalist movements and the absolute poverty of the economies. In all three cases the initiative lay outside the country involved: in Britain where there was some anxiety to have done with the last vestiges of formal colonial control; in tropical Africa where newly independent countries also pressed for the complete decolonisation of Africa; and above all in the Republic of South Africa which saw ways of controlling the territories whether as independent or as colonial states. There had, of course, been independence movements in the protectorates, and they were especially active in the 1960s; but the dynamism for political change was to be found elsewhere. The position and prospects of the ex-protectorates are best considered in the final chapter.

Political developments north of the Zambezi were also very different from those to the south. With the impending break-up of Federation, and

Joshua Nkomo and the Rev. Ndabaningi Sithole, leaders of the Zimbabwe African People's Union and the Zimbabwe African National Union

closely following the failure of Union Minière and the Federal Government to keep Moise Tshombe in power in secessionist Katanga, the forces of white supremacy were in disarray in the early 1960s. Furthermore, Britain retained ultimate and real control over the Governments of Northern Rhodesia and Nyasaland, and Britain had suffered too many reverses in attempting to contain nationalist movements in Asia and tropical Africa, to welcome another encounter in Central Africa as well. There the United National Independence Party led by Dr Kaunda, and the Malawi Congress Party led by Dr Banda, swept to power and to independence in 1964. Neither party enjoyed the mass support of ZANU or ZAPU, nor of ANC nor P-AC; but against imperial control less power was required than against settler regimes.

One of the strangest paradoxes of the recent history of Southern Africa is that armed and effective resistance has been most obvious and powerful in the least developed of the territories, namely the Portuguese possessions. That anomaly is partly explained by the fact that Africans in the Portuguese territories were never tempted to waste their time and skill in manoeuvring within legal limits to bring about constitutional reform. There was so little scope for such activity in the Portuguese possession – or even in Portugal for that matter – that opposition was necessarily unconstitutional. The Portuguese conquest was also comparatively recent – 1915 at the earliest in most of Angola, and 1908 at the earliest for most of Mozambique – so that violent methods were fairly fresh in people's memories. In 1959 armed liberation movements began to be effective in Angola and Mozambique – and Portuguese Guinea – while nationalists elsewhere in Southern Africa (and in most of the rest of tropical Africa) were still committed to non-violent methods. Having the longest experience of guerilla warfare, it was these liberation movements which devised the techniques required: extensive political education before a shot could be fired in a military campaign; provision for the education of children and adults, the marketing of produce, and the availability of medical and other social services. They appreciated the fact that political slogans – even the slogan of political independence – were not enough to mobilise the peasantry. In Mozambique, Dr Edward Mondlane organised the Frente de Libertacao de Mozambique (Frelimo) until his assassination in 1969, and achieved the extraordinary feat of mobilising aid from both East and West, and setting up the infrastructure of government in the captured areas of northern Mozambique. The continuing success of Frelimo, and its smaller and more radical competitor Coremo, will largely depend upon the fate of the Cabora Bassa Dam project in the lower Zambezi, which the Portuguese hope will form the economic basis for substantial white settlement. In Angola, there are no less than three liberation movements, Roberto Holden's FNLA being the oldest and least radical, and the least successful so far. MPLA and UNITA, both depending heavily upon Eastern assistance, have been much more successful in taking over sections of inland Angola and establishing their own provisional administrations. It is in Guinea, a tiny enclave in West Africa, where liberation is conducted by one agency, the PAIGC, that the insurgents have been most successful so far in tying down thousands of Portuguese troops and instituting provisional governments in liberated areas.

By the early 1960s, then, throughout Southern Africa, the major African parties had restored to force in pursuit of freedom: in Malawi and Zambia the struggle was destined to be short and successful; in Rhodesia and South Africa long protracted; and the fate of the ex-protectorates, nominally independent, would be seen only when the result of the confrontation elsewhere became clear.

Chapter 19

Changing conditions of life

In the 1860s there were areas in which a relatively prosperous economy could be found, especially in the vicinity of Cape Town and to a lesser extent at the other colonial ports. Outside those enclaves living conditions for all races were very much alike. The vast majority of people lived mainly outside a cash economy, and therefore it was difficult for individuals to accumulate large quantities of capital. For the same reason few people could afford stone or brick houses, or the products of industry imported into South Africa – and if they could afford to make large purchases they tended to buy firearms and ammunition. Some Tswana lived in large urbanised groups, but they were exceptional and most people lived at great distances from dense settlement. Afrikaners, meeting every three months for the celebration of communion and for other social purposes, congregated at rural villages; for most Africans the chiefly courts performed the same function. Life, in other words, was overwhelmingly rural, the economies were very localised, and inequalities of wealth rather limited. By the 1860s the introduction and extensive breeding of sheep for the sale of wool on the world market was already making a difference to the lives of white farmers in the Cape and in the Orange Free State. Otherwise the pre-industrial economy offered few opportunities for great prosperity, except around the ports, where individuals could enter quite fully into a world-wide economic system.

By the 1960s the social and economic life of South Africa had been transformed almost beyond recognition, and therefore it is useful to try to identify precisely what changes have taken place. The most obvious transformation is associated with the development of mineral production, and the growth of secondary industries associated with mining. By the late 1960s at any given time there were half a million Africans employed in the mining industry. Since the mining industry employs Africans almost exclusively on the basis of migrant labour on contract for perhaps nine months at a time, the figure of half a million is an index of a colossal impact on family life. African families may well continue to consider a rural area as 'home', but even then they are economically dependent upon labour in the urban, industrial areas. At least half a million other Africans were employed at any given time in manufacturing, and a further half million

in government or government-owned enterprises, while it is difficult to estimate the numbers employed in commerce, the building industry, or domestic labour. What can be said, however, is that there must be precious few Africans in Southern Africa who earn their living entirely outside the 'modern' sector of the economy. Even employment on white-owned farms, a relatively rural and not very modern activity, means heavy dependence upon wage employment; while the locations (or Bantu homelands as the Government prefers to describe them) generally have to import food, since they are too overcrowded and send away too many able-bodied men to the industrial areas, to be self-supporting. What has happened is that the whole African population has been absorbed into a modern, cash economy, while the old rural economies have withered away.

It is certainly true that cash incomes in the modern sector are strikingly high by comparison with cash incomes elsewhere in Africa, and the point is frequently made by government apologists. The picture is, however, less attractive than the statistics would suggest. A monthly wage of less than R 18 (£9) in mining, with accommodation and food provided, sounds quite sufficient; in the government service the monthly average is nearly R 24 (£12), and in manufacturing it is nearly R 50 (£25) usually without fringe benefits. In order to grasp the significance of these figures, however, two other factors have to be taken into account. In the rest of Africa, where Africans have usually retained possession of the land, a family can often

Contrasting ways of life: Cape Town, with the Houses of Parliament in the foreground; an African shanty town near Johannesburg and a new African location

support themselves simply from the land, and cash income from migrant labour provides the wherewithal for school fees, taxes, and other demands. In Southern Africa the case is different, since the cash income must provide almost the whole income for the whole family. Secondly, the curbing of trade unions for Africans, and the general adoption of economic paternalism regarding African workers, has resulted in the almost complete exclusion of Africans from wage negotiations. It may therefore be supposed that the wages offered are the minimum required for Africans to sustain life in a modern, cash economy. It is difficult otherwise to explain how white miners have won a salary structure which gives them an average wage of R 280 (£140), which is fifteen times as great as the African wage (though without the food and accommodation offered to Africans in their compounds). What we have is an apparent paradox, whereby Africans earn rather more in cash than Africans in independent Africa, but are nevertheless im-poverished, since they live entirely within a cash economy, and have no land to fall back on to supplement their cash incomes.

Naturally, Africans are by no means alone in having been absorbed into a modern economy. By 1970 nearly 90 per cent of the white population lived in urban areas, and can therefore be assumed to be part of the modern economy, while the remainder, as farmers, were usually dependent upon urban markets for a steady income. The figure for Indians was almost as high, while for Coloureds the figure was a little more than two-thirds. These statistics also high-light a further feature, namely the active discouragement of Africans from settling permanently in urban areas. Indians had become urbanised before restrictions were imposed, while Coloureds in the Cape were also largely urbanised before legislation imposed difficulties. One consequence of this discrimination is that although everyone has been absorbed into a modern industrial economy, relatively few Africans have had access to the educational, recreational and other facilities of town life. Another related factor is that whites, as permanent city-dwellers, and as full members of the political systems, have been able to organise themselves very effectively into trade unions and professional associations, while Africans – as migrants and as non-members of the political systems – have not. Coloureds and Indians, despite political difficulties, have been able to take advantage of their relative security in towns to organise relatively effective trade unions and other organisations. In other words the process of urbani-sation has been unequal from one racial group to another, and therefore the opportunities offered by urbanisation have not been equally available to all. During the 1960s the Government made determined efforts to segregate urban Africans into peri-urban locations, of which Soweto outside Johannesburg is the best-known example. The time and distance involved in transport, combined with the long hours of employment in the industrial areas, and the strict government control over urban African life, have all restricted the benefits which Africans might otherwise have derived. There is seldom time for recreation, seldom money for education, and little opportunity for family life even when both parents are permitted to live together.

An extremely important political consequence follows from the absorption of Africans into a wage economy. If we consider some of the most disruptive anti-colonial movements in colonial Africa during the twentieth century, we would perhaps list Mau Mau in Kenya, riots against agricultural regulations in Northern Rhodesia and Nyasaland, Kimbanguism in the Belgian Congo, the activities of the U.P.C. in Cameroun, and perhaps the cocoa boycott in the Gold Coast. These were instances of rural radicalism, whereby the activities of peasants wrenched the initiative from the colonial administrators. Somewhat similar movements occurred in Zululand, Pondoland and Sekhukhuneland in South Africa in the 1950s – but the dependence of the rural Africans upon urban wages reduced their capacity for long-term rebellion. Similarly, as we have seen, strikes by urban employees have been complicated not only by government hostility and the opposition of non-African workers, but to a great extent by the dependence of most African workers upon a regular wage packet. Precisely because African workers find it impossible to save money out of their wages, long-term strikes have become impossible to organise. In other words, two political weapons used by Africans in the anti-colonial struggles of most of Africa have been impossible to wield in the South African situation. Immediate and impromptu explosions of passion, such as have often occurred after train accidents (when the poor material used in the construction of African railway carriages fails to protect passengers) indicate the level of frustration, but do not offer a means of attaining a political goal.

Paradoxically, economic development in South Africa as a whole has been accompanied by a relative decline in African skills. As has happened almost throughout Africa, the introduction of imported iron and steel goods (and in South Africa the local manufacture of these goods) meant a decline in iron-smelting and iron technology as a whole, since local smiths have been unable to compete with mass production. Again, the restrictions placed upon African land-holding, the growth of dense rural populations, and the migration of able-bodied men to urban employment, has probably involved an absolute decline in the skills required for cultivating and pastoralism. Within the traditional economy therefore, efficiency has declined while the skills of the modern industrial economy and skilled employment in industry have normally been reserved for white workers. In theory the learned professions have been open to all races, and certainly there have been Africans who have overcome all difficulties to qualify as doctors, lawyers, academics and so on. Legislation in the 1960s, however, has tended to operate against non-white professional people. The rationale of much legislation is that skilled Africans (either professional or technical) should find employment in the relevant 'homeland'; but in practice the homelands are so poor that they cannot sustain significant numbers of professional or technical people. It is generally accepted that skilled workers and professional people find it easier than unskilled migrant workers to exercise influence over employers and governments. The relative decline of technical skills among Africans is therefore not only an economic but also a political event. The same can be said of the consistent exclusion of non-whites from opportunities to train as soldiers, air-force pilots, sailors, armed police, or indeed for any of the armed forces.

It might be thought that the creative arts would not be affected by legislation; and to a great extent it is true that legislation has not directly affected the work of artists, except that censorship inhibits (and sometimes suppresses) work which has any bearing upon political problems. A more important influence upon artists is the kind of society in which they live, and the kind of life they are obliged to lead. The long and elaborately composed novels of Nigeria or Ghana have no counterpart in South Africa, for at least two major reasons: one is that almost no African writer has the leisure or the time to write at such length, and must restrict himself to short stories. Similarly the extended dramatic poetry of modern Ugandan authors has no counterpart, since Africans in South Africa have little opportunity for the sustained concentration required. Secondly, precisely because the South African government encourages Africans to live intellectually in a long-vanished 'tribal' ethos, few Africans have seen much merit in writing about rural life. To some extent radical white novelists, poets and academics have filled the gaps: but the important point is that the quality of African writing in South Africa reveals a great deal about the life of those who try to write for a living.

Economic and political forces, then, can be seen to have broken down the social, political and economic organisations of nineteenth-century South Africans. The same forces have tended to reform South Africans as atomised members of a modern industrial economy, which makes extravagant demands upon the time, labour and thinking of South Africans, especially those restricted to the least rewarding levels of employment. During the 1950s the South African government perceived a great danger in that trend, namely that, just as white citizens thought of themselves as whites, so Africans might identify themselves as Africans, irrespective of language or 'tribe'. The subsequent Bantu homelands legislation may be seen as an attempt to 'retribalise' an African population which had largely discarded tribal identities as irrelevant to most day-to-day problems. This, of course, is only one of innumerable occasions when political power has been used to attempt to over-ride economic forces. The fact that the new 'tribal authorities' have often very dubious claims to historical authenticity is obvious: at the same time it is clear that governmental policies have had some effect upon African attitudes. For most economic and social purpose 'tribal authorities' are probably irrelevant: but the creation of subordinate political systems in which tribal identities are positively encouraged may well have undermined the sense of 'African-ness' which was emerging so strongly in the 1950s. Here it is worth mentioning a point that is made elsewhere in the book: that Chief Kaiser Matanzima was heavily out-voted in the first Transkei election, but won a majority of seats in the second general election. There are, of course, many other factors involved in Transkei elections, but it would still seem as if large numbers of Africans in the Transkei have had their political ambition channelled away from 'dangerous' nationalist politics to relatively harmless local politics, even though the Transkei government excercises almost no independent power, and has extremely few political gifts to bestow upon loyal supporters. On the other hand it is difficult to see quite how even an ingenious government can divert the energies and ambitions of urban Africans into the rigmarole of 'tribal' politics – and despite government opposition, no way has been discovered of stemming the tide of Africans away from the rural areas into the more lucrative urban settlements. The grant of restricted and partly imaginary political rights to a life-long resident of Soweto, in a rural area which he may never have visited, is not likely to be important.

In any case, social and economic trends are more difficult to alter than political forms. It may be relatively easy to transform a man from being politically an 'African' to a 'Zulu': but it is infinitely more difficult to transform him from a speaker and writer in English, into a man who thinks consistently in Zulu; and almost impossible to change the habits of a modern industrial man into those of the peasants who were his ancestors. 'Re-tribalisation' in other words, would seem an impossible programme to accomplish.

Chapter 20

Imperial factors

Imperial power in Southern Africa was obviously considerable in the nineteenth century: equally obviously it has declined since then, to the point where formal imperialism can nearly be discounted in Southern Africa in the 1970s. The extinguishing of formal imperialism is therefore one of the most significant changes to have taken place during the past century, and several episodes during that process deserve attention.

British imperial control, having exercised an easy supremacy in Southern Africa until the 1870s, was over-shadowed by the development of colonial power in the Cape from the 1870s onwards, and by Afrikaner power based upon the Transvaal from the 1880s onwards. Despite the massive intervention of British troops and administrators during and after the South African War of 1899–1902, that supremacy could not be re-established, except by the permanent deployment of massive military force. Such an expensive remedy was also, by the twentieth century, unnecessary. British economic and strategic interests were not injured by the formation of Union, nor by successive Union governments. The transfer of power from Imperial to Colonial and Afrikaner hands nevertheless left substantial responsibilities with the Imperial Government. We should therefore consider how Britain has contrived to divest itself of these remaining responsibilities.

The most substantial of these sub-continental responsibilities lay in Nyasaland, Northern and Southern Rhodesia. Northern Rhodesia and Nyasaland were consistently governed on an East African model rather than a South African: that is to say that settler influence upon administration was often very great indeed, but that the settlers never quite achieved a formalisation and entrenchment of that influence. As a result, the destinies of those territories could be determined by British governments, without too much regard for settler interests. The position in Southern Rhodesia was rather different, since the settlers had already entrenched themselves in power under the Chartered Company, by the time the Imperial Government took direct control after the expiry of the Company's charter.

The Central African Federation scheme of the 1950s was essentially an Imperial attempt to create a local coalition to which power could be transferred, without creating a second South Africa, but without permitting majority rule. It took an astonishingly long time for the Imperial Government to realise that there was no middle way between these two 'extremes', and that 'partnership' could not function without the willingness of the settlers to regard Africans as full partners. In order to abandon responsibility therefore, a different compromise became necessary, whereby the nationalism of Malawi and Zambia was legitimised by the negotiation of separate independence for the two states and a decision regarding Southern Rhodesia was postponed, on the grounds that it was too difficult to deal with. While Malawi and Zambia nationalism should not be under-rated, it is important to bear in mind that they were successful partly because they offered alternative governments, in an area which Britain was no longer anxious to govern directly. Nationalism having come to power in West and East Africa, a formal colonial empire in South-Central Africa was obviously an anachronism which was becoming somewhat embarrassing in Westminster.

Rhodesia presented a much thornier problem. Again, the Imperial Government desired to rid itself of responsibility, but was anxious to do so with a measure of dignity and the appearance of fairness to the inhabitants of the colony. Since the settlers were firmly in control of the armed forces, the economy and the political structure, a dignified and fair imperial exit could not be accomplished without armed intervention. On the other hand Rhodesia had become a settler colony precisely because of its inaccessibility from London, and its proximity to South Africa. These circumstances made Imperial intervention as difficult and potentially hazardous in the 1960s as at any earlier time. Undecided between dignity and irresponsibility, the Imperial Government allowed the initiative to fall into the hands of the Rhodesia Front, within which an increasingly militant and racialist leadership took office.

When Ian Smith's Government declared Rhodesia to be independent, on 11th November 1965, the new alignment of forces in Southern Africa was revealed very clearly. The Imperial Government, trying at all moral cost to avoid thinking about Rhodesia, had already declared that force would not be used in the event of Unilateral Declaration of Independence (UDI). South Africa and Portugal, having made no official comment, were believed to be willing to provide military assistance to the Smith regime in the event of a British armed intervention. It is likely that no such decision had been taken by that time, but the South African Government, at least, would be compelled by white South African opinion to make some military gesture. Rhodesia itself had a small but reliable army, and had inherited the aeroplanes of the Federal Government. Independent African states, having themselves no military power with which to intervene successfully, were reduced to requesting the Imperial Government to intervene. These requests were similar to those of the ANC in South Africa after Union: in both cases the appeals reflected the inability of the appellants to do anything themselves, and a misplaced faith in the willingness of Britain to act on their behalf.

The economic sanctions applied to Rhodesia, first by Britain and later by the United Nations, have affected the economy of Zambia quite severely, but appear to have had little effect upon Rhodesia, except to inhibit the growth of their economy. Ian Smith remains Prime Minister while Harold Wilson has returned to the opposition. Constitutionally, Rhodesia declared itself to be a republic in 1970, and in real political and economic terms has formed useful alliances with South Africa, the Portuguese, and a variety of international traders who have helped to find loop-holes in the sanctions barrier. It seems safe to say that Rhodesia will not be transformed into Zimbabwe by means of imperial efforts, though other approaches may prove more effective.

The devolution of power in the three High Commission territories of Bechuanaland, Basutoland and Swaziland may also be regarded as a deliberate shelving of imperial responsibilities. Since 1910 Britain had been content to allow the economies of these three territories to fall increasingly under South African control. Political independence, by itself, was unlikely to change that dependent relationship. Conversely, the removal of imperial presence was likely to expose the territories to a more direct and pervasive South African influence. It was even suggested at the time that the independence of the territories might be a retrograde rather than a progressive step. Nevertheless the last of these three polities – Swaziland – became independent in 1970, leaving Britain without formal colonial responsibilities in Africa except in Rhodesia. That formal imperial factor has almost been extinguished, except for one responsibility which the British Government has continued to ignore, in the hope that it will go away.

The eclipse of German Imperial power was a much more abrupt performance. Despite some diplomatic pressure during the 1920s and 1930s, Germany was not permitted to regain her colonies, which had been parcelled out amongst the victors of the First World War – Britain and France in West Africa, Britain and Belgium in East Africa, and South Africa in South-West. It is significant that even in 1919 South Africa was in a position to fill part of the vacuum left by the removal of an imperial administration.

The decline of Portugal, on the other hand, has been the result of a much more serious and prolonged struggle. When guerilla warfare broke out in the African provinces of Portugal during the late 1950s and early 1960s, Portuguese power was very fragile indeed. In that crisis, however, the Portuguese were able to discover some very useful allies and strategies. Membership of the North Atlantic Treaty Organisation, for example, entitled Lisbon to purchase the most sophisticated fire-arms and anti-guerilla weapons of western Europe and America. Close proximity to South Africa encouraged the formation of formal and informal alliances, since the fate of South Africa and of Portuguese Africa are so obviously related. Most significantly, the Portuguese Government also decided to bring in as many non-African settlers as possible, calculating that colonial power would make an effective bastion for the imperial presence. That decision also reflected the hopelessness of winning any substantial and reliable number of Africans to the Portuguese civilising cause. Dr Caetano's decision of 1970 to create regional governments in the African provinces took the policy a step further. As has happened everywhere else in Africa, colonists have compelled the imperial authorities to yield a share of political power, in exchange for supporting imperial interests. Portugal, in other words, came to the conclusion that imperial power was no longer sufficient to defend imperial interests: those interests must therefore be defended by a combination of Portuguese colonists, South Africans, and NATO weapons.

If South Africa was able to step into the vacuum left by the British in the protectorates and Rhodesia, by the Germans in South-West Africa, and by the Portuguese in Angola and Mozambique, it is interesting that the South African Government failed to move into the vacuum left by the Belgians in the Congo. When the Congo became independent in 1960, with Patrice Lumumba as Prime Minister, it looked as if that massive country and its considerable mineral wealth might be added to the anti-apartheid scales. The wealth of the country, however, was concentrated in Katanga province, where Moise Tshombe established a secessionist regime assisted by a variety of curious allies. One of these was Union Minière, the mining company which owned the copper industry. Another was the expiring Central African Federation, and tacit and military support was provided by South Africa as well. Conor Cruise O'Brien described Katanga correctly as an extension of the white supremacist states, with a thin but expensive veneer of African front-men.

In response to Lumumba's appeals, the United Nations intervened to suppress the breakaway regime, but the UN force in the Congo was placed in a rather ambiguous position by the veiled approval which Britain and France extended to the Tshombe Government. Though the secession was ultimately brought to an end, Lumumba was assassinated in peculiar circumstances, and the Congo passed into a long political crisis which threatened to dismember the state altogether. A variety of leaders – including Tshombe himself, and the Commander-in-Chief, General Mobutu – tried in vain to bind the Congolese together. Eventually, in 1965, Mobutu took over absolute control, and brought order to the Congo, working from the capital at Kinshasa outwards to the outlying provinces. In 1970 he presented himself as the only candidate in the presidential election, and was duly confirmed in office. However, the disastrous experience of the Congo in its first years of independence, and the prolonged struggle to dismiss the white mercenaries upon whom Mobutu relied for several years, all discouraged the Congo from any further involvement in external affairs. The government's anxiety to encourage foreign investment in the country means that Belgian Imperial power has not been transformed into Belgian neo-colonial control. On the other hand, the Congo is unlikely to become the platform for liberation movements which Lumumba anticipated.

Finally, the relationship between South Africa and the declining French Imperial power deserves some consideration. When President de Gaulle offered the African colonies a choice between continuing association with France, or immediate independence in 1958, Guinea was the only state to choose instant independence. The immediate withdrawal of all French personnel and assistance illustrated de Gaulle's annoyance, and inhibited other colonies from following suit. A radical and militant anti-colonial movement had been suppressed in the French Cameroons during the 1950s,

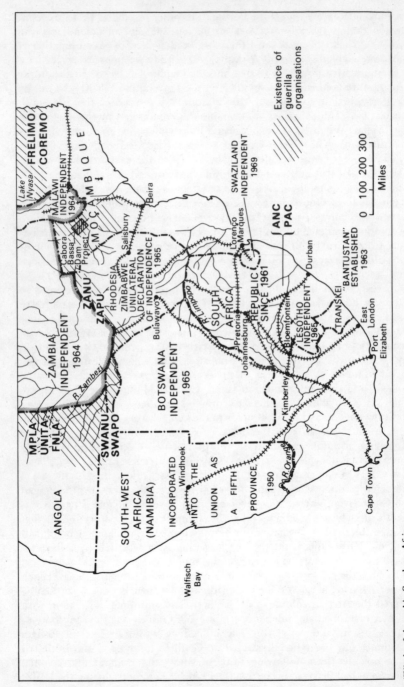

'Winds of change' in Southern Africa

and anti-colonial nationalism was not strongly developed in any part of French Africa (except Algeria) by the time the decision was faced. In consequence, France was able to allow independence to devolve upon a series of very small, economically weak, and politically quiescent communities. The links between metropolitan France and her ex-dependencies often remained surprisingly close, and the foreign policies of the new states remarkably unadventurous.

Among these communities South African emissaries seem to have been active throughout the late 1960s. In 1970, the Malagasy Republic accepted economic aid from South Africa, and at the same time Ivory Coast, Gabon, and a few less important states announced their willingness to start a 'dialogue' between independent Africa and Pretoria. Whether or not such meetings ever take place (and whether or not they would find any topic for discussion) the pronouncements suggest that Francophone Africa might prove fertile ground for further South African diplomacy, leading possibly to the investment of South African capital, managerial skills and diplomats in parts of West Africa.

It would, of course, be over-optimistic to suppose that formal imperialism has entirely vanished from Africa. On the other hand the decline of formal imperialism has often left room for informal influence on behalf of powers which have not traditionally been regarded as imperialist. It is in these partial vacuums that South African diplomacy has been busy and sometimes modestly successful, since the winds of change began to blow.

Chapter 21

Nationalisms

The departure of imperial governors and their entourages has left the Southern African stage in possession of a variety of forces which may roughly be described as nationalist, though that description is not always helpful in understanding the nature and purposes of the groups involved. Comparison and contrast between these various nationalisms may illustrate the nature of contemporary Southern African affairs, and may even allow some consideration of their future prospects.

Afrikaner nationalism undoubtedly occupies the centre of the stage. Whether a movement deserves the description of nationalist, when its purpose is to perpetuate the complete authority of an ethnic minority in a plural society, is neither here nor there. Afrikaner leaders may not be dedicated to the creation of a South African nation, but they lead a disciplined and determined movement. The problems involved in sustaining such a movement are two-fold: how to preserve internal unity despite urbanisation and the economic differentiation of the Afrikaner community; and how to order the lives of other communities so that their own may prevail. We should now consider how those two problems have been tackled.

A sense of pan-Afrikaner destiny, as we have seen, developed in the Afrikaner diaspora during the mid-nineteenth century, and spread from there to the more numerous Afrikaners of the Cape Colony. The provocation of the Jameson Raid, and the trials of the South African War translated that sense of destiny into collective action: yet Cape Afrikaners were for the most part uninvolved in fighting the war, and some Afrikaners from all the states of the sub-continent took the part of the Imperial Government. Afrikaner unification was only formally achieved in 1911, when the four provincial Afrikaner parties amalgamated into the South African National Party. It was almost immediately disrupted when Hertzog was expelled and carried most of the Free State Afrikaners with him to form the National Party. Afrikaner unity, so close in 1910, was again within reach during the early 1930s, but again the dream faded when Malan led his followers out of the Government and created the Purified Nationalist Party. Only from 1948 onwards, when Malan's Nationalists came to power, did Afrikaner unity again come within the realm of practical politics. Even as late as the 1960s, significant minorities of Afrikaners adhered to an old United Party loyalty, though those minorities have steadily dwindled.

214

Economic differentiation has also threatened to disrupt Afrikaner unity. Particularly, the flow of Afrikaners from the rural areas to the urban slums, during the first fifty years of the twentieth century, threatened to drain Afrikaners away from their political nationalism into identifying with the other urban white workers. The Broederbond, a secret society which became prominent during the 1930s, set about the task of preserving the loyalty of these potential refugees from nationalism. Afrikaner organisations were set up to work parallel with English-speaking social organisations: Afrikaner equivalents of the Boy Scouts, the Red Cross, debating societies and so on, all served to protect urban Afrikaners from over-exposure to non-nationalist influences. Afrikaner trade unions were set up, to serve the same purpose, and to ensure that white workers would not contemplate an alliance with workers of other colours. Traditional dances, purporting to date back to the Trek, were also invented as a measure of the determination of Afrikaner leaders to prevent the de-nationalisation of their urban followers. In short, a whole life-style was developed, where none had existed before.

A further challenge emerged during the 1960s, when Dr Verwoerd persuaded the party to adopt his particular tactics in dealing with internal and external opponents of the government. Afrikaner leaders were required to feign a certain degree of courtesy in their dealings with independent African Presidents, and with the African collaborators within the country. At the same time, a new group of people, Afrikaner investors, supported the government in its attempts to form alliances with African leaders in independent tropical Africa. These developments placed a terrible strain upon the loyalty and the mental habits of the more conservative members of the party. Albert Hertzog, son of a Prime Minister and himself a Cabinet Minister, found such behaviour intolerable, and regarded it as compromising the essential interests of Afrikaners. During 1969 he led a break-away of the 'verkrampte' (conservative, or constricted) members of the party, accusing the majority of 'verligte' (enlightened, or pragmatic) sympathies. Though his new party failed to win a single seat during the 1970 elections, it distracted the Government so severely that, for the first time since 1934, it failed to win any new seats in parliament, and indeed lost a few to the startled United Party. The existence of a continuing division between 'verkrampte' and 'verligte' points of view within Afrikanerdom suggests that Afrikanerdom may in future be further troubled by difficulties in reconciling different interest groups as they emerge. The absence of a plausible parliamentary opposition means that there is no immediate danger in division, since there is no real risk of non-Afrikaners coming to power by constitutional means.

The methods adopted in dealing with other national groups, or with quasi-national movements, are more interesting. By 1948, as we have seen the Government was divided between those who regarded 'apartheid' as nothing more than a useful election tactic, and those who were more or less committed to the establishment of territorial separation of the races as much as possible. Until the death of Prime Minister Strijdom in 1956, the former group prevailed, legislating in greater and greater detail a policy which was straight-forward white supremacy. As a sop to the ideologues, however,

Dr Verwoerd, Prime Minister, 1958–66, architect of the South African Republic and the Bantustan policy

the Government appointed a commission of enquiry, under Professor Tomlinson, to enquire into the best way of regulating race relations, particularly in the rural areas. That commision reported in 1956, much to the embarrassment of the Government. The Tomlinson Commission report recommended territorial division of the land into white and non-white regions. The hundreds of fragments of African reserve land were to be consolidated into seven substantial land areas, each destined to become a 'homeland' for one of the major African ethnic groups – Venda, North Sotho, South Sotho, Tswana, Zulu, and the inhabitants of the Transkei and the Ciskei. It was further recommended that the Protectorates (whose independence was not at that time expected) should be incorporated or allied to the closest South African reserve.

Observing the desperate poverty of the African reserves, the Commission asserted that an annual investment of £104,000,000 would be required, if the reserves were ever to support their inhabitants. The inhabitants of these areas would enjoy full citizenship within the relevant 'homeland', but would be treated as foreign visitors elsewhere. Once the reserves were viable economically, migrant labour to the 'white' areas would become less necessary and pose less of a problem to the state. It seems likely that a thorough application of the Tomlinson Commission's recommendations would have transformed the South African situation beyond recognition. Homelands which were economically and politically viable would be under no obligation to supply the necessary flow of unskilled migrant labour to the industrial and manufacturing industries. That result was precisely what the Government wished to avoid, and for that reason the report was profoundly embarrassing. Instead of the annual grant of £104,000,000, the Government in 1956 granted a total of £3,500,000 for one year only. The political recommendations were shelved, and might well have been forgotten entirely.

By 1959, however, the impending independence of large parts of tropical Africa, and the heightened criticism of the Union at the United Nations and elsewhere, forced the Government to look again at the Tomlinson report. The fact that Dr Verwoerd was by then Prime Minister no doubt facilitated the change of heart, since Verwoerd had earlier been associated with the ideologues of the South African Bureau of Racial Affairs. He certainly took the credit for initiating a new policy, and he may well have deserved whatever credit is due. At any rate, some gesture was required in order to pacify foreign criticism, and a modification of the Tomlinson report was produced as a blueprint for Bantu Homelands in the future – a policy now better known by the term Bantustans.

The Transkei was the obvious place to start. African territory in the Transkei was relatively compact, whereas other potential Bantustans were criss-crossed by substantial areas of white-owned land. The population density of the Transkei was also so great that there was practically no risk of its becoming economically viable and independent. The Transkei also possessed a tradition of local participation in administration. The Transkeian Territorial Authority, better known as the Bunga, dated from the late nineteenth century. Its composition was a mixture of elected and chiefly members, and through long association between the Bunga and the central Government the latter was sure of a certain number of loyal collaborators. Finally, the Xhosa, Mfengu, Thembu, Mpondo and other ethnic components of the Transkei were divided amongst themselves to the point where concerted action against the central Government was extremely unlikely.

When the Government enacted permissive legislation in 1959, and let it be known that a Bunga request would be well received, the Bunga duly requested 'self-government' as defined in the legislation. Chief Kaiser Matanzima was able to persuade and coerce other Government chiefs and elected members that 'self-government' might prove real, and that the Government was determined to grant it anyway. The central Government then drafted a constitution for the Transkei, and enacted it in 1963. In the ensuing elections Matanzima's supporters won perhaps seven seats, compared to perhaps 38 won by supporters of Chief Victor Poto, the Paramount chief of the Mpondo, and once member of the Native Representative Council. However, the elected members sat in the same house as the appointed chiefs, who gave overwhelming support to Matanzima, and enabled him to gain a tiny majority in the assembly. Matanzima became Chief Minister, and the Government had won a notable victory in contriving the election of the man most closely identified with their points of view. Poto, on the other hand, was believed to be hostile towards separate development in general, and towards the Transkeian version in particular.

Although the leaders of the Transkeian Government have the titles of ministers, their powers correspond more closely to those of rural district councillors. The central Government can (and does) control the Transkeian Government in a variety of powerful ways. For one thing, the legislature is composed of 109 members, of whom only 45 are elected. The other members are chiefs appointed by the Government, which reserves the right to dismiss them. Since the chiefs are by no means universally popular in the Transkei, the Government is the only reliable support which they possess, and they are unlikely to turn against their employers. Again, the Transkeian Government is prohibited from legislating on a large number of subjects including foreign policy, military resources, national communications and the security services. In other words, the really sensitive areas of decision-making are severely closed to them.

Perhaps the most severe constraint upon the independence of the Transkei is in finance. Though the Transkei is an agricultural and pastoral area, it has to import much of its food, and is the reverse of viable in economic affairs generally. In consequence, revenue is extremely restricted. When Matanzima introduced his first budget in 1964, he revealed that the Government would need to spend some £8,000,000 in order to pay for education, roads, the civil service and other basic necessities of administration. Revenue would amount to rather less than £2,000,000. The central Government would therefore have to pay about three-quarters of the budget. Holding the purse-strings, the central Government has little to fear from the local assembly.

It became fashionable to regard Matanzima simply as a Government stooge, with no mind nor will of his own. That view would seem to be mistaken. By 1959 he had come to the conclusion that the African political parties were doomed to fail in their attempts to change the nature of the South African Government. If that were the case, then it was absurd to continue along the same path, and it made more sense to accept the half-loaf offered by the Nationalist party, than to do without political bread altogether. In that opinion he seems to represent a significant strand in contemporary African thinking, both within and outside South Africa. In 1968, for example, the second general election was held in the Transkei and this time Matanzima won a majority of the elected seats, while holding on to the loyalty of the chiefly members.

Matanzima has come to exercise slightly more authority than his puppet status would suggest was possible. His electoral victory, for example, makes him slightly less dependent upon support from Pretoria, than was true before 1968. Secondly, as the first African Chief Minister in South Africa, he is an important weapon in the Government's propaganda armoury. It would be extremely embarrassing if Matanzima were provoked to state that separate development is not working even in the Transkei. There are slight indications that he is prepared to use the relative freedom which his peculiar status gives him. Even before the second election he pressed the Government to alter its policy on the medium of instruction in schools. It was Government policy to insist upon mother-tongue instruction, in theory to preserve traditional African values, but more importantly to restrict the access of school-children to dangerous knowledge and ideas. Matanzima requested that education should instead be conducted in English, and the Government was obliged to yield to him on that point. A series of marginal financial concessions have also been made, though nowhere near enough to make the Transkei a viable economy.

The relationship between the Bantustan policy and the demands of foreign policy appears to be very close indeed. The 1959 legislation was passed at a time when foreign and domestic criticism were severe, and the Bantustan blueprint was used to try to dispel the disastrous image of the South African Government after Sharpville. No further moves were made in that direction until 1970, when the Government's 'outward-looking' foreign policy began to pay dividends in Francophone Africa. Concessions once made can hardly be revoked without embarrassing the foreign policy planners, and therefore concessions have been made only with considerable reluctance. The assassination of Dr Verwoerd may also have contributed to delays in executing the Bantustan policy, since he alone had the political charisma (as the initiator of the Republic in 1961) to quieten the doubts of verkrampte critics. Most important of all, foreign policy does not require that Bantustans be constructed, it only requires that they should be accepted as a blueprint for ultimate action. Bantustans in the future are just as good as Bantustans in the present, to soothe critics of the Government. They are also much less risky. The Zulu and Tswana separate institutions, therefore, have developed at a much slower pace.

Though the Bantustan policy has not been implemented with much enthusiasm, it is consistent with Government policy regarding race relations as a whole. That policy might be described as divide and rule. It is assumed that Africans ought to belong to tribes, and that they can be reabsorbed into tribal units despite the long period of migrant labour and urbanisation. Education has therefore been provided along ethnic lines from the primary school to the university level. Graduates of the University College for the Zulu may be expected to be less able to bring about inter-ethnic and inter-racial movements than graduates of non-racial institutions. Loyalty to the 'traditional' tribal units is also fostered by the policy of undermining the security of urban residents. Though some 5,000,000 Africans are urban residents, they are conceived of as temporary visitors, who may exercise political and residential rights only in some distant Bantustan. The fact that some people have been absent from the homeland for several genera-tions, and may not even speak the language, is conveniently overlooked. It is for this reason that South African governments have striven to preserve and revive tribal sentiment while Africans inside and outside the country are trying to suppress it.

In the late 1960s the elaborate institutions of separate representation were extended to the Indian and Coloured communities. The South African Indian Council, an advisory and nominated body created in 1964, was modified by legislation of 1968 to become a body of 25 Government-nominated members, with provision that some members in the future might be elected. Since the Indian community is not located in one territorial location, and since the Council appears to have no greater power than its pre-1968 parent, the policy appears to be designed for ethnic tidiness rather than any more positive purpose. The same may be said of the establishment of a Coloured Persons Representative Council, for which the first elections were held in 1969. As in the Transkei, the Government retained the power to nominate a proportion of members in addition to the elected members, and that power became necessary when Tom Swartz, the Government's leading supporter in the Coloured community, not only lost his own seat but led his party to a massive defeat at the polls. The Government was still able to nominate Swartz and enough of his supporters to form a majority in the new Council. Neither the Coloured nor the Indian community has a territorial base, though legislation has permitted the Government to reserve employ-ment for different races in different regions. In that way, Coloured people have been allowed a monopoly of non-white employment in the Western Cape, from which the African residents are to be returned to their 'home-lands'; and Indians have been barred from employment in Zululand in exchange for a free run in certain categories of employment in parts of Natal. With the enactment of those pieces of legislation, the theoretical framework of separate development and separate representation may be said to be complete, and every community has some real or imaginary representation either now or in the foreseeable future. Whether that framework ensures representation or economic or social development is another matter altogether.

The scheme has naturally been extended to South-West Africa, though less swiftly and less thoroughly. The relative absence of urbanisation and of an Indian community, and the large size of the Coloured communities, involve some marginal differences in the application of the separate development policy; but those differences arise out of the situation rather than the minds of the administrators.

Not surprisingly, the Rhodesian regime has emulated certain features of the South African scheme for heading off African nationalism. On various formal occasions before and especially after UDI, a collection of chiefs has been paraded before the television cameras in ceremonial splendour, to testify that 'their people' have full confidence in whatever happens to be Government policy at the time. The trick is simple, and reasonably successful: to the outside world, familiar with the colonial image of Africans as dutiful subjects of tribal chiefs, these chiefs are the spokesmen of African opinion; in reality they are salaried civil servants of the incumbent regime, whose hostility to Government policy would certainly lead to dismissal and might lead to worse trouble. Implicit in the Rhodesian 'apartheid' constitution of 1968 is the belief that the nationalists can be split into tribal parts, each of which will grow hostile towards the other. If they succeed in that policy, they will restore to the sub-continent the conditions of mutual suspicion which characterised the days following the Mfecane. That is what is particulary ominous about the Rhodesian situation: ultimately white minority rule will probably be overthrown, but by that time the Zimbabweans may have been re-divided into Shona and Ndebele component parts.

The Bantustans in South Africa and the Homelands in Rhodesia are not the only examples of new kinds of 'independence' in the sub-continent. In many ways Chief Kaiser Matanzima in the Transkei has the advantage over Chief Leabua Jonathan of Lesotho. Lesotho enjoys more of the trappings of independence – its own flag, anthem, sovereign status, seat in the United Nations and membership of the Commonwealth. On the other hand the limitations on Matanzima's freedom of action are clearer, and his policies therefore more understandable by the mass of the people. Whereas the ordinary Mosotho may be bewildered and annoyed that Lesotho's independence has brought no visible advantage except to a few diplomats and Government leaders, no Transkeian is misled into believing that his local Government has much power to make decisions. It follows that there can be greater comprehension and rapport between rulers and people in the Transkei than in Lesotho. Similarly, the independence of Lesotho can be interpreted as a blow to the nationalist cause, since one of the first measures of the new independent Government was to expel leaders of ANC and P-AC who had sought refuge and a political haven in the British Protectorate. Undoubtedly the British were reluctant to provide refuge to these dangerous exiles, but at least they had permitted them to find political asylum. The independent state of Lesotho proved less able to resist the South Africans than the Protectorate had been. On the other hand, it is a sad commentary on British neglect of the High Commission Territories in general, that Lesotho was poorer and less viable and less united in 1970 than it had been in 1870 when Moshoeshoe I died. Whether the damage can be repaired after independence, and while the Southern African complex is dominated by South Africa, is an extremely dubious proposition. If it is impossible (as it seems) for Malawi to break the economic bonds, and if it is impossible for Zambia to adopt an unambiguous policy towards the South, how much more difficult must it be for the internal hostages? What this amounts to is a conviction amongst Afrikaners that tribalism is compatible with Afrikaner interests, and that 'independence' without economic power can also be contained.

English-speaking white South Africans do not pose a nationalist threat, by any stretch of terminology or imagination. Economic differentiation has divided them much more than Afrikaners, and the electoral system makes it improbable that they will achieve political power. Their status may be compared with that of the bijwoners (see chapter 13) of the early twentieth century, living on Afrikaner land, enjoying the privilege of almost equal status with the landlord, and distinguished sharply from the African labourers. Throughout the 1960s small numbers have abandoned the United Party in the hope of wielding influence within the governing party. That trend was especially pronounced from 1965 (when UDI in Rhodesia demonstrated that Afrikaners were better allies of Smith than the British Government would be) to 1970 (when Hertzog forced the Government into an extremely Afrikaner-exclusive position). Though none of the Government's English-speaking recruits have occupied more than decorative positions, the trend continues.

The Government's experience in re-tribalising its own citizens, and in subverting the political sovereignty of its immediate neighbours, could conceivably be applied to the problems of foreign relations. Africa abounds in new states whose political independence is not matched by economic viability. The economic boom which vitalised South Africa's economy from 1960 to 1969 has provided not only a self-sustaining growth, but also surplus funds with which to assist friendly foreign states. A well developed military and internal security machine can also be lent to unpopular rulers elsewhere in the continent. The first independent African state to be won to a more co-operative attitude was Malawi, which is a particularly interesting case.

When Malawi became independent in 1964, President Banda seemed the archetypal African nationalist leader. Despite a long absence from the country as a medical practitioner in London, he had kept in contact with potential nationalist leaders, and had been summoned back to Nyasaland by them to assume the leadership of the Nationalist party. Like Nkrumah of Ghana, he went to gaol in 1959, was released in 1960, led the Malawi Congress Party to electoral victory in 1961, and became the first president of the country in 1964. Only then did differences of opinion emerge which divided him from many of his cabinet colleagues. For one thing, the President did not pursue a policy of complete and immediate Africanisation, since he believed that expatriate administrators still had a part to play. He also came to the conclusion that Malawi could not afford to sever relations with South Africa, which provided employment for tens of thousands of Malawians every year. The cheapest available manufactured goods were also those produced nearby in South Africa. Malawi's chronic budget deficits, and its capital intensive projects, both required the assistance of some friendly and wealthy power. These issues crystallised into a cabinet crisis and within two months of independence six cabinet ministers resigned. One of them – Chipembere – subsequently tried to invade the country and expel its president. Though Dr Banda's dispute with his earlier colleagues has compelled him to state his position strongly, it does seem to be true that he has little alternative to his South African alliance. What some other African leaders object to, is not so much his policies, as the enthusiasm with which he adopts them and attempts to convert other leaders to accept them.

If Malawi nationalism can be diverted to suit South Africa's interests, it is little wonder that the same is true in Lesotho. The independence of Basutoland, as the independent kingdom of Lesotho, necessarily brought another independent state into the South African orbit. For almost a century after the establishment of a British protectorate over the remains of Moshoeshoe's kingdom, the Basotho took comfort in the fact that they were politically better placed than their kinsmen within the Union. The real problem therefore, namely the increasing dependence of the country upon the South African economy, was not greatly emphasised. Under the protectorate also, chiefs were sufficiently honoured to make them accept their country's dependent situation. The only considerable political movement – Josiel Lefela's Commoners' League, founded in 1919 – found itself opposed to the chiefs as much as the British officials. The exceptional conservatism of the Catholic clergy, whose position is immensely powerful, has also tended to stifle a radical view of the predicament of the Basotho community. When formal national politics were lauched in late 1950s, they were very different in tone and purpose from the Commoners' League. The Catholic Church encouraged the adoption of violently anti-Communist policies, and the chiefs quickly fell to the formation of political factions. Power was likely to fall to whichever politician could obtain the support of the Catholic Church, a substantial group of chiefly factions, and a source of campaign funds in a country where transport is difficult and expensive. The Basutoland Congress Party, founded in 1959 out of a combination of political leaders, soon fell under the influence and leadership of Ntsu Mokhehle, a graduate of Fort Hare and a close friend of many members of the South African ANC Youth Wing. To make the BCP politically competitive, it was necessary for Mokhehle to sever his connections with the ANC, since Basutoland conservatives considered the ANC to be a manifestation of Communism. Even then, conservatives were able to discover some indiscreet observations by BCP leaders, with which to level a charge of being Communist-sympathisers and therefore hostile to established religion. Mokhehle therefore lost the 1965 independence elections, and although his party probably won the 1970 elections, his opponents were by then too firmly in power to allow the elections to proceed to a conclusion.

The man who did grasp the realities of the power struggle was chief Leabua Jonathan. He formed the Basutoland National Party in 1959, on the issue that the BCP was alienating the chiefs, and soon he acquired the support of the Catholic hierarchy in a programme which accused the BCP of being Communist and hostile to chieftancy and Christianity. That clerical support began to dwindle after the internal 1960 elections, when it moved behind a short-lived anti-communist league. Though there certainly was a Communist Party in Basutoland, it appears to have been even less powerful than its South African counterpart; nevertheless the clergy and some of the chiefs determined to pursue a policy reminiscent of the crude and sweeping anti-Socialist policies of America in the 1950s and South Africa since 1948. Jonathan, in any case, had to look around for fresh sources of support and campaign funds. Shortly before the 1965 elections he found his source in the South African Government, which provided much of the required backing for the crucial 1965 election. Winning 42 per cent of the votes, Jonathan's party crept into power with 31 of the 60 seats – small, but still a majority.

Soon after the election, the new Government fell foul of the young king, Moshoeshoe II, who had terminated his Oxford studies in 1960 to return and enter politics. Jonathan's family had long been hostile to the ruling dynasty, and in 1960 he encouraged the Regent, who was unpopular, uneducated and unprogressive, to hold on to the throne; and it was not surprising that conflict would resume when Jonathan became Prime Minister. The conflict dragged out, with Moshoeshoe II under restriction, until he went into exile early in 1970, leaving the remaining powers of the monarchy in the hands of Jonathan's nominee. He returned late in 1970, once he had agreed to remain passive politically. The other major difficulty was the continuing popularity of the major opposition group, Mokhehle's BCP. Despite Mokhehle's prickly temper and authoritarian attitudes, he attracted a considerable degree of support from Basotho who grew tired of Jonathan's humble attitude towards South Africa and continuing failure to discover any remedy to Lesotho's chronic poverty. The BCP may well have won the 1970 election, but Jonathan was able to use the power of the Government to declare an emergency, cancel the election results, and rely upon military power and his South African allies for continuing support. In addition to an obvious economic dependence upon South Africa therefore Lesotho has become directly dependent in politics as well. Any government in Lesotho would be vulnerable to South Africa: the BNP Government is especially so, having over-ruled the people's decision and sent the king into exile as well.

The other two protectorates moved to independence with less political disturbance. Within a year, Bechuanaland had become the independent republic of Botswana, with Seretse Khama's Bechuanaland Democratic Party winning no fewer than 28 of the 31 seats. Seretse Khama had risen to fame by marrying an English girl in 1948, thereby incurring the wrath of the South African Government and being deposed from the paramountcy of the major ethnic group, the BamaNgwato. Personal vindictiveness however plays no part in his politics, and Botswana's relations with South Africa have been characterised by quietness and even coolness. Botswana differs from Lesotho in several important respects, so far as South Africa is concerned. Though almost entirely surrounded by South Africa, South-West Africa and Rhodesia, Botswana shares a border of some 500 yards with Zambia. That border is important for psychological rather than material reasons, though it has certainly been used as an escape route for South African refugees. Again, though Botswana is desperately poor, it is less directly dependent upon South Africa than is Lesotho, and can anticipate some economic benefits from selling cattle to meat-starved Zambia and from the development of the mining industry. Most important, however, is the fact that the Government enjoys a very widespread support from its citizens. These range from Afrikaner farmers to pastoralists and Bushman hunting-gathering groups, and from the political left to the political right. Without an army, and unwilling to enter any disreputable bargain with South Africa, the Government has sustained a massive popular support, and won the 1969 elections just as convincingly as those of 1965. Economic aid has not been negotiated from South Africa, nor have full diplomatic relations been established. Botswana has contrived to retain a modicum of self-respect in a very trying situation. If, as the Government hopes, mineral resources can be exploited on a large scale, and transport to Zambia facilitated, the country may achieve some degree of real independence.

Swaziland was the last of the three to reach independence – in 1969. Politics had for many years become personalised by the entry of the Ngwenyama, Sobhuza II, into active political life. He has been Ngwenyama since 1899, so that his reign exceeds 70 years. By 1969 he was very firmly in control of events, and was able to ensure that his party – Imbokodvo – won all the seats in the independence elections. Whether the political system can survive intact when Sobhuza is succeeded by another Dlamini seems doubtful; meanwhile the Government certainly enjoys massive support from all races, and from all but a few educated Swazi who regret the absence of radicalism in the independent Government. Swaziland may be expected to follow in the path of Botswana rather than Lesotho, at least during the reign of Sobhuza II. Nevertheless the links between the South African Government and those of the ex-protectorates are so close that the most that can be expected of the client Governments is neutrality in the event of large-scale unrest or warfare.

Clearly the most significant opposition faced by South Africa's Government and allies is presented by the guerilla movements of the sub-continent. Since the major powers are extremely unlikely to intervene in South Africa, any hope for change must centre upon these indigenous movements. They represent forms of nationalism very different from those welcomed by Pretoria. They are the lineal descendants of the ANC and P-AC in South Africa, and of ZANU and ZAPU in Rhodesia. Some light may be thrown on their nature by looking once more at their origins.

One of the important ways in which modern South African history has differed from that of the rest of the continent is that the issue of 'independence' has not loomed as large in the minds of articulate Africans, but has been subordinated to the rather different ambition of freedom. Unlike independence movements elsewhere in Africa, African political leaders in South Africa and Rhodesia have been operating within political systems which were already independent of metropolital control, and which were dominated by racial minorities. By the time the African National Congress was founded in 1912, South Africa was already very largely 'independent', whereas most of its citizens were conspicuously unfree. For many years the ANC concerned itself with two very limited aims: to preserve African rights from further encroachment, and if possible to infiltrate the area of social, economic and political privilege to which some middle-class Africans had already been partially admitted. The leadership of the ANC therefore ordinarily comprised respectable professional men – ministers of religion, doctors, lawyers – whose interests were close to the heart of ANC. Equally important, little attempt was made to mobilise mass support, either by espousing popular causes or by recruitment campaigns. Naturally the ANC was most conspicuous when existing African rights were threatened, as they were first by the Natives Land Act and in 1935 by the Hertzog bills relating to political and economic rights. When there was no great issue to defend, the ANC tended to decline into a moribund organisation.

When the Second World War broke out, however, the extent and depth of African grievances and ambitions were too great to be contained within the old structure. Young men were recruited first into the semi-autonomous Youth Wing, and after the war into the Congress itself. These younger men were impatient of the respectability of Congress, and had more precise ideas about what objects the ANC ought to pursue. They rejected the existing emphasis of the ANC upon the rights of the professional minority, and thought in terms of emancipating the whole African population from discriminatory restrictions. Similar developments were taking place elsewhere in Africa, as improvement associations were obliged to cope with more ambitious projects advanced by younger men. In the South African context, this involved the acceptance of 'African Claims' formulated by the Youth Wing and accepted by the whole ANC in 1945. The claims amounted to a demand for complete democracy without regard for race or colour. It is perhaps curious that African movements elsewhere in the continent at the same time were moving towards a more exclusively African emphasis, while South African radicalism took the anti-racialist line.

Despite this advance, the ANC was neither as united nor as militant as might be supposed. Amongst the Youth Wingers were many who insisted that non-Africans could not normally be trusted as allies of the African cause, and who therefore deplored the alliance of the ANC with the Indian Congress and the Congress of Democrats and the Coloured People's Organisation. At the same time, the ANC was seldom able to initiate political movements, and more often had the rôle of supporting movements initiated by other people. It certainly helped to initiate the Passive Resistance Campaign in 1952, and the anti-Pass campaign in 1960; but between these campaigns the initiative often lay with rural communities who independently rose against the state (in the northern Transvaal, for example, and in Pondoland); and with urban groups (as for example the residents of Johannesburg locations who organised a boycott of bus companies to protest against increased fares). This inability to lead produced severe frustrations. The Africanists within Congress suspected that the ANC was being restrained and destroyed by its non-African allies: conversely the organisers of campaigns suspected that the factionalism of the ANC contributed to the poor responses of many groups of people. As happened elsewhere in Africa, the militancy of disorganised people forced the formal political party to adopt more militant policies in order to preserve the initiative in affairs. But the harassment of the ANC by the South African government during the 1950s very effectively prevented it from taking any remedial action, and there was no way of relieving the tension within the movement. Eventually in 1958 it split in two: the ANC lost its Africanist Wing, who formed the Pan-Africanist Congress under the leadership of Robert Sobukwe.

Though these separate organisations existed for only two years before they were both banned and forced underground, they did differ in important respects, and were animated by different visions of what 'freedom' should be pursued. The P-AC rejected the socialist notions of the ANC, along with the non-African allies of the movement, and thought in terms of a more 'African' community than the ANC had in mind. In practice, and especially after it was suppressed, the P-AC modified its hostility to non-Africans, and even admitted non-African members, so long as they were not 'socialist'. In time, even the hostility to 'foreign ideologies' was modified. Again, the P-AC thought of itself as more militant than the ANC – though in practice it faced the same difficulty of keeping pace with localised resentful communities. Essentially the ANC and P-AC differed in the emphasis they placed, and it is more sensible to regard the division as a consequence of frustration, rather than profound disagreement about principles and methods. The emergence, in the 1960s, of African collaborators in the separate development programme, underlined the point that by no means all Africans could be assumed to favour a prolonged and probably violent struggle for emancipation.

A further significant difference lies in the fact that the ANC (and RBVA in Rhodesia) were both concerned to protect existing African rights from erosion by governmental pressure. The tactical position helps to explain the essentially defensive approach to politics, which characterised both political organisations before the second world war. On one hand the African leaders were attempting to conserve their remaining privileges from destruction, and on the other hand attempting to democratise the existing political structure. Conservatism and liberalism were therefore the most striking personal characteristics of the moderate leadership. Similarly, to counter the racialism of the Government, African leaders proposed a non-racial approach to politics, economics and society. In all these respects the leadership in Southern Africa differed in emphasis from African leaders north of the Zambesi river. They operated in the tradition of Moshoeshoe rather than Shaka, but more important they operated entirely within the legal and ideological limits established by the white community. Radicals laboured in vain, for example, to commit the ANC to the policy of a black republic.

These characteristics have, to a remarkable degree, continued to distinguish African political leadership in Southern Africa, even though they failed to turn away the prejudice and rapacity of successive governments. It took a tremendous volume of provocation in the 1950s, as we have seen, to radicalise the African movements into militant, mass-supported organisations. Even then, the kind of political organisation formed north of the Zambesi was not entirely applicable to the south, since the governments in the south were so much more powerful, and the aims of the leaders not entirely identical. Instead of describing ANC, P-AC, ZAPU and ZANU as African nationalist parties, it would seem more accurate and appropriate to describe them as democratic movements, committed to differing degrees to political and economic equality.

In a move obvious sense the use of 'nationalist' can also be questioned. Just as the governments of the supremacist states have perceived that their interests are intertwined and indivisible, so have the militant leaders understood the inseparability of the Southern African issues. It makes little sense to divide forces and scatter them around the sub-continent in trivial numbers. In consequence, each of the national movements has entered into alliance with other national movements: indeed this has proved easier than the formation of alliances between two or more movements from the same nation. The racial frontier, from the Congo to Mozambique, has become much more meaningful than the frontiers between the supremacist states.

The outcome of the contest between these forces will probably depend upon the degree of assistance which independent African countries can provide to the guerilla movements. If the guerillas have to depend very heavily upon eastern aid, it is likely that the supremacist states will be able to obtain equivalent aid from certain western powers. The prospects for a concerted Pan-African effort do not seem very promising. The inability of the Organisation of African Unity to mobilise African opinion and resources during the Nigerian civil war, and during the Portuguese raid on Guinea in 1970, suggests that the OAU is itself too divided in aim to be an effective force. The continuing inability of independent African states to create an African High Command suggests that national interests continue to override continental ambitions, in the minds of most African leaders. Guerilla movements have found allies in particular African states – particularly Tanzania and Zambia, despite the vulnerability of these countries to Southern African military strength. Individual African states, however, simply do not enjoy the economic, military or perhaps political power to decide the issue single-handed. The goal of African unity seems no closer today than it did in 1960, and until that goal is attained, the supremacist states will probably be able to contain the guerilla movements.

Conversely, the South African Government can expect further rewards from its 'outward-looking' foreign policy, so long as national interests continue to divide independent Africa. Pretoria strategists doubtless hope to establish South African hegemony over most of the continent south of the Sahara, and it would be unduly bold to dismiss that ambition as unattainable. On the other hand it seems unlikely that Africa, having shed the formal imperialism inherited from the nineteenth century scramble, will ever submit to a twentieth-century informal imperial yoke. When President Banda and other 'moderate' African leaders claim that they are trying to kill apartheid by kindness, they are repeating the aspiration of the African National Congress in its infancy. Just as the ambitions and methods of African leaders within South Africa have changed, so closer experience of the supremacist states may bring the African independent leaders to a more realistic understanding of the problems of the sub-continent. Then the tradition of Shaka may be added to the tradition of Moshoeshoe, into a formidable power.

A note on sources

The present text has concentrated on providing one way of synthesising the material which already exists, dealing with South Africa and her neighbouring countries since 1800. For the text to be most useful, it should be read in conjunction with as many other sources as possible. However, a plural society such as South Africa has naturally produced a very uneven historiography, in which writers have interpreted historical events from a very wide variety of different perspectives. Historians have also made full use of their right to select whatever information seems to them to be relevant to their purposes. 'Raw information' has therefore to be tracked down from a large number of published sources, and each of the possible approaches deserves some consideration. What follows is an attempt to guide the unwary reader through the perils of this profuse and contradictory body of material. For convenience, we have grouped together the schools of interpretation which are most obvious in the historiography, even though this method of classification is somewhat arbitrary, and even though many of the historians may resent being classified in the way that we think they approach their subjects.

The first significant attempts to assemble material for historical purposes were made by white settlers on the Cape's eastern frontier, and it seems reasonable to talk of a 'frontier' interpretation of the events which those historians describe. Foremost among these was G. M. Theal, who assembled the archives of the Cape colony and of Basutoland, and published massive and comprehensive treatments of those materials. He was inclined to assume that, in case of conflict, the frontier settlers were generally in the right, and the frontier Africans usually in the wrong, while the Cape Town Government was generally ill-informed about frontier conditions. Nevertheless he did not fall into the habit of many later historians, of regarding Africans as being essentially without history, and a great deal of valuable information may be gleaned from his many published volumes, despite his consistent bias. Indeed the consistency of that bias adds to his value as a source. A. T. Bryant's works on early Natal and Zulu history fall into the same category, with much the same strength and weakness. By and large that view of South African history has died out, though A. F. Hattersley's volumes on Natal history may be regarded as 'second-generation frontier' in their orientation.

A very large proportion of South African scholars have concerned themselves with the role of Portuguese and British imperial power in the subcontinent. These writers have not always assumed that the imperial authorities were justified in their activities, but they have usually assumed that imperial officials held the initiative in South African affairs. The work of Eric Axelson on the Portuguese is amongst the best of this 'imperial' school. British imperial activity has been studied much more thoroughly, perhaps because the archival material is so much more accessible. British 'imperial' historiography flourished powerfully at the turn of the century, inspired by the imperial intervention during and after the South African War. More recently, a less 'committed' group of scholars has turned its attention to the problems of imperial power in South Africa. Perhaps the best of these is Galbraith, *Reluctant Empire*. Sections of *Africa and the Victorians* by R. E. Robinson and J. Gallagher are also extremely relevant to understanding the imperial role in South African history.

Afrikaner historiography is relatively less varied and less voluminous than anglophone history: for one thing, fewer Afrikaners have enjoyed the time, money and academic incentive required for scholarship; for another, Afrikaner historians have been very closely involved in the political fortunes of Afrikaners in politics, and have devoted much of their talent to justification of contemporary Afrikaner power. F. van Jaarsveld's study of *The Origins of Afrikaner Nationalism* transcends these limitations, and is very useful both for its own subject and for comparative purposes. A more characteristic work is edited by Muller and described as *Five Hundred Years of South African History*. Africans are restricted as much as possible to an appendix, and it is clear from the text that the authors consider Africans very lucky to have been allowed even so marginal a position.

A school which has been much more widely published and read, may be described as 'liberal' in the South African meaning of the term. The progenitor of this school was W. M. MacMillan, whose best-known work is *Bantu, Boer and Briton*. Among his successors have been C. W. de Kiewiet and E. A. Walker, who dominated South African historiography in the 1930s and 1940s. More recently they have been emulated by Clem Goodfellow, J. S. Marais, L. M. Thompson, and G. M. Carter. It is a curious feature of this school that it is related to the earlier 'imperial' school, to which Walker and de Kiewiet, for instance, might be said to belong. Part of the explanation may be that the scholarship of these writers has enabled them to see through the obfuscating language of politicians, to the realities of oppression. That vision, in turn, suggests that South African affairs have moved from bad to worse because of the extinction of the imperial factor. Also, antipathy towards the aspirations of Afrikaner nationalism can easily lead to acceptance of imperial power as the only historically effective restraint upon settler and Afrikaner oppression. More important than the frequent link between the 'imperial' and 'liberal' schools is the fact that liberal scholars, though extremely scrupulous in their use of sources, have generally been very conservative in their methodology. Most have denounced the mythology that white rule is really in the interests of everyone else; but few have gone further than criticise and analyse white historical initiatives. Since most of the documentary material for South African history has been written by white people, for other white people to read, a concentration on documentary evidence tends to produce the history of the white communities. Liberal scholars, like their conservative and nationalist rivals, have accepted that the historical initiative has usually rested within the white communities. That assumption is, of course, often correct, but it is an assumption which limits the vision of the scholars.

The volume of determinist interpretations is astonishing, in view of the ineffectiveness of determinist philosophies in South African politics. Perhaps the imbalance is the result of the retreat of determinists from their political failures into historical analysis. A powerful piece of geographical determinism is S. Agnew and Pollock's *Historical Geography of South Africa*, a work distinguished by many interesting insights but marred by an enthusiasm for explaining every historical event in terms of exclusively geographical causes. A less ambitious, but more convincing publication is S. Neumark's analysis of the economy of the Cape frontier, to which the present writers owe much inspiration.

However, the bulk of the determinist writing is Marxist in inspiration. J. A. Hobson, at the turn of the century, was probably the first, and possibly the best. It was in these early works that he traced a connection between capitalism and imperialism, a connection which has been accepted by all subsequent Marxist (and many other) analysts of imperial history. Roux and Professor and Mrs Simons have published works whose greatest strength lies in their recollection of radical politics from the 1920s onwards, but which fail to account for the fact that colour has been more important than class, in determining the attitudes of South Africans to each other. The same criticism may be made of Sachs's *Anatomy of Apartheid*, and Bunting's *Rise of the South African Reich*. These works are remarkable collections of information, but they fall short of Hobson's capacity to explain South African events in economic determinist terms. It should also be noticed that these works tend to focus upon some very obscure radical thinkers and activists, as the heroes of the South African drama. That, of course, could be said of most of the schools of interpretation considered so far. Afrikaner historians have seized upon Afrikaner worthies, liberals upon Cape liberal politicians, and imperialists upon imperial heroes (and villains). However, the fact that Afrikaners, liberals and imperialists have on various occasions exercised power and initiatives, makes those emphases slightly less arbitrary than the selection of radical heroes.

What may be described as 'Africanist' interpretations have been slow to develop. For one thing, few Africans have enjoyed the leisure and the equipment with which to work. These few, also, have often belonged to a political and social élite, a circumstance influencing the way they approach their subjects. J. H. Soga, for example, in his *South-Eastern Bantu*, allows the fact of being one of the first African missionaries to govern his approach. The historical traditions of the Xhosa are tacked on to the end of pre-history which is derived directly from the Old Testament. Jabavu, in *The Black Problem*, gives greater weight to the ideas and interests of the Cape's African élite than their numbers and power would justify. As compilations of evidence, these works are invaluable, but as guides to interpreting history they are less than perfect. Later generations of African writers have similarly lacked the time, the resources and the professional training to compose historical works. The autobiographies of many African leaders concentrate on immediate political problems, rather than historical perspectives. Historical interpretation is therefore more often implicit than explicit. Nevertheless the works of S. T. Plaatje, Albert Luthuli, Jordan Ngubane, Nelson Mandela, Govan Mbeki, and in Rhodesia Ndabaningi Sithole, contain a wealth of information and ideas. In the same category is the autobiography of Clements Kadalie, which was published only in 1970.

If there is an 'African point of view' of South African history, it has therefore to be found in the work of predominantly non-African scholars, particularly social anthropologists and students of religion, many of whom have worked in vernacular, in great depth, and with sympathy and integrity. Among anthropologists, Monica Wilson, Hilda Kuper, Max Gluckman, Hammond-Tooke, A. Vilakazi and D. H. Reader are deservedly well-known; and among students of religious studies B. G. M. Sundkler. The military historian, D. H. Morris, might also be considered in this context.

The history of South Africa, however, should be something more than the sum of its racial and ethnic parts. The task of composing an interpretation of the history of this plural society is particularly taxing, since so many different kinds of influence and power, from so many different directions, have come into conflict with each other. Before our knowledge of African participation had reached its present limited volume, the task was still comparatively easy. It is now nearly impossible. For example, J. D. Omer-Cooper's work on the Mfecane, a period in which European influence upon African events was limited, succeeds in painting a convincing picture of that massive event. De Kiewiet and Walker, who wrote under the impression that African initiatives on white history were very limited, also succeed in assembling elegant and convincing portraits. Dr S. Marks, binding together the variety of influences which contributed to the Bambatha disturbances in Natal and Zululand, has been strikingly successful – but the work is limited to a relatively small time and space. The recent Oxford History of South Africa, which attempts to write the comprehensive history of South Africa using every available source of information, is less successful. This may be partly because so few of the contributors are historians, but it is more likely that the very size of the task has overwhelmed the contributors. The volumes are invaluable as sources of information, however, and have justly become essential reading.

Further reading on the history of South Africa and the neighbouring states might usefully include some of the following titles, arranged in order of price and region.

Inexpensive
Portuguese East Africa:
  J. Duffy, *Portugal in Africa,* London 1961; Cambridge, Mass. 1962.
  E. Mondlane, *The Struggle for Mozambique,* London and
    New York 1969.
Malawi and Zambia:
  B. M. Fagan (ed.), *A Short History of Zambia,* Oxford 1967;
    New York 1968.
  T. O. Ranger (ed.), *Aspects of Central African History,* London
    and Evanston, Ill. 1968.
Rhodesia:
  T. O. Ranger, *ibid.*
  T. O. Ranger, *The African Voice,* London 1970.
  N. Sithole, *African Nationalism,* Oxford and New York 1959.
South-West Africa:
  R. First, *South West Africa,* London 1963.
South Africa and the old High Commission territories:
  C. W. de Kiewiet, *A History of South Africa, Social and Economic,*
    Oxford and New York 1941.
  L. M. Thompson, *Politics in the Republic of South Africa,*
    Boston 1966.
  E. Roux, *Time Longer than Rope,* London 1964.
  C. Kadalie, *My Life and the ICU,* London and New York 1970.
  M. Benson, *The African Patriots,* London 1963.
  J. Halpern, *South Africa's Hostages,* London 1965.
  G. Mbeki, *South Africa: The Peasant Revolt,* London
    and New York 1964.
  P. N. S. Mansergh, *South Africa 1906–1961,* London 1962.

More expensive but worth acquiring
Portuguese East Africa:
  J. Duffy, *Portuguese Africa,* Harvard and Oxford 1959
Malawi and Zambia:
  E. Stokes and R. Brown, *The Zambesian Past,* Manchester
    and Evanston, Ill. 1966.
  R. Rotberg, *The Rise of Nationalism in Central Africa,* Harvard
    and Oxford 1966.
Rhodesia:
  R. Gray, *The Two Nations,* London 1960.
  T. O. Ranger, *Revolt in Southern Rhodesia,* Oxford
    and Evanston, Ill. 1960.
South-West Africa:
  H. Vedder, *South-West Africa in Early Times,* London
    and New York 1966.
  H. Bley, *South-West Africa Under German Rule,* London 1971.
South Africa and the old High Commission territories:
  J. D. Omer-Cooper, *Zulu Aftermath,* London 1966.
  B. Bunting, *The Rise of the South African Reich,* London 1964.
  T. R. H. Davenport, *The Afrikaner Bond,* Cape Town
    and New York 1966.

L. M. Thompson and M. Wilson (eds.), *Oxford History of South Africa*, 2 vols.

E. Walker, *A History of Southern Africa*, London 1957.

M. Ballinger, *From Union to Apartheid*, Cape Town 1969; New York 1970.

S. Marks, *Reluctant Rebellion*, London 1969.

J. S. Marais, *The Cape Coloured People*, Johannesburg 1957.

J. Galbraith, *Reluctant Empire*, Berkeley, Calif. and Cambridge 1961.

R. E. Robinson and J. Gallagher, *Africa and the Victorians*, London 1961.

A. Luthuli, *Let My People Go*, London and New York 1962.

J. Ngubane, *An African Explains Apartheid*, London 1963.

N. Mandela, *No Easy Walk to Freedom*, London and New York 1965.

H. J. and R. E. Simons, *Class and Colour in South Africa*, London 1969.

I. Schapera, *Western Civilisation and the Natives of South Africa*, London 1934.

B. G. M. Sundkler, *Bantu Prophets in South Africa*, London and New York 1961.

A. Vilakazi, *Zulu Transformations*, Natal 1962; Mystic, Conn. 1965.

Finally, in order to feel something of the texture of South African life, the rich source of novels should be considered. Alan Paton, Ezekiel Mphahlele, Peter Abrahams, Olive Schreiner, all merit reading for their own sake, and all illuminate aspects of South African life.

Index

THE AUTHOR: Donald Denoon was born in Scotland and moved as a child to South Africa, where he went to school and later received his first degree from the University of Natal. After obtaining his Ph.D. degree from Cambridge in 1965, he returned to Africa and since that time has lectured in history at Makerere University. Dr. Denoon is well known for his scholarly articles on Southern African history.

DATE DUE

DEC. 9 1987

DEMCO 38-297